汉字入门

李 刚 著

清华大学出版社
北京

内 容 简 介

本书是根据国际中文教育教学特点及要求编写的，涵盖HSK(汉语水平考试)三级所需的大部分词汇和部分四级词汇。本书分为五课内容，包括汉字的基本知识、自然崇拜、五行、目见耳闻和母子情深。

学习汉字的过程，就像儿童搭积木，由单块积木拼装成一个完整的造型，正如由象形字或指事字"创造性地"组合成会意字和形声字。本书紧紧抓住汉字造字法，引导读者通过汉字结构规律和语境感悟字形、字义，使其在学习汉字时自然地联想到自己的生活经历，从而产生共鸣，进而主动探索汉字结构，还汉字表形、表意之原始形式。

本书作为国际中文教育汉字教学的教材，内容丰富、通俗易懂，既可作为国际中文教育初级教学的参考书，也可作为对中国传统文化感兴趣的外国朋友的自学读物。

本书封面贴有清华大学出版社防伪标签，无标签者不得销售。

版权所有，侵权必究。举报：010-62782989，beiqinquan@tup.tsinghua.edu.cn。

图书在版编目(CIP)数据

汉字入门/李刚著．—北京：清华大学出版社，2023.1
ISBN 978-7-302-62301-4

Ⅰ.①汉… Ⅱ.①李… Ⅲ.①汉语－对外汉语教学－教材 Ⅳ.① H195.4

中国版本图书馆 CIP 数据核字 (2022) 第 253151 号

责任编辑：	施　猛　王　欢
封面设计：	常雪影
版式设计：	方加青
责任校对：	成凤进
责任印制：	宋　林

出版发行：清华大学出版社

网　　址：http://www.tup.com.cn，http://www.wqbook.com
地　　址：北京清华大学学研大厦 A 座　　**邮　　编**：100084
社 总 机：010-83470000　　**邮　　购**：010-62786544
投稿与读者服务：010-62776969，c-service@tup.tsinghua.edu.cn
质 量 反 馈：010-62772015，zhiliang@tup.tsinghua.edu.cn

印 装 者：三河市铭诚印务有限公司
经　　销：全国新华书店
开　　本：185mm×260mm　　**印　　张**：18.25　　**字　　数**：410 千字
版　　次：2023 年 1 月第 1 版　　**印　　次**：2023 年 1 月第 1 次印刷
定　　价：68.00 元

产品编号：066055-01

我的语言的局限意味着我的世界的局限。
The limits of my language mean the limits of my world.

——路德维格·维特根斯坦 (1889—1951)，奥地利哲学家
— Ludwig Wittgenstein (1889—1951), Austrian philosopher

序

  为满足国际中文教育教学的需要，沈阳大学国际教育学院组织教育教学经验丰富的教师编写了中国传统文化教育系列教材。这些教材既是我校中国传统文化教育研究所的研究成果，也是我校国际中文教育教学实践的结晶。《汉字入门》是本套系列教材之一。

  汉字是世界上现存的唯一被普遍使用的古老文字，至今闪烁着智慧的光芒，广泛而深远地影响着中国周边国家和地区。大约在公元前1300年，古老的中国就已经出现了甲骨文。历经几千年的演变，现在很多汉字的字形与字义发生了变化，因此，很多外国朋友在学习汉语时，因为汉字的繁多复杂而倍感困惑。知其然，就要知其所以然。本书从甲骨文的象形字开始探究，通过对几百个有代表性的常用汉字的详细解说，让人们了解汉字究竟是怎么演变来的，并附以脍炙人口、耳熟能详的锦言妙语，可帮助读者加深对神秘方块字的理解，提高正确使用汉字的能力，促进对古老东方文化的体悟。中华文化博大精深，相信神奇的汉字探究之旅将处处是惊奇，处处是惊喜！

  《汉字入门》是一本写给汉语初学者的书，作者辛勤耕耘数载，我是以十分欣悦的心情来看待国际教育学院这一教学成果的，相信这一成果将会在我校来华留学生教育事业上发挥积极作用。如果能在一定程度上改善初学汉语的学习条件，降低学习汉语的难度，帮助外国朋友认识汉字和学会书写汉字，使其在愉快和轻松的气氛中学习汉语，并能取得良好的学习效果，是我们最大的荣幸。同时，希望本书能为促进中外文化交流、增进中外友谊和相互了解尽一份微薄之力。

王晓初 教授

沈阳大学副校长

2022年7月

前　言

　　《汉字入门》是一本写给没有汉语基础的"真正"初学者的书。常言道："万事开头难。"汉字是表意文字，字形和字义密切相关。作者以汉字造字法为切入点，帮助读者了解汉字的构造，由形表意、由易到难、由简到繁，将繁多的汉字梳理成一幅幅情境画卷。全书共分五课，内容包括：汉字的基本知识、自然崇拜、五行、目见耳闻、母子情深。本书条理清晰、简单易懂、栩栩如生、引人入胜。一书在手，读者能在阅读中习得汉字知识，解决入门难的问题。

1. 本书特色

　　本书是根据国际中文教育教学的特点编写的教材，遵循汉字文字学的认知规律，注重书写，注重介绍汉字的演变发展过程，注重介绍文字源流，注重介绍汉字在实际生活中的应用，并且充分引导读者发挥想象力和洞察力，努力还原中国古代社会活动，通过汉字生动形象地反映古代社会活动的实际情况。本书严格遵循国际中文教育教学词汇大纲要求，涵盖 HSK(Hanyu Shuiping Kaoshi，汉语水平考试) 三级所需大部分词汇和部分四级词汇。

　　孟子提出："故事半古之人，功必倍之。"合适的教材或读物会启发我们的感悟能力与形象思维，帮助我们学得更快、更好。帮助读者增强汉语听说读写的能力，增强中西文化对比的能力，增强对中国传统文化和当代文化的领悟能力，都是我们孜孜以求的目标。汉字是千百年来中国劳动人民智慧的结晶，也是人们生活方式的体现。本书力求充分利用读者的生活经验、固有知识和想象力，借鉴中国古人的生活智慧、哲学、美学，帮助读者理解每个汉字。汉字像儿童的积木一样，象形字或指事字好比积木的零件，能够"创造性地"组合成会意字和形声字(有的是会意兼形声字，有的是形声兼会意字)，这样理解会使学习汉字变得容易而有趣。在实际教学中，我们紧紧抓住汉字造字法，让学生通过汉字的结构规律和语境感悟字形、字义，容易使学生自然地联想到自己的生活经历，在开启智慧大门的同时，也拓展了思维，产生了共鸣，不知不觉地去探索汉字的结构，还汉字表形、表意之原始形式。

2. 内容结构

　　第一课简明地介绍汉字的基础知识：汉字的基本笔画，汉字笔画的书写顺序，汉字的演变，汉字的造字法。

　　从第二课到第五课，每一课都从读写基本汉字开始，按照象形字、指事字、会意字和形声字的顺序进行讲解。对每一个字的阐述都从书写开始，因为汉字的笔画和书写一向被认为是汉语学习的难点，所以每个字下面都留有田字格，方便读者练习书写。

在对每个字进行全面解读时，按照形体演变的历史顺序排列字体，最多列出八种字体，即甲骨文、金文、篆书、隶书、楷书、行书、繁体字、简化字，使读者对每一个字的形体演变过程一目了然、印象深刻。接下来要指明这个字是象形字、指事字、会意字还是形声字。依照文字的形体演变，对甲骨文、金文或篆书形体进行分析，找出象征意义。如果是象形字或指事字，作为"标准件"备用。如果是会意字或形声字，则注重对汉字的结构和形义的分析，当然也包括发音。有的参照《说文解字》进一步精讲字义，指出造字本义，进而补充说明近引申义及远引申义，同时探求它的本义与近引申义乃至远引申义的关联。这样不仅拓展了词汇范围，而且有助于读者从中看出汉字词义的发展规律。全面解读力求简洁明了、清晰明确、通俗易懂，解读本身也是极好的阅读或研读资料。

针对部分汉字，本书附以插图，通过插图形象地说明文字，生动、逼真、直观，可帮助读者理解与本汉字及关联词汇有关的语境。最后匹配的词汇、短语和锦言妙语更为重要，所选词汇是 HSK 三级或四级必备词汇，短语中的成语能反映生活智慧、脍炙人口、精炼、生动、富有哲理，具有浓厚的文化色彩和历史内涵，是本字的灵魂。锦言妙语耳熟能详、朗朗上口、诙谐幽默、实用性强，还具有声律美、民族和地域特征。本书通过以上方法，尽可能勾勒本字的全貌，使其有模有样、有声有色，好似一个"演员"以一种直透生命本质的表演方式活跃在舞台上。

3. 课时安排

《汉字入门》共讲解了近两百个基本汉字，字与字的语义或多或少相互关联，形成四个主题，各个主题独立成章，又章章相扣，互为基础。学生可在一个学期内完成对本书的学习，总共需要大约 72 课时。如果可用课时较多，教师也可根据学生的接受能力自行增加内容。

4. 教学思想和教学方法

无论学习哪一种语言，其意义都非常重大，学习汉语也不例外。如何在课堂教学中激发学生的学习兴趣，调动学生的主动性呢？注重与学生保持思想交流至关重要。教学材料的选择和编辑，课堂气氛的营造，恰如其分的案例教学，与学生保持积极的互动，鼓励他们在课堂上大胆表达，尽量照顾到每一个学生，根据学生的实际情况调整学习进度和教学内容，循序渐进安排教学内容，这些都是教师基本功的体现。教学是一门艺术，努力激发学生的好奇心，保持吸引力，保证教学顺利进行下去，都需要合理的方法。在教师的耐心传授和支持鼓励下，学生会逐渐培养起学习汉语的能力和信心。

在生活中，培养学生使用汉语的习惯是学好汉语的有效途径。学生还可以结合自己的生活阅历，多交流、多探讨，学习效果自然好。

5. 教学用具

象棋、文房四宝(笔、墨、纸、砚)、折叠纸扇和醒木、竹简、木制积木、弹弓、竹制弓箭、凸凹透镜、茶及茶具、瓷器、20 元人民币(背面图案为桂林山水)、稻穗、谷穗、铃铛、圆规、木制曲尺、习字田字格、橡皮、铅笔、钢笔、圆珠笔、便利贴、写字板、识字卡、新华字典、石臼等。

本书在写作过程中，曾得到王晟伟、李伟权、马可欣、刘永安、任福洪几位教师的指导和关怀，又承蒙美籍英语教师杰西卡·沃恩、科德尔·唐纳德、艾伦·达戈、爱华和贝宁籍汉学学者卡宗的审阅，他们提出了很多宝贵意见，王毅老师为本书题写书名，在此一并表示感谢！

本书部分词语、习语及翻译引自曹亚民主编的《汉英大辞海》(中国中医药出版社，2002 年)，在此表示诚挚的感谢！

本书部分插图由李笑来绘制创作，部分图片来自网络，出版时未能找到相关版权人，请相关版权人看到本书及时与作者本人联系，在此表示感谢！

清华大学出版社施猛老师对本书的出版给予了热情的支持、付出了艰辛的努力，在此表示衷心的感谢！

由于本人学识水平有限，本书难免存在疏漏，敬请海内外学者及读者不吝赐教，慷慨批评指正，以便对本书做进一步的修改。

反馈邮箱：wkservice@vip.163.com。

作者

2022 年 7 月

[目录]

第一课　汉字的基本知识
LESSON 1　The Basic Knowledge in Learning Chinese Characters

一、汉字的基本笔画……………… 002
二、汉字笔画的书写顺序………… 002
三、汉字的演变…………………… 003
甲骨文 …………………………… 004
金文 ……………………………… 005
篆书 ……………………………… 006
隶书 ……………………………… 007
楷书 ……………………………… 008
行书 ……………………………… 008
草书 ……………………………… 009
四、汉字的造字法………………… 009
象形字 …………………………… 010
指事字 …………………………… 010
会意字 …………………………… 010
形声字 …………………………… 011

第二课　自然崇拜
LESSON 2　Nature Worship

一、读写基本汉字………………… 014
象形字 …………………………… 014
　象 ……………………………… 014
　日 ……………………………… 015
　月 ……………………………… 016
　人 ……………………………… 017
　大 ……………………………… 018
　田 ……………………………… 019
　王 ……………………………… 020
　小 ……………………………… 022
　雨 ……………………………… 023
　云 ……………………………… 024
　力 ……………………………… 025
　气 ……………………………… 027
　乞 ……………………………… 028
　电 ……………………………… 029
　申 ……………………………… 030
　山 ……………………………… 031

| 石 | ………………………………… | 032 |
| 玉 | ………………………………… | 034 |

指事字………………………………… 035
元	…………………………………	035
旦	…………………………………	036
夕	…………………………………	037
太	…………………………………	038

会意字………………………………… 039
早	…………………………………	039
天	…………………………………	040
明	…………………………………	041
晶	…………………………………	042
名	…………………………………	043
从	…………………………………	045
众	…………………………………	046
佃	…………………………………	047
男	…………………………………	047
夯	…………………………………	049
尖	…………………………………	049
少	…………………………………	050
劣	…………………………………	052
因	…………………………………	052
囚	…………………………………	054
困	…………………………………	054
雷	…………………………………	055
动	…………………………………	057
岩	…………………………………	058
危	…………………………………	059

形声字………………………………… 060
像	…………………………………	060
星	…………………………………	061
时	…………………………………	062
雪	…………………………………	063

汽	…………………………………	065
吃	…………………………………	065
伸	…………………………………	067

二、注解………………………………… 068
三、反义词……………………………… 070
四、汉字的偏旁部首…………………… 071
五、HSK 试题选做 …………………… 075
六、朗读与书写练习…………………… 076

第三课 五行
LESSON 3　The Five Elements

一、读写基本汉字……………………… 080
象形字………………………………… 080
火	…………………………………	080
白	…………………………………	081
木	…………………………………	083
禾	…………………………………	084
土	…………………………………	085
水	…………………………………	086
泉	…………………………………	088
川	…………………………………	089
州	…………………………………	091
鱼	…………………………………	092
网	…………………………………	093

指事字………………………………… 094
一	…………………………………	094
二	…………………………………	095
三	…………………………………	096
四	…………………………………	097
百	…………………………………	098
中	…………………………………	100
本	…………………………………	101
末	…………………………………	102

片	103	霾	138

会意字 ········· 105
   伙 ········· 105
   炎 ········· 106
   灭 ········· 107
   灶 ········· 108
   黑 ········· 109
   墨 ········· 111
   树 ········· 112
   林 ········· 113
   森 ········· 114
   焚 ········· 115
   东 ········· 116
   休 ········· 117
   体 ········· 118
   尘 ········· 119
   坐 ········· 120
   里 ········· 122
   埋 ········· 123
   金 ········· 124
   泵 ········· 125
   渔 ········· 126
   鲁 ········· 127
   仁 ········· 128
   原 ········· 130

形声字 ········· 131
   橡 ········· 131
   柏 ········· 132
   坦 ········· 132
   坛 ········· 133
   地 ········· 134
   城 ········· 136
   冲 ········· 137

二、注解 ········· 139
三、反义词 ········· 142
四、汉字的偏旁部首 ········· 143
五、HSK 试题选做 ········· 152
六、朗读与书写练习 ········· 153

第四课　目见耳闻
LESSON 4　What Is Seen and Heard

一、读写基本汉字 ········· 156

象形字 ········· 156
   口 ········· 156
   舌 ········· 157
   牙 ········· 158
   齿 ········· 159
   目 ········· 160
   眉 ········· 161
   自 ········· 162
   耳 ········· 164
   面 ········· 165
   首 ········· 167
   心 ········· 168
   页 ········· 169
   须 ········· 170
   而 ········· 171
   长 ········· 172
   欠 ········· 174

指事字 ········· 175
   甘 ········· 175
   旦 ········· 176
   十 ········· 177
   廿 ········· 178
   旬 ········· 179

上 ·················· 180
　　下 ·················· 181
　会意字 ················ 182
　　品 ·················· 182
　　吞 ·················· 183
　　古 ·················· 184
　　合 ·················· 185
　　甜 ·················· 187
　　见 ·················· 188
　　眼 ·················· 189
　　泪 ·················· 190
　　相 ·················· 191
　　冒 ·················· 193
　　咱 ·················· 194
　　息 ·················· 194
　　臭 ·················· 195
　　闻 ·················· 197
　　奄 ·················· 198
　　志 ·················· 199
　　忑 ·················· 199
　　卡 ·················· 200
　　烦 ·················· 201
　　嚣 ·················· 202
　　吹 ·················· 203
　形声字 ················ 204
　　睛 ·················· 204
　　想 ·················· 205
　　念 ·················· 207
　　聪 ·················· 208
　　闷 ·················· 209
二、注解 ················ 210
三、反义词 ·············· 212
四、汉字的偏旁部首 ······ 213

五、HSK试题选做 ········ 218
六、朗读与书写练习 ······ 220

第五课　母子情深
LESSON 5　Great Affection between Mother and Son

一、读写基本汉字 ········ 224
　象形字 ················ 224
　　母 ·················· 224
　　每 ·················· 225
　　女 ·················· 226
　　丫 ·················· 227
　　儿 ·················· 228
　　子 ·················· 230
　　夫 ·················· 231
　　父 ·················· 233
　　巳 ·················· 234
　　厶 ·················· 235
　　身 ·················· 236
　　幺 ·················· 237
　　囟 ·················· 237
　　凹 ·················· 238
　　凸 ·················· 239
　指事字 ················ 240
　　八 ·················· 240
　　要 ·················· 241
　　呆 ·················· 243
　会意字 ················ 244
　　好 ·················· 244
　　孬 ·················· 245
　　姓 ·················· 246
　　妇 ·················· 247
　　幼 ·················· 248

保	249	雹	263
孕	250	饱	264
育	251	份	265
包	252	扒	266
规	253	吩	267
兄	255	二、注解	268
公	256	三、反义词	270
分	258	四、汉字的偏旁部首	270
脑	259	五、HSK试题选做	272
形声字	261	六、朗读与书写练习	274
奶	261	**后记**	277
私	262		

第一课
LESSON 1

汉字的基本知识
The Basic Knowledge in Learning Chinese Characters

一、汉字的基本笔画 The Basic Strokes of Chinese Characters

一般来说,我们把横(一)、竖(丨)、撇(丿)、捺(㇏)、点(丶)、提(㇀)这六种笔画称为汉字的基本笔画,其他笔画都是由这六种笔画演变而来的,也称为派生笔画。六种基本笔画 (six basic strokes of Chinese characters) 如表1-1所示。

表1-1 六种基本笔画

序号	笔画	笔画名称	例字
1	一	横 (héng)	一、二、三、土、王
2	丨	竖 (shù)	十、山、中、串、工、木、个
3	丿	撇 (piě)	白、八、太、乞、鸟、毛、手、力
4	㇏	捺 (nà)	人、入、大、八
5	丶	点 (diǎn)	亩、门、主、广、六、这
6	㇀	提 (tí)	我、北、打、地、河、冰、习

二、汉字笔画的书写顺序 The Order of Strokes for Writing Chinese Characters

汉字笔画的书写顺序,即笔顺。先写什么,后写什么,应遵循一定的笔顺规则。只有按照合理的笔顺来写汉字,才能写得漂亮,才能提高书写速度。七项笔顺基本书写规则 (seven basic rules of writing order of strokes) 如表1-2所示。

表1-2 七项笔顺基本书写规则

一般规则	例字	书写顺序
先横后竖	十	横、竖
	丰	横、横、横、竖
先撇后捺	人	撇、捺
	八	撇、捺
从上到下	三	横、横、横
	李	横、竖、撇、捺、横撇、竖钩、横
从左到右	川	撇、竖、竖
	树	横、竖、撇、点、横撇、点、横、竖钩、点
先外后里	问	点、竖、横折钩、竖、横折、横
	用	撇、横折钩、横、横、竖

（续表）

一般规则	例字	书写顺序
先进"人"后关门	田	竖、横折、横、竖、横
	国	竖、横折、横、横、竖、横、点、横
先中间后两边	小	竖钩、撇、点
	水	竖钩、横撇、撇、捺

补充规则

1. 关于"点"

(1) 点在上、左上，应先写，如"户、主、头、六、亥、宀"等。

(2) 点在内、右上，应后写，如"叉、瓦、试、犬、发、我"等。

2. 关于两面包围结构的字的书写顺序

(1) 上左、上右包围结构，先外后里，如"左、右、有、石、旬、司、氧、岛、枭"等。

(2) 左下包围结构，先里后外，如"辶"字旁的"远、辽、过、这、边"等。

3. 关于三包围结构的字的书写顺序

(1) 缺口向上，先里后外，如"山、画、齿"等。

(2) 缺口向下，先外后里，如"内、凤、网、同、周"等。

(3) 缺口向右，先上后里再左下，如"区、医、巨、匠、匪"等。

三、汉字的演变　Evolution of Chinese Characters

中华文明源远流长，汉字是记录中华民族文明的重要工具，已沿用近六千年。汉字是世界上最古老的文字之一，是由图画发展而成的表意文字。中国人熟悉的仓(cāng)颉(jié)造字说法广为流传，相传仓颉是黄帝时期的造字史官，有"双瞳四目"，法力无边，是个不食人间烟火的"神人"。

仓(cāng)颉(jié)

然而，考古学家通过深入研究，越来越相信汉字是劳动人民的伟大创造。汉字从无到有，从少到多，每个字都闪烁着智慧的光芒。据考证，在新石器时代，中国人就开始使用汉字了，现代汉字是从甲骨文（刻在龟甲和兽骨上的卜辞）、金文演变而来的。《康熙字典》（公元1716年）收录的汉字有四万多个，通用的汉字大约有八千个。（《辞海》）

从古到今，汉字一直影响着亚洲其他国家的文字，如日本、韩国、越南等。

汉字的演变可划分为古文字阶段和今文字阶段。隶书对古文字形体进行了重大变革，因而成了古今文字的分界线。隶书以前是古文字阶段，主要包括甲骨文、金文、篆书；隶书以后是今文字阶段，主要包括隶书、楷书、草书和行书。

甲骨文
Oracle Bones

甲骨文是指商周时代（商，公元前1600年—公元前1046年；周，公元前1046年—公元前256年）刻在或者书写在龟甲和兽骨上的文字，也称"卜辞"。甲骨文最初出土于河南安阳附近的小屯村的殷墟。考古证明，殷墟正是商王朝最后的都城，因此，商王朝也称殷商王朝。

卜 (bǔ) 骨 (gǔ) 刻 (kè) 辞 (cí)

在殷商王朝，人们非常崇拜神，笃 (dǔ) 信 (xìn) 占 (zhān) 卜 (bǔ)。占卜者会将占卜的问题刻写在乌龟壳或牛羊骨头上，向神灵问询天气、家庭成员的命运、田猎、征战等方面的问题，然后将这些乌龟壳或牛羊骨头放在金属棒上烘烤，直到有裂纹出现。裂纹就像中国汉字卜、兆的缩影，也许汉字"卜""兆"就是这样得来的。占卜师会根据裂纹解释吉凶祸福，再将释义写在龟甲和兽骨头上。这些文字都是殷商王朝，人们利用龟甲和兽骨占卜吉凶时，写刻的卜辞和与占卜有关的记事文字。

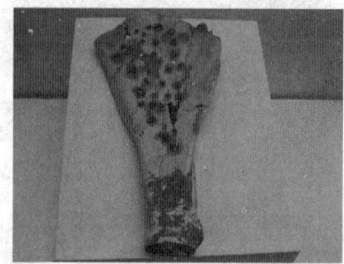

卜骨，新石器时代，龙山文化（公元前2500年—公元前1900年）
Oracle bone, Neolithic, Longshan Culture (2500 BC-1900 BC)

有趣的是，这些距离现在已有三千多年甚至更长历史的古文字，到了1899年才被清朝末年的王(wáng)懿(yì)荣(róng)发现。王懿荣是翰林院大臣，又是个青铜器收藏家，对于古文字很有研究。有一天，他得了疟疾，有个朋友帮他抓了不少中草药材，其中一味药是龙骨。王懿荣不经意间发现龙骨上有许多规律的符号。这些符号与古代文字有着千丝万缕的联系。于是，他买下所有龙骨，并对这些龙骨反复推敲、拼合、整理。依据深厚的金石功底，他了解到这些龙骨是龟甲和兽骨。又经过考订，他确认这些甲骨上所刻的符号是我们祖先创造的古老文字。王懿荣因此被公认为甲骨文的最早发现者。

王(wáng)懿(yì)荣(róng)
(1845—1900)
Wang Yirong, Chinese politician and scholar, was
the first to recognize the oracle bones
as ancient writing in 1899.

迄今为止，已挖掘出带有文字的甲骨十六万至十七万片，已发现的甲骨文单字约有三千五百个，已经考释认识的约有两千个，其中有大批的形声字。可以说，甲骨文是最古老而又成系统的汉字。

同时，这一发现有力地证明了商王朝的真实存在。此外，一些也许当时没及时雕刻的用毛笔书写的甲骨文也足以证明毛笔在当时普遍被使用。(《百科全书》)

金文 Bronze Script

金文是中国古代铸或刻在商周时期青铜器上的文字。古人称铜为"吉金"，所以称铜器上的文字为金文。青铜器以钟和鼎较为著名，因此金文又称钟鼎文。商代金文的字体和甲骨文相近，被看作甲骨文的进一步发展，但字数较少。周武王灭商纣王后，建立周朝。周朝分西周和东周。西周的金文数量大，艺术水准高，是历史上金文的鼎盛时期。西周第十二个帝王宣王靖时的《毛公鼎》有499个字，大多记载了祭祀、征伐、契约等相关的事情，其史料价值很高。至今发现的不重复的金文单字约有三千个，其中近两千字已经被考释出来。

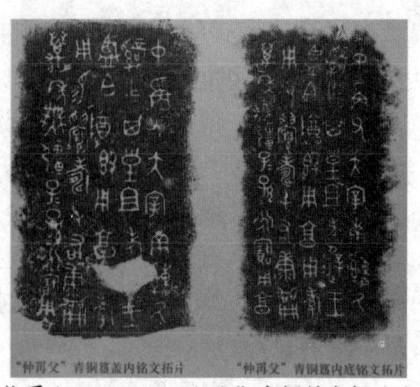

"仲爯(chèn、chēng)父"青铜铭文拓(tà)片

金文书法富有浓郁的地域色彩：南方以楚系文字为代表，影响遍及汉淮两岸及长江中下游地区，字形工整修长，线条宛转灵动；东方以齐国文字为代表，影响波及齐鲁大地，其字体秀丽，线条挺拔遒劲；西方则以秦国文字为代表，影响力随着秦国领土的扩张而逐渐远播四方，其字体开张宽博，线条浑厚苍雄。金文铭辞字体于战国末年逐渐接近小篆字形。

金文书法
Jinwen calligraphy

篆 书
Seal Script

郭沫若认为，篆书其实就是"官书"。篆书可分为大篆和小篆，大篆的真迹就是"石鼓文"，与小篆接近，小篆也叫"秦篆"。秦始皇(公元前259年—公元前210年)统一中国后(公元前221年)，采取宰相李斯(公元前284年—公元前208年)的建议，废除异体，而创秦篆，统一了全国的文字，对汉字的规范化起了很大作用。小篆一直在中国流行到西汉末年(约公元8年)，才逐渐被隶书所取代。

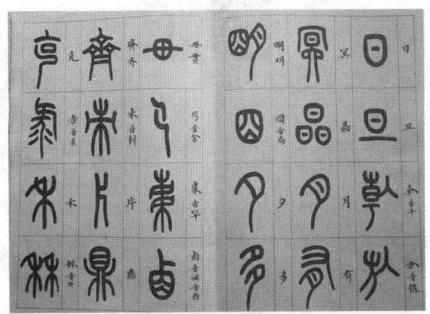

篆体书法
Seal character calligraphy

现在人们刻制印章时,依然热衷于采用篆书或金文。

隶书
Official Script

隶书始于战国时代(公元前475年—公元前221年),在秦朝得以发展,普遍使用于汉朝,所以隶书也称为"汉隶"。隶书是由篆书简化演变而成的,在结构上,改象形字为笔画字,以便书写,可使书写速度更快。如果把汉字的形体分为古今两大类,隶书以前称为"古",隶书开始而后则称为"今",所以说隶书是古今汉字的分水岭。隶书奠定了楷书基础,是汉字发展史上的一大进步、一个转折点,它使中国的书法艺术进入一个新境界。

隶书《西岳华山庙碑》(部分)
Official script, Huashan Mountain temple monument

楷书
Regular Script

  楷书也叫正书，由隶书逐渐演变而来，更趋简化，字形由扁改方，笔画中简省了汉隶的波势，下笔时藏锋，收笔时用回锋，起笔或略顿，收笔宜顿笔或提笔，横平竖直，方方正正，工工整整。《辞海》解释，因其笔画平直、形体方正、严谨端正，可作楷模，故名楷书。它始于汉末，魏晋以后大为流行，通行至今，长盛不衰。如今，楷书仍是现代汉字手写体的参考标准，也发展出另一种手写体——钢笔字。

自书告身帖（传为颜真卿墨迹）
Own Writing(Yan Zhenqing's ink)

行书
Semi-cursive Script

  行书，也叫行楷，相传是在后汉末年所创。它在楷书的基础上产生，是介于楷书、草书之间的一种字体。它的出现，弥补了楷书书写速度太慢和草书难以辨认的不足。"行"是"行走"的意思，它不像草书那样潦草，也不像楷书那样端正。实际上，它是楷书的草化或草书的楷化。

  晋朝书圣王羲之（公元303—361年）将行书的实用性和艺术性完美地结合起来，并把行书推到了相当成熟的高度。

王羲之《兰亭序》（部分）
Wang Xizhi, Lan Ting Xu

草书
Cursive Script

草书是书写便捷、便于速记的一种字体,始于汉初,当时通行的是草隶,即"草率的隶书",其存字之梗概,运笔放纵,字迹潦草,有草创之意,故称草书。后来逐渐发展,形成一种具有艺术价值的"章草"。草书往往上下字之间的笔画牵连相通,末笔与起笔相呼应,通篇神采飞扬,彰显个性,但不太熟悉的人有时不易辨认。

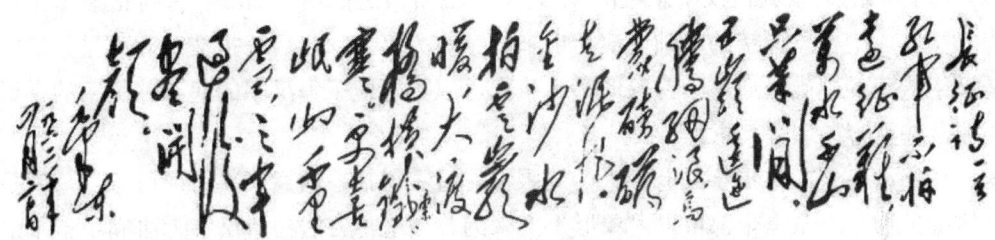

毛泽东《七律·长征》
Chairman Mao, Qilu Long March

四、汉字的造字法 The Formation of Chinese Characters

六书是汉代对汉字进行分析而归纳出来的系统。"六书"在东汉(公元25—220年)许慎编著的《说文解字》中被系统地阐述。《说文解字》,简称《说文》,是中国最早的系统分析汉字字形和考究字源的语文辞书,也是世界上最早的字典之一。它开创了部首检字的先河,后世的字典大多采用这个方式。《说文解字》为我们保存了上古丰富的文字资料,保存了汉字的形、音、义,是研究甲骨文、金文不可缺少的重要工具书,特别是《说文解字》对字义的解释保存了最古的含义,对我们理解古书的词义更有帮助。总而言之,《说文解字》是科学文字学和文献语言学的奠基之作,在中国语言学史上有极其重要的地位。

"六书"即象形、指事、会意、形声、转注、假借。现在人们通常认为转注和假借不是造字法,而是用字法。在汉字的造字法中,形声用得最多,大量汉字就是通过形声法造出来的,形声字的数量约占汉字总数的90%。

象形字
Pictographic Characters

　　文字是人们根据实际生活的需要，经过长期的社会实践慢慢丰富和发展起来的。象形字也叫表意文字，是汉字形体构造的基础，来自图画文字。象形是把客观事物的形体描绘出来的一种造字方法，如自然现象、人、动物或植物、生产工具和生活用具等。它是一种最早出现的造字方法，有时只勾画客观事物的大体特征，它也只能表示具体事物，都是名词。这些文字是按照实物的形状描绘出来的，所以称为"象形字"。

　　象形字的数量约占汉字总数的 4%，但它的价值之高不言而喻。古时把象形字称为"文"，把在象形字的基础上演化出来的字称为"字"，后统指文字，可见象形字是汉字造字的基础。通过学习象形字，我们可以更好地了解汉字的起源、汉字的字形构造，并更容易理解其意思。

　　然而，古老的象形字具有很大的局限性。且不说抽象的意义"无形可象"，就是具体的事物，也不是全都可以"象形"出来的。用这种方法构造汉字无法满足记录语言的需要，于是指事字和会意字应运而生。

指事字
Self-explanatory Characters

　　指事字是指用特征性符号组合成字表示某种意思，或加注指事符号在象形字的某个部位。这种造字法便于记忆，也能表达象形字表达不了的抽象意思。例如，上 (shàng)、下 (xià)、刃 (rèn)、本 (běn)、末 (mò)、八 (bā)、兀 (wū 或 wù)，等等。

　　"上"字，在甲骨文中将表示"天"的北端写得较短，表示朝天的方向；"下"字，在甲骨文中将表示"地"的南端写得较短，表示朝地的方向。

　　"刃"字是指事字，在甲骨文中，在象形字"刀"的刃口加上一个点，指出这里是刀刃，表示刀口所在的位置。这一个点就是指示符号，因而构成了"刃"字。

　　"本"和"末"的含义正好相反，"木"的根部所在之处为"本"，"木"的树梢所在之处为"末"。成语"舍本逐末"就是指做事不从根本上着手而在细枝末节上费功夫。

　　汉字里指事字比象形字还少，《说文解字》中，指事字只有 125 个，常用的有 50 个左右。

会意字
Associative Compound Characters

　　会意字是把两个或两个以上的象形字或指事字组合起来，通常表示一种新的、抽象的字意。例如，休 (xiū)、好 (hǎo)、東/东 (dōng)、集 (jí)、林 (lín)、字 (zì)、炎 (yán)、闩 (shuān)、息 (xī)，等等。

具体来说，"休"字是由"人"（亻，单立人部）和"木"左右组成，表示一个人靠着一棵树正在休息。

"好"字是由"女"和"子"组合而成，表示一个男人成了家并有了孩子，是一件极好的事情。

"東/东"字是由"木"和"日"组合而成，表示太阳初升之时阳光透过树木照射过来，表明日出东方。

"集"字是由表示鸟的"隹"和"木"上下组合而成，表示树上有很多只鸟。

《说文解字》中收会意字1167个。会意字大致分为以下两类。

(1) 两个象形字或指事字重复组合，多是左右并列结构，或者三字重叠，呈塔形的上下结构。例如，从 (cóng)、众 (zhòng)、林 (lín)、森 (sēn)、炎 (yán)，等等。

(2) 图形式会意，一般由两个或两个以上的象形字或指事字构成。例如，家 (jiā)、坐 (zuò)、安 (ān)、开 (kāi)、灭 (miè)、明 (míng)、公 (gōng)、尖 (jiān)、甜 (tián)、看 (kàn)、采 (cǎi)，等等。

形声字
Phono-semantic Compound Characters

形声字是在象形字、指事字和会意字的基础上形成的。在《康熙字典》中，形声字的数量占汉字总量的90%左右，它由表示意义的形旁和表示声音的声旁组合而成。形声字早在甲骨文中就已被广泛应用，是最多产的造字方式。形旁一般由象形字或指事字担任，声旁可以由象形字、指事字和会意字充当。

形声字的形旁表意，声旁表声，左右结构居多。例如，熄 (xī)，"火"字为形旁，表示与火有关；"息" (xī) 为声旁，熄发"息"的声音。嫁 (jià)，"女"字为形旁，表示与女人有关；"家" (jiā) 为声旁，嫁 (jià) 的发音与家 (jiā) 相似。形声字有时为上下结构，如简 (jiǎn)、雹 (báo)、想 (xiǎng)。

我国对汉字进行改革后，采用汉字简化方案，使书写变得简单。1986年重新发布的《简化字总表》实收2274个简化字。如今中国大陆通行的简化汉字已经成为中国人生活的一部分，而中国的香港、澳门、台湾地区仍旧沿用繁体字。古今汉字虽然形体不同，却一脉相承，都是具有象形意味的表意文字。

第二课
LESSON 2

自然崇拜
Nature Worship

天下难事，必作于易；天下大事，必作于细。
——老子

Solve a difficult problem by attacking its weakest link; Do a great deed by attending to minor details.
— Lao Zi

一、读写基本汉字 Read and Write Basic Chinese Characters

象形字
Pictographic Characters

象 xiàng (elephant) 　【部首】豕　【笔画】十一画

ノ ⌒ 丨 フ ー ノ) ノ ノ ㇏
撇、横撇/横钩、竖、横折、横、撇、弯钩、撇、撇、撇、捺

甲骨文	金文	篆书	隶书	楷书	行书	简化字
Oracle Bones	Bronze Script	Seal Script	Official Script	Regular Script	Semi-cursive Script	Simplified Character

"象"是象形字。"象"的甲骨文写作 、，金文写作 、，形似一头长着大鼻(bí)子的大象。大耳、长鼻、长牙是象的突出特征。象是陆地上现存最大的动物，主要生活在非洲和亚洲。"象"本义指长鼻子大象，也指象牙。

想象力是介于感性和知性之间的先天能力，是人在已有形象或图案的基础上，在头脑中创造出新形象的能力，由此"象"引(yǐn)申(shēn)为相似(sì)、类似、如同之义，指仿(fǎng)效(xiào)，象形，经过演变，也指代现象、形象、气象、象征、印象。

象 (xiàng)

词或短语 Words & Phrases

大象	dàxiàng	elephant
象形字	xiàngxíngzì	pictographic character
想象力	xiǎngxiànglì	imaginative power; imagination
象棋	xiàngqí	Chinese chess

LESSON 2 Nature Worship • 第二课 自然崇拜

锦言妙语 Proverbs & Witticism

春回大地，万象更新 chūn huí dàdì, wànxiànggēngxīn
Spring comes round to the earth again and everything looks fresh and joyful.

大象走路——稳重 dà xiàng zǒu lù——wěnzhòng
An elephant walks steadily.

日	rì (the sun)	【部首】日　【笔画】四画
	丨 𠃍 一 一 竖、横折、横、横	

甲骨文	金文	篆书	隶书	楷书	行书	简化字
☉ ⊖	⊖	⊖	日	日	日	日
Oracle Bones	Bronze Script	Seal Script	Official Script	Regular Script	Semi-cursive Script	Simplified Character

"日"是象形字。"日"的古文字形似太(tài)阳(yáng)。"日"本义指太阳。因为有太阳的时候是白天，所以"日"引申指白天，又引申指地球自转一周的时间，即一昼(zhòu)夜(yè)，相当于24小时。太阳是地球上最重要的生命能量来源。

太(tài)阳(yáng)

词或短语 Words & Phrases

节日	jiérì	festival; holiday
生日礼物	shēngrì lǐwù	birthday gift
日记	rìjì	diary
日期	rìqī	date

- 015 -

锦言妙语 Proverbs & Witticism

日久见人心 rì jiǔ jiàn rén xīn
A long task proves the sincerity of a person. || It takes time to know a person.

日有所思，夜有所梦 rì yǒu suǒ sī, yè yǒu suǒ mèng
You will dream of at night what you think about in the day.

不争一日之短长 bù zhēng yí rì zhī duǎn cháng
Don't strive for only temporary superiority.

月	yuè (the moon)	【部首】月　【笔画】四画
	ノ 乛 一 一 撇、横折钩、横、横	

甲骨文	金文	篆书	隶书	楷书	行书	简化字
Oracle Bones	Bronze Script	Seal Script	Official Script	Regular Script	Semi-cursive Script	Simplified Character

"月"是象形字。"月"的古文字形似半月。"月"本义指月(yuè)亮(liang)，引申指月份。

月(yuè)亮(liang)

词或短语 Words & Phrases

月亮	yuèliang	the moon
一年分十二个月	yì nián fēn shí èr gè yuè	One year is divided into twelve months.
日积月累	rìjī-yuèlěi	accumulate day by day and month by month

锦言妙语 Proverbs & Witticism

月是故乡明 yuè shì gùxiāng míng
The moon over the home village is brighter.

月有阴晴圆缺 yuè yǒu yīn qíng yuán quē
The moon may be dim, bright, full, or wane.

近水楼台先得月 jìnshuǐlóutái xiān dé yuè
A waterside tower gets the moonlight first. ‖ Those on the waterfront are the first to enjoy the rising moon — a person in a favorable position gains special advantages.

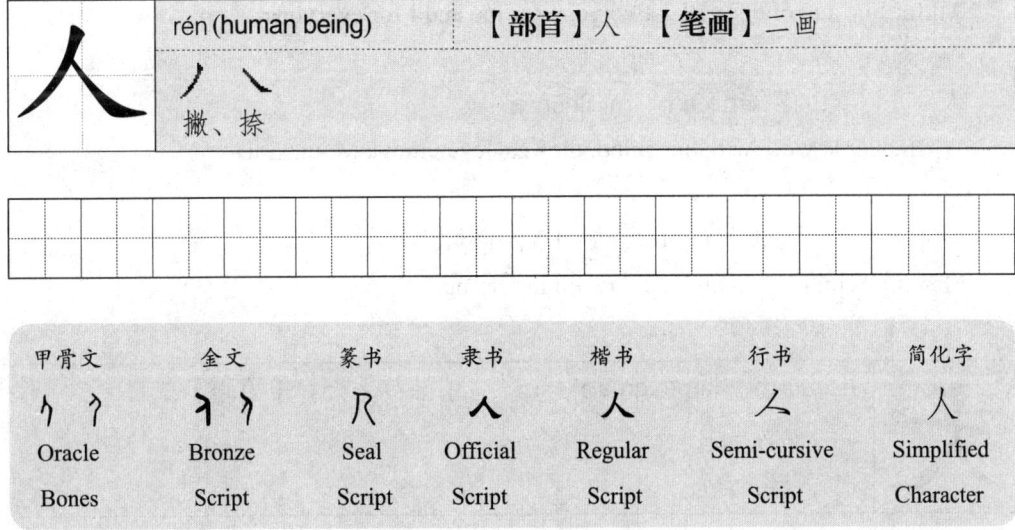

"人"是象形字。甲骨文的"人"写作 ⺅ ⺅，金文的"人"写作 ⺅ ⺅，皆形似一个侧向站立的人，两只手还向前下方伸出，好像在劳作。《说文解字》提及："人，天地之性最贵者也。""人"本义指有理性思维，能直立行走，能制(zhì)造(zào)并使用工具进行生产劳动的高等动物。

"人是宇宙的精华，万物的灵长。""人"在古代也指老百姓。现在，"人"也指人的品质、性格、名誉，常见词如人品、人格、丢人。

耕(gēng)田(tián)图(tú)

词或短语 Words & Phrases

人类	rénlèi	human beings
人才	réncái	person with ability
别人	biérén	others
客人	kèrén	guest
人民币	rénmínbì	Renminbi(RMB)
人杰地灵	rénjié-dìlíng	a remarkable place producing outstanding people

锦言妙语 Proverbs & Witticism

人人为我，我为人人 rénrén wèi wǒ, wǒ wèi rénrén
All for one and one for all. ‖ Everyone for me and I for everyone.

人心齐，泰山移 rén xīn qí, Tài Shān yí
When people work with one mind, they can even move Mount Tai.

人凭志气，虎凭威 rén píng zhìqì, hǔ píng wēi
Man relies on his will and the tiger on his strength.

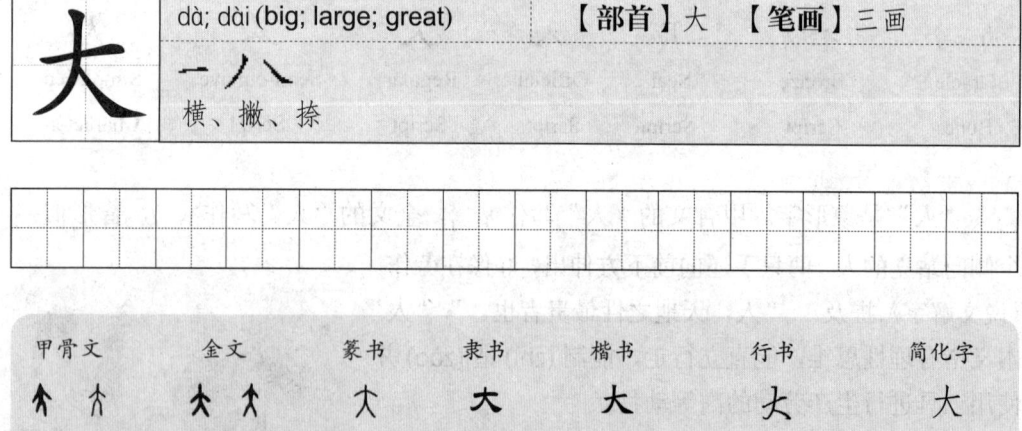

"大"是象形字。古文字的"大"形似一个两手平伸、两脚分开的顶天立地的成 (chéng) 年 (nián) 人，它表示抽象的大。《说文解字》："天大、地大、人亦大。" "大"

本义指"大小"的"大",与"小"相对。

"大"又读 dài,大 (dài) 夫 (fu),是对医生的尊称。

"大"字图示

词或短语 Words & Phrases

大学	dàxué	college; university
大度	dàdù	generous; magnanimous
大吃大喝	dàchī-dàhē	eat and drink extravagantly

锦言妙语 Proverbs & Witticism

大河有水小河满,大河无水小河干 dà hé yǒu shuǐ xiǎo hé mǎn, dà hé wú shuǐ xiǎo hé gān

When the main stream is low, the small streams run dry-individual well-being depends on collective prosperity.

大事化小,小事化了 dà shì huà xiǎo, xiǎo shì huà liǎo

Turn big problems into small ones and small ones into no problems at all.

举大事者必以人为本 jǔ dà shì zhě bì yǐ rén wéi běn

The success of every great enterprise depends upon humanity.

田   tián (field; farmland; cropland)   【部首】田   【笔画】五画

丨 フ 一 丨 一
竖、横折、横、竖、横

甲骨文	金文	篆书	隶书	楷书	行书	简化字
田 毌 田	田	田	田	田	田	田
Oracle Bones	Bronze Script	Seal Script	Official Script	Regular Script	Semi-cursive Script	Simplified Character

"田"是象形字。甲骨文中的"田"写作田、毌、田，形似一片阡 (qiān) 陌 (mò) 纵 (zòng) 横 (héng) 的田地，例如水稻田。"囗"(wéi) 像田地的四周边界，里面的"十"像通往四面八方的田埂。"田"本义指已 (yǐ) 经 (jīng) 耕种的土地。

水 (shuǐ) 稻 (dào) 田 (tián)

词或短语　Words & Phrases

田地	tiándì	field; farmland
水稻田	shuǐdào tián	a rice field
农田	nóngtián	farmland; cultivated land
田园荒芜	tiányuán huāngwú	fields and gardens turn to a jungle

锦言妙语　Proverbs & Witticism

崽卖爷田心不痛　zǎi mài yé tián xīn bú tòng

A prodigal son squanders the family fortune recklessly.

王	wáng (king)　　【部首】王　【笔画】四画
	一 一 丨 一
	横、横、竖、横

甲骨文	金文	篆书	隶书	楷书	行书	简化字
Oracle Bones	Bronze Script	Seal Script	Official Script	Regular Script	Semi-cursive Script	Simplified Character

"王"是象形字。金文的"王"写作王、王、王，形似刃部朝下的斧(fǔ)钺(yuè)。斧钺象征实力和权威，在中国古代，使用特大战斧的将帅叫"王"。秦汉以后，封爵的最高一级为王。

有人说，三横(héng)画(huà)分别代表天、地、人，而能够参(cān)悟、贯通这三者的人，就是王。孔子也说"能以一贯三者为'王'"。

在中国百家姓中，王姓较为常见。

斧(fǔ)

词或短语 Words & Phrases

国王　　　　　guówáng　　　　　king

秦(qín)始(shǐ)皇(huáng)
（公元前259年—公元前210年）

王位　　　　　wángwèi　　　　　throne; crown
王法无情　　　wángfǎwúqíng　　　The law knows no mercy.

锦言妙语 Proverbs & Witticism

王婆卖瓜，自卖自夸 Wáng Pó mài guā, zì mài zì kuā
All his geese are swans.

王者以民为天，而民以食为天 wángzhě yǐ mín wéi tiān, ér mín yǐ shí wéi tiān
The king considers the people as his heaven, and the people consider food as their heaven.

成者为王，败者为寇 chéngzhě wéi wáng, bàizhě wéi kòu
He who succeeds becomes the king, and he who fails becomes an outlaw.

小	xiǎo (small; little; tiny)	【部首】小　【笔画】三画
	↓ 丿 丶 竖钩、撇、点	

甲骨文	金文	篆书	隶书	楷书	行书	简化字
Oracle Bones	Bronze Script	Seal Script	Official Script	Regular Script	Semi-cursive Script	Simplified Character

"小"是象形字。甲骨文的"小"写作 ⺌、川，金文的"小"写作 小、ハ，都是由三个像沙(shā)粒(lì)那么大的小点组成的，用以表示物体之小。"小"本义为细(xì)碎(suì)的尘沙微粒。

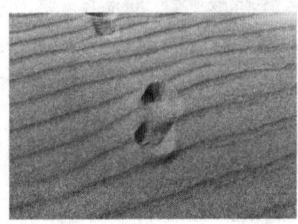

沙(shā)漠(mò)

词或短语　Words & Phrases

小米　　　　xiǎomǐ　　　　　　millet

小(xiǎo)米(mǐ)

小费　　　　xiǎofèi　　　　　　beer-money; tip
小吃街　　　xiǎochījiē　　　　　snack street

小心眼儿	xiǎo xīnyǎnr	petty minds; narrow-minded
小题大做	xiǎotí-dàzuò	make a fuss over a trifle; a storm in a teacup

锦言妙语　Proverbs & Witticism

小不忍则乱大谋　xiǎo bù rěn zé luàn dà móu
A little impatience spoils great plans.

大处着眼，小处入手　dà chù zhuó yǎn, xiǎo chù rù shǒu
Keep the general goal in view and set one's hand to specific jobs.

大事做不来，小事又不做　dà shì zuò bù lái, xiǎo shì yòu bú zuò
Be incapable of doing great things, yet disdain minor tasks.

雨　yǔ (rain)　【部首】雨　【笔画】八画

一　丨　㇆　丨　丶　丶　丶　丶
横、竖、横折钩、竖、点、点、点、点

甲骨文	金文	篆书	隶书	楷书	行书	简化字
Oracle Bones	Bronze Script	Seal Script	Official Script	Regular Script	Semi-cursive Script	Simplified Character

"雨"是象形字。甲骨文和金文的"雨"字皆形似从天空降 (jiàng) 落 (luò) 的水滴。"雨"字形顶部的"一"像天，"冂"像云团，水 (shuǐ) 滴 (dī) 零落其间。《说文解字》："雨，水从雲 (云字繁体) 下也。""雨"本义为下雨。

雨 (yǔ)

词或短语　Words & Phrases

下雨	xià yǔ	rain

大雨	dàyǔ	heavy rain
小雨	xiǎoyǔ	small rain
雨过天晴	yǔguò-tiānqíng	After a shower, the sky has cleared.
挥汗如雨	huīhànrúyǔ	be perspiring like rain

锦言妙语　Proverbs & Witticism

一场秋雨一场寒　yì chǎng qiūyǔ yì chǎng hán
After each autumn rain, it becomes colder than before.

好雨知时节，当春乃发生　hǎo yǔ zhī shíjié, dāng chūn nǎi fāshēng
The good rain knows its season. When spring arrives, then it comes.

经风雨，见世面　jīng fēngyǔ, jiàn shìmiàn
Experience wind and rain, and see the ways of the world.

云　yún (cloud)　【部首】厶　【笔画】四画

一 一 厶 丶
横、横、撇折、点

甲骨文	金文	篆书	隶书	楷书	行书	繁体字	简化字
Oracle Bones	Bronze Script	Seal Script	Official Script	Regular Script	Semi-cursive Script	Traditional Character	Simplified Character

甲骨文的"云"写作云、云，金文的"云"写作云，都是象形字，形似天上的云朵回(huí)旋(xuán)转动。空中的小水滴形成云，有云才有雨。篆文加"雨"为"雲"，变成了会意字。"云"是"雲"的本字。《说文解字》："云，山川气也。"简化字的"云"省去了雨字头。"云"本义为云气，即天上的云彩(cǎi)，又用以形容多，如云集。

云 (yún)

词或短语 Words & Phrases

白云 　　　　báiyún 　　　　　　white cloud

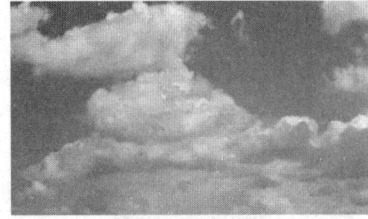

白 (bái) 云 (yún)

乌云 　　　　wūyún 　　　　　　dark cloud

乌 (wū) 云 (yún)

云集 　　　　yúnjí 　　　　　　gather; come together in clouds
云开日出 　　yúnkāi-rìchū 　　　the sun scatters the clouds

锦言妙语 Proverbs & Witticism

拨云雾见青天　bō yúnwù jiàn qīngtiān
Clear the clouds and see the sky.

天有不测风云，人有旦夕祸福　tiān yǒu bú cè fēngyún, rén yǒu dànxī-huòfú
In nature there are unexpected storms and in life unpredictable vicissitudes. ‖ The fortunes of men are as unpredictable as the weather.

云行雨施，天下平也　yúnxíngyǔshī, tiānxià píng yě
Only when the emperor is benevolent to the people can peace prevail.

甲骨文	金文	篆书	隶书	楷书	行书	简化字
丿丶	丿丶	丙丙	力	力	力	力
Oracle Bones	Bronze Script	Seal Script	Official Script	Regular Script	Semi-cursive Script	Simplified Character

"力"是象形字。甲骨文的"力"写作丿丶，形似强壮的手臂，也像中国古代耕(gēng)地用的农具耒(丿、丙)(lěi)。"力"本义指耒，耕田需要用力，由此引申指力量、力气。

耕(gēng) 田(tián) 图(tú)

词或短语 Words & Phrases

力气	lìqi	physical strength
能力	nénglì	capacity; ability
努力	nǔlì	make great efforts; strive
想象力	xiǎngxiànglì	imaginative power
力大如牛	lìdàrúniú	as strong as a bull
力不从心	lìbùcóngxīn	be unable to do as well as one would wish
力挽狂澜	lìwǎnkuánglán	to do one's utmost to save a desperate situation

锦言妙语 Proverbs & Witticism

心有余而力不足 xīn yǒu yú ér lì bù zú
Be more than willing, but lacking in strength. ‖ The mind is willing, but the body is weak.

争取更大的胜利 zhēngqǔ gèng dà de shènglì
To struggle hard for a still greater victory.

LESSON 2 Nature Worship • 第二课 自然崇拜

| 气 | qì (air; gas) ノ 一 一 乙 撇、横、横、横折弯钩/横斜钩 | 【部首】气 【笔画】四画 |

甲骨文	金文	篆书	隶书	楷书	行书	繁体字	简化字
Oracle Bones	Bronze Script	Seal Script	Official Script	Regular Script	Semi-cursive Script	Traditional Character	Simplified Character

"气"是象形字。甲骨文的"气"写作三，形似天上云气飘(piāo)浮(fú)，三条长短不一的横线与"三"相似，代表天地之间的气流。"气"本义指云气，即一切流动的气体。《说文解字》："气，云气也。"今"氣"简化为"气"。

雾(wù) 气(qì)

词或短语 Words & Phrases

天气	tiānqì	weather
空气	kōngqì	air
气候	qìhòu	climate; weather
气味	qìwèi	smell; flavour
生气	shēngqì	be angry; be annoyed
骨气	gǔqì	moral integrity; backbone
谢谢	xièxie	Thank you!
不客气	bú kèqi	Not at all. ‖ Don't mention it.
气急败坏	qìjíbàihuài	utterly discomfited

锦言妙语 Proverbs & Witticism

气可鼓不可泄 qì kě gǔ bù kě xiè
Morale should be boosted, not dampened.

靠运气不如靠勇气 kào yùnqì bù rú kào yǒngqì
It is better to trust to valour than to luck.

人争一口气，佛争一炷香 rén zhēng yì kǒu qì, fó zhēng yí zhù xiāng
A man needs self-respect, and Buddha needs incense.

乞	qǐ(beg)	【部首】乙 【笔画】三画
	ノ 一 乞	
	撇、横、横折弯钩/横斜钩	

甲骨文	金文	篆书	隶书	楷书	行书	简化字
三	≒	㇉	乞	乞	乞	乞
Oracle Bones	Bronze Script	Seal Script	Official Script	Regular Script	Semi-cursive Script	Simplified Character

"乞"是象形字。"乞"与"气"同源，后分化。甲骨文中的"气"字，本义指云气，还表示乞求的意思。"乞"，甲骨文写作 三，金文写作 ≒，篆书写作 ㇉，隶书写作 乞，将篆书的 ㇉ 减去一横，表示呼吸局(jú)促(cù)，求人气短。"乞"本义指向人求(qiú)讨(tǎo)、乞求、请求。

乞(qǐ)讨(tǎo)

词或短语 Words & Phrases

乞丐	qǐgài	beggar; pauper
乞求	qǐqiú	beg; implore; supplicate
乞讨	qǐtǎo	go begging

LESSON 2　Nature Worship ● 第二课　自然崇拜

锦言妙语　Proverbs & Witticism

族大有乞儿　zú dà yǒu qǐ ér
There may be beggars in any big clans. ‖ There are black sheep in every fold.

乞丐永远不会破产　qǐgài yóngyuǎn bú huì pòchǎn
A beggar can never be bankrupt.

一次做乞丐，永远是乞丐　yí cì zuò qǐgài, yóngyuǎn shì qǐgài
Once a beggar, always a beggar.

电	diàn (electricity; lightning)	【部首】田　【笔画】五画
	丨　フ　一　一　乚	
	竖、横折、横、横、竖弯钩	

甲骨文	金文	篆书	隶书	楷书	行书	繁体字	简化字
Oracle Bones	Bronze Script	Seal Script	Official Script	Regular Script	Semi-cursive Script	Traditional Character	Simplified Character

　　"电"是象形兼会意字。甲骨文的"电"写作 ，形似闪电。金文的"电"写作 ，上部形似下雨，下部形似闪电，表示雨天闪电。闪电是一种自然现象，是在雷雨暴风天气产生的一道道明亮夺目的闪光。今"電"简化为"电"。"电"本义指闪电。现在，"电"多指电力，是物质中存在的一种能。

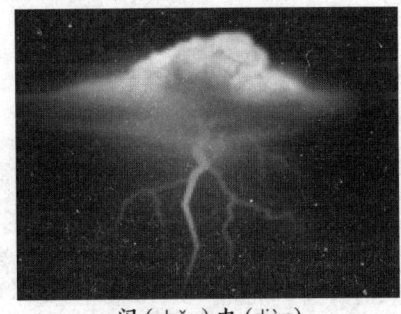

闪 (shǎn) 电 (diàn)

词或短语 Words & Phrases

电话机 diànhuàjī telephone

电 (diàn) 话 (huà) 机 (jī)

电影 diànyǐng movie; film; motion picture

看 (kàn) 电 (diàn) 影 (yǐng)

电视机	diànshìjī	TV set
电灯	diàndēng	electric light
电脑游戏	diànnǎo yóuxì	computer game
电梯	diàntī	elevator; lift
电子邮件	diànzǐ yóujiàn	e-mail
太阳能发电	tàiyángnéng fā diàn	solar electrical energy generation

 shēn (express; clarify)　【部首】田　【笔画】五画

丨 乛 一 一 丨
竖、横折、横、横、竖

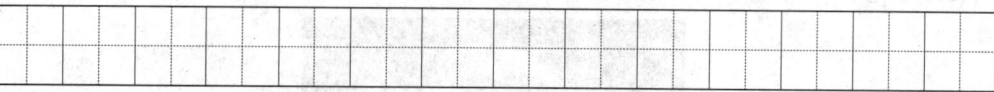

甲骨文	金文	篆书	隶书	楷书	行书	简化字
Oracle Bones	Bronze Script	Seal Script	Official Script	Regular Script	Semi-cursive Script	Simplified Character

闪 (shǎn) 电 (diàn)

"申"在甲骨文和金文中是象形字。甲骨文的"申"写作 ，形似曲 (qū) 折 (zhé) 的闪电。"申"本义指闪电，后用"电"字表示闪电。"申"的常用义指伸开、伸直、伸展 (zhǎn)、展开 (kāi)，引申指说 (shuō) 明 (míng)，即把表达的意 (yì) 思 (si) 展开。

古代科学不发达，闪电对当时的人们来说还是很神秘的，所以古代也用作"神 (shén)"。

词或短语 Words & Phrases

引申	yǐnshēn	extend in meaning
申请	shēnqǐng	require; apply for
三令五申	sānlìng-wǔshēn	give repeated instructions

| 山 | shān (mountain; hill) | 【部首】山 【笔画】三画 |
| | 丨 乚 丨 竖、竖折/竖弯、竖 | |

甲骨文	金文	篆书	隶书	楷书	行书	简化字
Oracle Bones	Bronze Script	Seal Script	Official Script	Regular Script	Semi-cursive Script	Simplified Character

"山"是象形字。甲骨文的"山"写作 、 ，金文的"山"写作 、 ，形似山峦 (luán) 起 (qǐ) 伏 (fú)。"山"本义指山峰，指地面上隆 (lóng) 起 (qǐ) 高 (gāo) 耸 (sǒng) 的部分，多由土石构成。

桂 (guì) 林 (lín) 山 (shān) 水 (shuǐ)

词或短语 Words & Phrases

| 火山 | huǒshān | volcano |

火 (huǒ) 山 (shān)

冰山　　　　　bīngshān　　　　　　　iceberg

冰 (bīng) 山 (shān)

山穷水尽　　　shānqióng-shuǐjìn　　　to come to a dead end

锦言妙语　Proverbs & Witticism

山高挡不住太阳　shān gāo dǎng bú zhù tàiyáng
The highest mountains can't shut out the sun.

山外有山，天外有天　shān wài yǒu shān, tiān wài yǒu tiān
There are mountains beyond mountains, and heavens beyond heavens.

留得青山在，不怕没柴烧　liúdé qīngshān zài, bú pà méi chái shāo
As long as the green hills last, there'll always be wood to burn.

石	shí (stone; rock)	【部首】石　【笔画】五画
	一 ノ 丨 一 一	
	横、撇、竖、横折、横	

甲骨文	金文	篆书	隶书	楷书	行书	简化字
ᎮᎮ	ᎾᎾ	ᎦᎧ	ᎹᎺ	石	石	石
Oracle Bones	Bronze Script	Seal Script	Official Script	Regular Script	Semi-cursive Script	Simplified Character

"石"是象形字。甲骨文的"石"写作ᎦᎧ，它由ᎮᎮ(厂)和ᎹᎺ(石块)构成，形似山崖下有石块，表示山岩。"石"本义指山石、岩(yán)石。"石"是部首字，从"石"取义的字多与石头有关。

青(qīng)岛(dǎo)崂(láo)山(shān)

词或短语　Words & Phrases

石头	shítou	stone; rock
玉石	yùshí	jade
宝石	bǎoshí	precious stone; jewel
落井下石	luòjǐng-xiàshí	drop stones on someone who has fallen into a well

锦言妙语　Proverbs & Witticism

搬起石头砸自己的脚　bānqǐ shítou zá zìjǐ de jiǎo
Lift a rock only to drop it on one's own toes.

精诚所至，金石为开　jīng chéng suǒ zhì, jīn shí wéi kāi
Complete sincerity can affect even metal and stone. ‖ No difficulty is insurmountable if one sets one's mind to it.

摸着石头过河　mōzhe shítou guò hé
Crossing the river by feeling the stones. ‖ Be very careful in doing things.

玉	yù (jade)	【部首】玉　【笔画】五画
	一 一 丨 一 丶 横、横、竖、横、点	

甲骨文	金文	篆书	隶书	楷书	行书	简化字
Oracle Bones	Bronze Script	Seal Script	Official Script	Regular Script	Semi-cursive Script	Simplified Character

"玉"是象形字。甲骨文的"玉"写作 丰、丯，形似用绳子串 (chuàn) 起 (qǐ) 的宝玉，所连的玉块数量或三，或四，或五，后规范为三。后用"丶"，既表示玉有瑕 (xiá) 疵 (cī)，又可区别于"王"字。"玉"本义指美好的石头，也就是玉石。

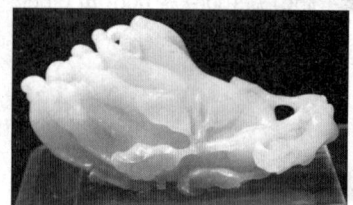

玉 (yù) 器 (qì)

词或短语　Words & Phrases

玉玺　　　　yùxǐ　　　　imperial jade seal

玉 (yù) 玺 (xǐ)

玉器　　　　yùqì　　　　jade articles; jadeware

玉石不分　　yùshíbùfēn

Make no distinctions between the jade and the stone — not to distinguish the good from the bad.

LESSON 2 Nature Worship • 第二课 自然崇拜

锦言妙语 Proverbs & Witticism

玉不琢，不成器 yù bù zhuó, bù chéng qì
An uncut gem does not sparkle.

金玉其外，败絮其中 jīn yù qí wài, bài xù qí zhōng
With gold and jade outside but rotten materials inside — a dandy but deceitful appearance. || Good-looking but empty-minded.

指事字 Self-explanatory Characters

元	yuán (first; leading; currency unit)	【部首】一 【笔画】四画
	一 一 丿 乚 横、横、撇、竖弯钩	

甲骨文	金文	篆书	隶书	楷书	行书	简化字
Oracle Bones	Bronze Script	Seal Script	Official Script	Regular Script	Semi-cursive Script	Simplified Character

"元"是指事字。甲骨文的"元"写作 、，金文的"元"写作 、，在"人"上加"二"，指出人体的最上部，即头部。"元"本义指人头，引申指居首、最上等的人，如元首、元帅、状元。

后来，"元"字又引申表示开始、第一，如元月、元旦。元月指每年的第一个月，元旦指每年的第一天。"元"也可用作货币单位，同"圆"。

元 (yuán) 旦 (dàn)(1月1日)

 Words & Phrases

元月   yuányuè   the first lunar month

元首	yuánshǒu	head of a state
元帅	yuánshuài	marshal; supreme commander
元气大伤	yuánqìdàshāng	greatly undermine one's constitution

旦 dàn (dawn; daybreak) 　【部首】日　【笔画】五画

丨 ㇇ 一 一 一
竖、横折、横、横、横

甲骨文	金文	篆书	隶书	楷书	行书	简化字
Oracle Bones	Bronze Script	Seal Script	Official Script	Regular Script	Semi-cursive Script	Simplified Character

"旦"是指事字。甲骨文的"旦"写作，金文的"旦"写作，"日"下加 ▢ 或 ●，形似水中倒影，指日(太阳)的影子，表示日(太阳)出天亮。旦，"日"在"一"上，"一"是指事符号，指代地面或海平面，表示太阳刚刚出地平线。"旦"本义指天亮、早晨。

日 (rì) 出 (chū)

词或短语　Words & Phrases

元旦	yuándàn	New Year's Day
旦夕祸福	dànxī-huòfú	unexpected good or bad fortune

锦言妙语　Proverbs & Witticism

人有旦夕祸福，月有阴晴圆缺 rén yǒu dànxī-huòfú, yuè yǒu yīnqíng-yuánquē

LESSON 2　Nature Worship • 第二课　自然崇拜

Men are subject to sudden changes of fortune as the moon is subject to the changes of being full and crescent, cloudy and clear.

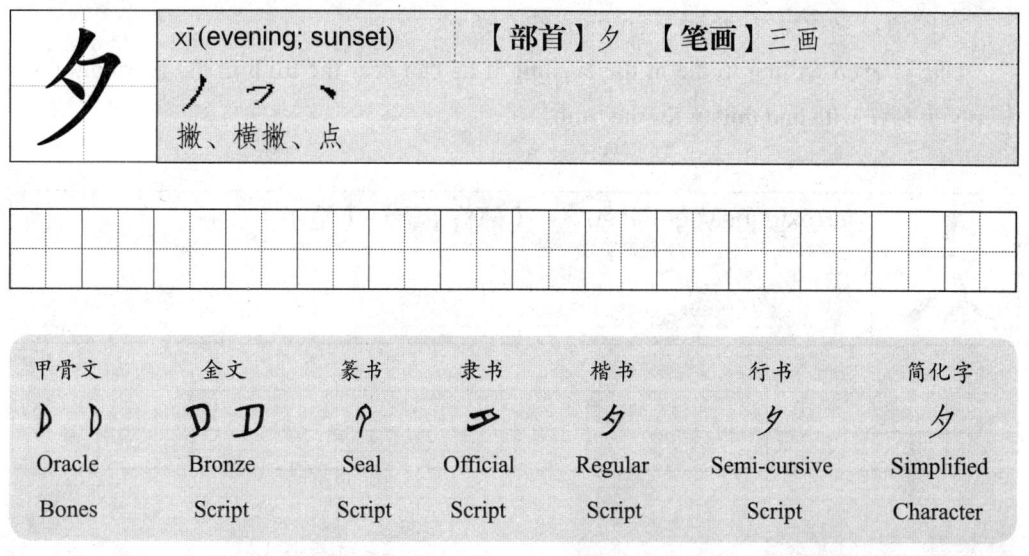

"夕"是指事字。甲骨文的"夕"写作 ᗞ、ᗞ，金文的"夕"写作 ᗞ、ᗞ，形似不完整的"月"。其中，短竖"丨"是指事符号，像半个"月"字，表示月亮刚出现时月光朦(méng)胧(lóng)、若隐若现。"夕"本义指傍(bàng)晚(wǎn)、黄昏，引申指夜晚。

除夕是农历年最后一天的晚上，即中国农历新年大年初一前夜。在甲骨文和金文中，"夕"还常常与"月"通用，这两个字都能表示月亮。

月(yuè)亮(liang)

词或短语　Words & Phrases

除夕	chúxī	Chinese New Year's Eve
夕阳西下	xīyáng xī xià	The sun is setting in the west.
一朝一夕	yìzhāo-yìxī	in one day

锦言妙语　Proverbs & Witticism

夕阳无限好，只是近黄昏　xīyáng wúxiàn hǎo, zhǐ shì jìn huánghūn
The setting sun has infinite beauty; only the time is approaching night-fall.

- 037 -

一万年太久，只争朝夕 yíwàn nián tài jiǔ, zhǐ zhēng zhāoxī
Ten thousand years is too long. Seize the day, and seize the hour.

朝闻道，夕死可矣 zhāo wén dào, xī sǐ kě yǐ
One is even willing to die in the evening if he can hear the truth in the morning. ‖ Be deeply in love with and thirsty for the truth.

金文	篆书	隶书	楷书	行书	简化字
太	大	太	太	太	太
Bronze Script	Seal Script	Official Script	Regular Script	Semi-cursive Script	Simplified Character

"太"是指事字。"太"与"大"本来是一个字，"太"的本义是大。"太"字是在"大"字下面加指事符号"丶"，以区别于"大"。"太"表示大的最高程度，即极大、无限大。

"太"字图示

 Words & Phrases

太极拳　　　　tàijíquán　　　　Tai Chi Chuan

太 (tài) 极 (jí) 拳 (quán)

太平洋　　　　Tàipíngyáng　　　the Pacific Ocean
太阳　　　　　tàiyáng　　　　　the sun

LESSON 2　Nature Worship • 第二课　自然崇拜

锦言妙语　Proverbs & Witticism

姜太公钓鱼，愿者上钩　Jiāng Tàigōng diào yú, yuànzhě shàng gōu
Like Jiang Taigong's fishing, the line has been cast for the fish that wants to be caught.

山高挡不住太阳　shān gāo dǎng bú zhù tàiyáng
The highest mountains can't shut out the sun.

会意字　Associative Compound Characters

早	zǎo (morning)	【部首】日　【笔画】六画
	丨 𠃍 一 一 一 丨 竖、横折、横、横、横、竖	

甲骨文	金文	篆书	隶书	楷书	行书	简化字
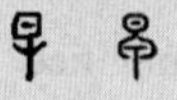 早 早	早	 早	早	早	早	早
Oracle Bones	Bronze Script	Seal Script	Official Script	Regular Script	Semi-cursive Script	Simplified Character

　　"早"是会意字。甲骨文的"早"写作 早，由 ⊙（日）和 屮（屮，小草）构成，表示旭日初升，草木沐（mù）浴（yù）在朝（zhāo）阳（yáng）之中。

　　篆书的"早"写作 早，上部形似"日"（太阳），下部形似"甲"，像种子发芽时，表皮开裂的样子。这里想表达的是，太阳冲破黑夜就是早晨。"早"本义指早晨、清晨，即太阳刚刚出来的时候，与"晚"相对。

"早"字图示

词或短语　Words & Phrases

| 早上好 | zǎoshàng hǎo | good morning |
| 早饭 | zǎofàn | breakfast |

- 039 -

锦言妙语 Proverbs & Witticism

早饭吃好，午饭吃饱，晚饭吃少 zǎofàn chīhǎo, wǔfàn chībǎo, wǎnfàn chīshǎo
A good meal for breakfast, a heavy meal for lunch, and a light meal for supper.

早睡早起，使人健康、富有、聪慧 zǎo shuì zǎo qǐ, shǐ rén jiànkāng、fùyǒu、cōnghuì
Early to bed and early to rise makes a man healthy, wealthy, and wise.

早起的鸟有虫吃 zǎo qǐ de niǎo yǒu chóng chī
The early bird catches the worms.

天	tiān (sky; heaven)	【部首】大　【笔画】四画
	一 一 ノ ㇏ 横、横、撇、捺	

甲骨文	金文	篆书	隶书	楷书	行书	简化字
Oracle Bones	Bronze Script	Seal Script	Official Script	Regular Script	Semi-cursive Script	Simplified Character

　　在古文字中，"天"都是会意字。金文的"天"写作 天、天，由"一"或一个椭圆形和"大"两部分会意而成，它指最 (zuì) 高 (gāo) 的部位。古文的"大"字，近似一个顶天立地的人的外形。人站立在大地上，头顶上就是高高的天空。

　　孔子从不把人的活动领域上升到天上，而是把人置于天地之间的某一中心位置。周朝所说的"天"就是商朝人心中的"帝"。

　　"天"本义指头顶，后转指天空。一日或一昼 (zhòu) 夜 (yè) 也被称为一天。

"天"字图示

词或短语 Words & Phrases

天气　　　　tiānqì　　　　　　weather; climate

晴天	qíngtiān	fine day
阴天	yīntiān	overcast sky; cloudy sky
蓝天	lántiān	blue sky
今天	jīntiān	today
明天	míngtiān	tomorrow
昨天	zuótiān	yesterday
天从人愿	tiāncóngrényuàn	Heaven has disposed matters according to one's wishes.

锦言妙语　Proverbs & Witticism

天下无难事，只怕有心人　tiānxià wú nán shì, zhǐ pà yǒu xīn rén
Nothing is difficult to a willing heart.

天下兴亡，匹夫有责　tiānxià xīng wáng, pǐfū yǒu zé
Everyone is responsible for his country's rise or fall.

天下之大，无奇不有　tiānxià zhī dà, wú qí bù yǒu
In the great world wonders never cease.

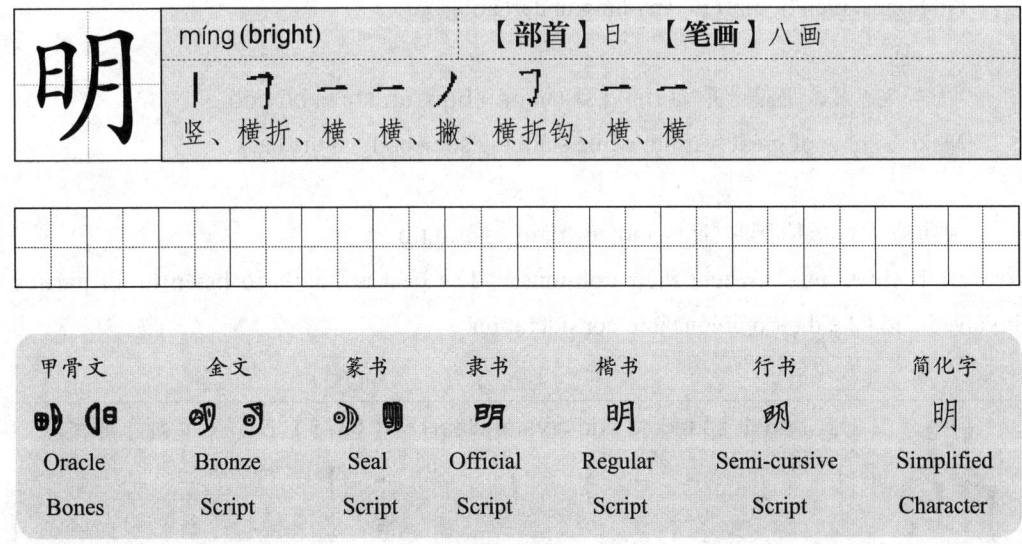

"明"是会意字。甲骨文的"明"写作 ☽日，由 日 (日) 和 ☽ (月亮) 构成，表示白天和黑夜发光的两个天体 (古人以为月亮在夜里发光)。"明"从"日"、从"月"，

日和月是最明亮的，故"明"表示明(míng)亮(liàng)的意思。"明"本义指光明，引申指人的眼睛明亮。"明"和"暗"相对。

天明是新一天的开始，所以"明"又表示下一段时间，如明天、明年。

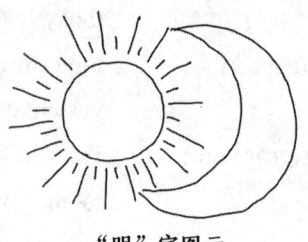

"明"字图示

词或短语 Words & Phrases

明白	míngbai	understand
明天	míngtiān	tomorrow
耳聪目明	ěrcōng-mùmíng	(of old people) have good ears and eyes
自知之明	zìzhīzhīmíng	self-knowledge

锦言妙语 Proverbs & Witticism

明人不做暗事 míng rén bú zuò àn shì
An honest man doesn't do anything underhand.

明是一盆火，暗是一把刀 míng shì yì pén huǒ, àn shì yì bǎ dāo
Make a show of great warmth while stabbing somebody in the back.

兼听则明，偏听则暗 jiān tīng zé míng, piān tīng zé àn
Both sides must present their opinions. ‖ The best policy is to listen to all parties involved and take their opinions into consideration.

晶	jīng (bright; sparkling and crystal-clear) 【部首】日 【笔画】十二画
	丨 𠃌 一 一 丨 𠃌 一 一 丨 𠃌 一 一
	竖、横折、横、横、竖、横折、横、横、竖、横折、横、横

LESSON 2 Nature Worship • 第二课　自然崇拜

甲骨文	金文	篆书	隶书	楷书	行书	简化字
🝰	🝰	晶	晶	晶	晶	晶
Oracle Bones	Bronze Script	Seal Script	Official Script	Regular Script	Semi-cursive Script	Simplified Character

"晶"是会意字。甲骨文的"晶"写作 🝰，由三个 ☉ (日，天体) 会意而成，表示众多闪烁发光的星体。"晶"在篆书中写作 晶，也是会意字，由三个 "日" 组成。"晶"本义指星，又指星光，引申为明亮、光亮，如亮晶晶。

星 (xīng) 空 (kōng)

词或短语　Words & Phrases

水晶　　　　shuǐjīng　　　crystal

水 (shuǐ) 晶 (jīng)

亮晶晶　　　liàngjīngjīng　　shining; sparkling

锦言妙语　Proverbs & Witticism

坚如水晶，亮如钻石　jiān rú shuǐjīng, liàng rú zuànshí
As solid as crystal and as brilliant as a diamond.

名	míng (name; reputation)	【部首】口　【笔画】六画
	ノ ⺈ 丶 丨 フ 一	
	撇、横撇、点、竖、横折、横	

甲骨文	金文	篆书	隶书	楷书	行书	简化字
Oracle Bones	Bronze Script	Seal Script	Official Script	Regular Script	Semi-cursive Script	Simplified Character

"名"是会意字。甲骨文的"名"写作，由 (口，呼叫)和 (夕，傍晚)构成，表示天黑时父母呼叫孩子的名字。"名"，从"夕"(月亮)、从"口"(嘴)，也可指天黑双方互相看不见，只好呼叫名字。"名"本义指呼叫名字，引申为名望，名声、名誉，又表示出名的、有名气的。

词或短语　Words & Phrases

名字	míngzi	name
报名	bào míng	enter one's name; sign up
有名的	yǒu míng de	famous; well-known
名誉	míngyù	reputation; fame
名闻天下	míngwéntiānxià	be world-famous; be well-known far and wide

锦言妙语　Proverbs & Witticism

名师出高徒 míng shī chū gāo tú
An accomplished disciple owes his accomplishment to his great teacher.

人怕出名猪怕壮 rén pà chū míng zhū pà zhuàng
A swine (hog) over fat is the cause of his own bane. ‖ Men are afraid of becoming famous, just as pigs are afraid of fattening.

山不在高，有仙则名；水不在深，有龙则灵
shān bú zài gāo, yǒu xiān zé míng; shuǐ bú zài shēn, yǒu lóng zé líng
Mountains are not famous for their height, but for the immortals, and rivers don't gain nimbus for their depth, but for dragons.

| 从 | cóng (follow) 丿、丶、丿、㇏ 撇、点、撇、捺 | 【部首】人　【笔画】四画 |

甲骨文	金文	篆书	隶书	楷书	行书	繁体字	简化字
Oracle Bones	Bronze Script	Seal Script	Official Script	Regular Script	Semi-cursive Script	Traditional Character	Simplified Character

"从"是会意字。甲骨文的"从"写作 ，形似一个人在前，一个人在后，表示跟(gēn)随(suí)。繁体"從"简化为"从"。"从"本义指跟从、随从，即两人相随而行，引申为顺从、听从。"从"用作副词时，表示从来、向来；用作介词时，表示由、自，如从今、从此。

跟(gēn)随(suí)

词或短语　Words & Phrases

跟从	gēncóng	follow
服从	fúcóng	obey; submit (oneself) to
从古到今	cóng gǔ dào jīn	from ancient times to the present

锦言妙语　Proverbs & Witticism

从无到有，从小到大　cóng wú dào yǒu, cóng xiǎo dào dà
Grow out of nothing and expand from small to large.

从群众中来，到群众中去 cóng qúnzhòng zhōng lái, dào qúnzhòng zhōng qù
Come from the masses, and go among the masses.

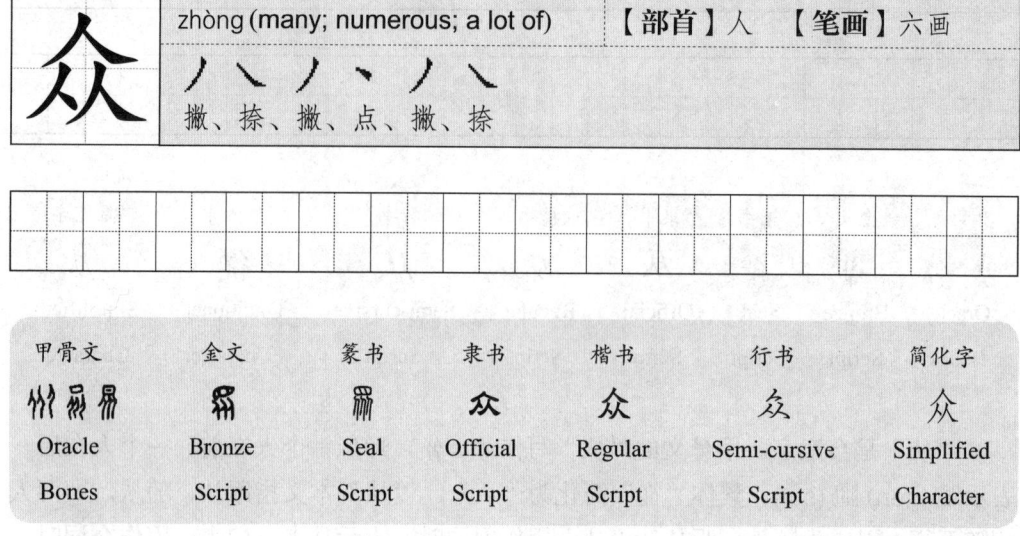

"众"是会意字。甲骨文的"众"可写作𠱃，这个字上部形似"日"（太阳），下部形似三个弯(wān)腰(yāo)劳作的人，合起来表示太阳出来后许多人都要劳动，即日出而作。甲骨文的"众"也可写作𠈌，由𠂉(从)和(从)构成，表示相随、同(tóng)行(xíng)的一群人，参考上文的"从"字。金文的"众"写作𠱃，从"目"、从三"人"，数字"三"在古时是众多的意思，像奴隶主瞪眼监视众奴隶劳动。简化字从三"人"，表示人多为众。"众"本义指人多。

词或短语 Words & Phrases

众多	zhòng duō	many; numerous
群众	qúnzhòng	the masses
观众	guānzhòng	audience
众口难调	zhòngkǒunántiáo	It's difficult to cater for all tastes.

锦言妙语 Proverbs & Witticism

众人拾柴火焰高 zhòng rén shí chái huǒyàn gāo
When everyone adds fuel, the flames rise high — great things may be done by mass efforts.

LESSON 2 Nature Worship • 第二课 自然崇拜

会当凌绝顶，一览众山小 huì dāng líng jué dǐng, yì lǎn zhòng shān xiǎo
Ah! To stand on the highest peak to see how tiny the rest of the hills are!

墙倒众人推 qiáng dǎo zhòng rén tuī
When a wall is about to collapse, everybody gives it a push — everybody hits a man who is down.

| 佃 | diàn (rent land from landlord) | 【部首】亻 | 【笔画】七画 |

丿丨丨 ㇆ 一 丨 一
撇、竖、竖、横折、横、竖、横

金文	篆书	隶书	楷书	行书	简化字
Bronze Script	Seal Script	Official Script	Regular Script	Semi-cursive Script	Simplified Character

"佃"是会意字。"佃"从"亻"(人)、从"田"(像农田)，田(tián)兼表声，表示人种(zhòng)田(tián)。"佃"本义指种田地，由种田引申指农民向地主或官府(土地占有者)租(zū)种(zhòng)土地，又指租种土地者，即佃户。

农(nóng)耕(gēng)壁(bì)画(huà)

 Words & Phrases

佃农   diànnóng   tenant farmer

| 男 | nán (man; male) | 【部首】田 | 【笔画】七画 |

丨 ㇆ 一 丨 一 ㇆ 丿
竖、横折、横、竖、横、横折钩、撇

甲骨文	金文	篆书	隶书	楷书	行书	简化字
Oracle Bones	Bronze Script	Seal Script	Official Script	Regular Script	Semi-cursive Script	Simplified Character

"男"是会意字。在甲骨文中，"男"从"田"（农田）、从"力"（ㄑ，耒，lěi）。"耒"是古人使用的一种木制的耕地农具，类似现在农耕用的耙(pá)犁(li)，合起来表示在田地里耕(gēng)作是力气活，因此农耕主要是男人的事。"男"本义指男人、男性、男子，与"女"字相对，又引申指儿子。

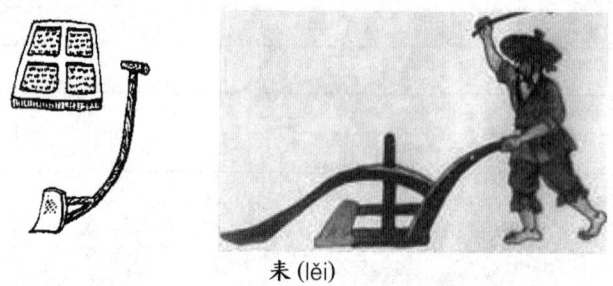

耒 (lěi)

词或短语　Words & Phrases

男人	nánrén	male; man; husband
男生	nánsheng	schoolboy
先生	xiānsheng	sir; gentleman
男耕女织	nángēng-nǚzhī	Men plough and women weave.

锦言妙语　Proverbs & Witticism

男儿有泪不轻弹，只因未到伤心处 nán'ér yǒu lèi bù qīng tán, zhǐ yīn wèi dào shāngxīn chù

A man does not easily shed tears until his heart is broken.

自古男儿当自强 zì gǔ nán'ér dāng zì qiáng

Since ancient times, men should always strive to become stronger.

男大当婚，女大当嫁 nán dà dāng hūn, nǚ dà dāng jià

Upon growing up, every male should take a wife and every female should take a husband.

夯	hāng (tamper; tamp)	【部首】大　【笔画】五画
	一 ノ 八 ㇆ ノ	
	横、撇、捺、横折钩、撇	

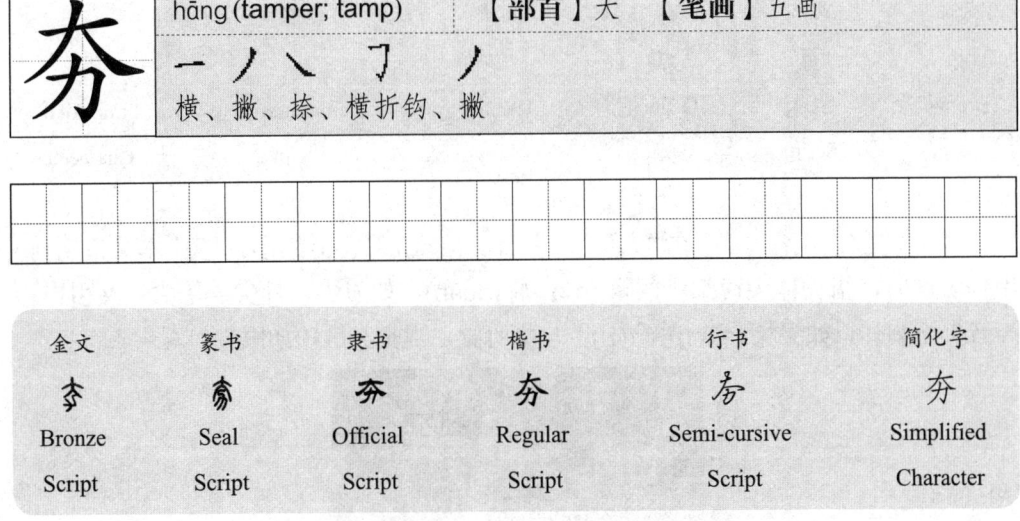

金文	篆书	隶书	楷书	行书	简化字
Bronze Script	Seal Script	Official Script	Regular Script	Semi-cursive Script	Simplified Character

"夯"是会意字。"夯"的上部是"大"、下部是"力",合起来表示用很大的力气扛起重物。"夯"本义指用力扛起重物,引申指用力扛起重物砸(zá)下去,即砸实地基的动作。砸地基的工具也称为夯,这时用作名词,如木夯、石夯。

夯(hāng)

词或短语 Words & Phrases

打夯机	dǎhāngjī	tamper
夯实	hāngshí	tamp; pun

尖	jiān (taper; sharp)	【部首】小　【笔画】六画
	丨 ノ 丶 一 ノ 八	
	竖、撇、点、横、撇、捺	

金文	篆书	隶书	楷书	行书	简化字
尖	尖	尖	尖	尖	尖
Bronze Script	Seal Script	Official Script	Regular Script	Semi-cursive Script	Simplified Character

"尖"是会意字。"小"在"大"上，表示顶(dǐng)部(bù)细小。"尖"本义指锐利；用作名词时，指物体尖锐细小的末(mò)端(duān)，如刀尖、针尖、笔尖；又引申指声音尖厉刺耳，如尖嗓(sǎng)子(zi)；也指听觉、视觉灵敏，如眼尖、耳尖。

笔(bǐ)尖(jiān)

词或短语 Words & Phrases

钢笔尖	gāngbǐ jiān	the tip of a pen; a pen point
塔尖儿	tǎ jiānr	the pinnacle of a tower
尖子生	jiānzishēng	top student
眼尖	yǎn jiān	have sharp eyes; be sharp-eyed

锦言妙语 Proverbs & Witticism

针尖大的窟窿，斗大的风　zhēnjiān dà de kūlong, dǒu dà de fēng
A big wind can blow through a small hole — a little leak will sink a great ship.

少　shǎo; shào (little; lack; young)　【部首】小　【笔画】四画

丨ノ丶ノ
竖、撇、点、撇

甲骨文	金文	篆书	隶书	楷书	行书	简化字
Oracle Bones	Bronze Script	Seal Script	Official Script	Regular Script	Semi-cursive Script	Simplified Character

"小"是"少"的本字,"少"在古文字中是会意字。金文的"少"写作ψ、ψ,承(chéng)续(xù)甲骨文的字形, ʼ ʼ ʼ ,由四个小点组成,表示细小、不多。"少"本义指数(shù)量(liàng)小、数量不多,如少数、少量、很少、多少。

"少"用作动词时,引申指缺少、丢失;又引申指时间短、不久;也可读shào,由时间短引申指年轻、年轻人,如少年儿童。

词或短语 Words & Phrases

少数人	shǎoshù rén	a small number of people
多少	duōshǎo	how much; how many
减少	jiánshǎo	reduce; decrease
缺少	quēshǎo	lack
少年儿童	shàonián értóng	children

锦言妙语 Proverbs & Witticism

少花钱,多办事 shǎo huā qián, duō bàn shì
Spend less money to accomplish more things.

少数服从多数 shǎoshù fúcóng duōshù
The minority is subordinate to the majority.

少壮不努力,老大徒伤悲 shào zhuàng bù nǔlì, lǎo dà tú shāngbēi
A man who does not work hard in his youth will be grieved when he grows old.

笑一笑,十年少 xiào yí xiào, shí nián shào
If you often smile, you will be ten years younger.

劣	liè (bad; substandard)	【部首】力　【笔画】六画
	丨ノ丶ノ𠃌ノ	
	竖、撇、点、撇、横折钩、撇	

金文	篆书	隶书	楷书	行书	简化字
少	劣劣	劣	劣	劣	劣
Bronze Script	Seal Script	Official Script	Regular Script	Semi-cursive Script	Simplified Character

"劣"是会意字。古代生产力落后，体力的大小是影响个人成败的关键因(yīn)素(sù)。"劣"从"少"、从"力"，表示缺(quē)乏(fá)力量、弱小，力少则弱。"劣"本义指力气弱小，引申为不好的、坏的、次(cì)等(děng)，如劣势、恶(è)劣。

词或短语　Words & Phrases

劣质产品	lièzhì chǎnpǐn	products of inferior quality
劣势	lièshì	inferior strength or position; disadvantaged
优胜劣汰	yōushèng-liètài	survival of the fittest

锦言妙语　Proverbs & Witticism

大浪淘沙，优胜劣汰　dàlàngtáoshā, yōushèng-liètài
Great waves sweep away the sand, and the competition eliminates the weak.

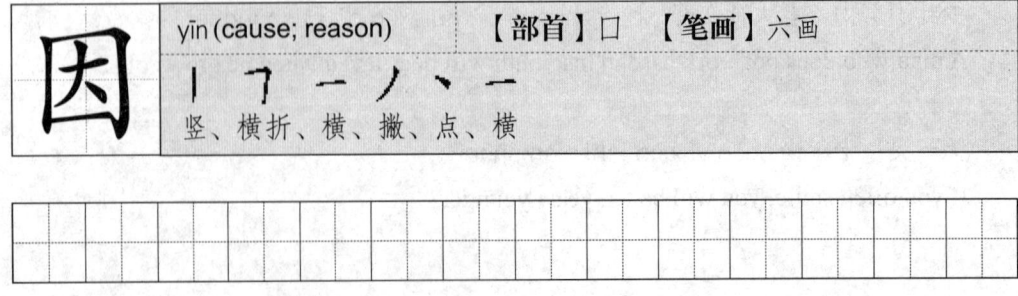

因	yīn (cause; reason)	【部首】口　【笔画】六画
	丨𠃌一ノ丶一	
	竖、横折、横、撇、点、横	

LESSON 2 Nature Worship • 第二课 自然崇拜

甲骨文	金文	篆书	隶书	楷书	行书	简化字
因	因	因	因	因	因	因
Oracle Bones	Bronze Script	Seal Script	Official Script	Regular Script	Semi-cursive Script	Simplified Character

  "因"是会意字。甲骨文的"因"写作囚，形似一个人（大）躺在席(xí)垫(diàn)（口）上。"因"本义指席子，引申为凭(píng)借(jiè)、依(yī)靠(kào)，后引申为原因。

  "因"在佛教中指能产生结果的原因。"因"表示人是改变周围环境的原因。"因"字蕴(yùn)含(hán)着人是原因的思想，体现了古人对人与环境之间关系的哲学思想。比如，草原上人、狼、牲畜和草之间的依存关系。

"因"字图示

词或短语 Words & Phrases

原因	yuányīn	reason
因为	yīnwèi	because; on account of
内因	nèiyīn	internal cause
外因	wàiyīn	external cause; exterior reason
因小失大	yīnxiǎo-shīdà	lose a great deal through trying to save a little
因材施教	yīncáishījiào	teach students in accordance with their aptitude
因祸得福	yīnhuò-défú	profit from a misfortune

锦言妙语 Proverbs & Witticism

  是非只为多开口，烦恼皆因强出头 shìfēi zhǐ wèi duō kāi kǒu, fánnǎo jiē yīn qiáng chū tóu

You get into trouble because you speak too much, and you get vexed because you strive to take the lead.

  只因一着错，满盘俱是空 zhǐ yīn yī zhāo cuò, mǎn pán jù shì kōng

A single false move loses the game — a wrong step leads to a total failure.

囚	qiú (prisoner; imprison)	【部首】囗 【笔画】五画
	丨 𠃌 丿 丶 一	
	竖、横折、撇、点、横	

甲骨文	金文	篆书	隶书	楷书	行书	简化字
Oracle Bones	Bronze Script	Seal Script	Official Script	Regular Script	Semi-cursive Script	Simplified Character

"囚"是会意字。甲骨文的"囚"写作，由（囗，封闭的空间）和（人，罪犯）构成，意思是拘禁罪犯或奴隶。"囚"从"囗"(wéi)、从"人"，表示把人关押起来。"囚"本义指拘(jū)禁(jìn)，后指囚犯，囚犯就是被拘禁在监狱里的人。

囚(qiú)犯(fàn)

词或短语 Words & Phrases

| 囚犯 | qiúfàn | prisoner; convict |
| 囚禁 | qiújìn | imprison; put... in jail |

困	kùn (be stranded; tired)	【部首】囗 【笔画】七画
	丨 𠃌 一 丨 丿 丶 一	
	竖、横折、横、竖、撇、点、横	

LESSON 2　Nature Worship ● 第二课　自然崇拜

甲骨文	金文	篆书	隶书	楷书	行书	简化字
困 困	困	困	困	困	困	困
Oracle Bones	Bronze Script	Seal Script	Official Script	Regular Script	Semi-cursive Script	Simplified Character

"困"是会意字。甲骨文的"困"写作 困，由表示门四框的 囗（囗 wéi）和 木（木）两部分构成。"困"本义指阻止门转动的木橛或门槛 (kǎn)。"困"从"囗"(wéi，古"围"字)，表示房屋四壁；从"木"(树)，表示树被围墙圈住无法自由生长。

无论是门橛、门槛，还是围墙，都起到限制作用，故"困"引申为障 (zhàng) 碍 (ài)，又引申为处 (chǔ) 境 (jìng) 艰难、窘 (jiǒng) 迫 (pò)，如困难、困苦、围困、困扰。此外，"困"也指疲乏想睡，如困乏、困倦，方言又指睡觉。

门 (mén) 槛 (kǎn)

词或短语　Words & Phrases

遇到困难	yùdào kùnnan	in trouble
解决困难	jiějué kùnnan	problem solving
困难重重	kùnnan chóngchóng	be plagued by numerous difficulties

锦言妙语　Proverbs & Witticism

鸟儿出牢笼——脱困 niǎor chū láolóng——tuō kùn
The bird is out of the cage — out of trouble

把方便让给别人，把困难留给自己 bǎ fāngbiàn ràng gěi bié rén, bǎ kùnnan liú gěi zìjǐ
Take on difficulties oneself and leave what is easy to others.

雷	léi (thunder)	【部首】雨　【笔画】十三画
	一、丶、㇀/㇆、丨、丶、丶、丶、丨、㇆、一、丨、一	
	横、点、横撇/横钩、竖、点、点、点、竖、横折、横、竖、横	

甲骨文	金文	篆书	隶书	楷书	行书	简化字
Oracle Bones	Bronze Script	Seal Script	Official Script	Regular Script	Semi-cursive Script	Simplified Character

"雷"是会意字。甲骨文的"雷"写作 ，由表示闪电的 和表示雷声的 会意组成，指云层放电时发出的响声。金文的"雷"写作 ，字的上部加 （雨）字会意，因为雷声和闪电之后通常会下雨，而后逐(zhú)渐(jiàn)简化成现在的"雷"字。"雷"本义指打雷。

雷 (léi) 电 (diàn)

词或短语 Words & Phrases

雷声	léishēng	thunderclap
春雷	chūnléi	spring thunder

锦言妙语 Proverbs & Witticism

雷声大，雨点小 léishēng dà, yǔdiǎn xiǎo
Loud thunder but small raindrops — much said but little done.

干打雷，不下雨 gān dǎ léi, bú xià yǔ
Thunder but no rain — much noise but no action. ‖ All talk and no cider.

久闻大名，如雷贯耳 jiǔwéndàmíng, rúléiguàněr
I have long heard of your great name, Sir, and it has been like thunder in my ears.

LESSON 2 Nature Worship • 第二课 自然崇拜

动	dòng (move)	【部首】力 　【笔画】六画
	一一厶、㇆丿	
	横、横、撇折、点、横折钩、撇	

金文	篆书	隶书	楷书	行书	繁体字	简化字
𤙹	䡖	動动	动	动	動	动
Bronze Script	Seal Script	Official Script	Regular Script	Semi-cursive Script	Traditional Character	Simplified Character

　　"动"是会意字。"动"从"力"、从"重",强调使用体力,表示用力搬动重物。"动"的简体字从"力"、从"云"(飘浮不定),表示用力移动。"动"本义指移动。现代汉语中,"动"指起身做事,特指人的行动,引申为心理上的感动、不平静。

登(dēng) 山(shān) 运(yùn) 动(dòng)

词或短语 Words & Phrases

体力劳动	tǐlì láodòng	manual labour; physical labour
体育运动	tǐyù yùndòng	sports
行动	xíngdòng	action
感动	gǎndòng	affect
动力	dònglì	motive power; driving force
动物	dòngwù	animals

锦言妙语 Proverbs & Witticism

动脑筋,想办法　dòng nǎojīn, xiǎng bànfǎ
Use one's brains to find a way out.

- 057 -

君子动口不动手 jūnzǐ dòng kǒu bú dòng shǒu
A gentleman uses his tongue but not his fists.

岩 yán (cliff; rock)　　【部首】山　【笔画】八画

丨 𠃊 丨 一 丿 丨 𠃍 一
竖、竖折/竖弯、竖、横、撇、竖、横折、横

甲骨文	金文	篆书	隶书	楷书	行书	简化字
Oracle Bones	Bronze Script	Seal Script	Official Script	Regular Script	Semi-cursive Script	Simplified Character

"岩"是会意字。甲骨文的"岩"写作 ，由 (山)和 (像众多石块)构成，表示布满石头的山。"岩"从"山"、从"石"，表示山石为岩。"岩"本义指高耸险(xiǎn)峻(jùn)的山崖，又转指岩洞。"岩"在现代指岩石。

山(shān)崖(yá)

词或短语　Words & Phrases

攀岩运动　　pānyán yùndòng　　rock climbing

攀(pān)岩(yán)运(yùn)动(dòng)

岩洞　　yándòng　　grotto or cavern

LESSON 2 Nature Worship • 第二课 自然崇拜

岩 (yán) 洞 (dòng)

危	wēi (danger; endanger)	【部首】厄 【笔画】六画
	ノ ⺆ 一 ノ 刁 乚	
	撇、横撇/横钩、横、撇、横折钩、竖弯钩	

金文	篆书	隶书	楷书	行书	简化字
Bronze Script	Seal Script	Official Script	Regular Script	Semi-cursive Script	Simplified Character

金文	篆书	隶书	楷书	行书	简化字
Bronze Script	Seal Script	Official Script	Regular Script	Semi-cursive Script	Simplified Character

　　"危"是会意字。篆书的"危"写作 ，由 (人) 和 (山) 构成，意思是人在高崖，身居险境。人在崖上为"危"，人在崖下为"厄"(è)。"厄"也是会意字，篆书的"厄"写作 ，由 (厂，石崖) 和 (屈服的人) 构成，表示人在山崖下的洞中蜷 (quán) 曲 (qū) 着身子，无法伸展。"厄"的本义指遇 (yù) 到 (dào) 困难。

危 (wēi)

厄 (è)

词或短语 Words & Phrases

危险	wēixiǎn	dangerous; risk
厄运	èyùn	misfortune; bad luck
危机意识	wēijī yìshí	crisis consciousness
危机四伏	wēijīsìfú	be plagued by crises; a crisis of danger lurks in four corners
危在旦夕	wēizàidànxī	be at death's door; in imminent danger

锦言妙语 Proverbs & Witticism

危急存亡之秋　wēijí cúnwáng zhī qiū
A time when national existence hangs in the balance. ‖ In critical time. ‖ Period of national crisis.

形声字
Pictophonetic Characters

像 xiàng (resemble; likeness of sb.)　【部首】亻　【笔画】十三画

丿 丨 丿 ㇇ 丨 𠃌 一 丿 ㇉ 丿 丿 丿 ㇏
撇、竖、撇、横撇/横钩、竖、横折、横、撇、弯钩、撇、撇、撇、捺

金文	篆书	隶书	楷书	行书	简化字
像	像 像	像	像	像	像
Bronze Script	Seal Script	Official Script	Regular Script	Semi-cursive Script	Simplified Character

"像"是形声兼会意字。篆书的"像"写作像，由亻(人)和象(象)构成，从"亻"(人)、从"象"(相似)，象兼表声。《说文解字》："像，形象相似。""像"本义指比照人物做成的图形。现在"像"用作名词，依然表示比照人物制作的图画、图形、雕(diāo)塑(sù)等，如画像、肖像、塑(sù)像、音像制品；引申泛指类(lèi)似(sì)、相似、如(rú)同(tóng)，如他俩长得太像了。

LESSON 2　Nature Worship　•　第二课　自然崇拜

两 (liǎng) 只 (zhī) 大 (dà) 熊 (xióng) 猫 (māo)

 **Words & Phrases**

画像　　　　huàxiàng　　　　portrait; portrayal

Proverbs & Witticism

困难像弹簧，你弱它就强　kùnnan xiàng tánhuáng, nǐ ruò tā jiù qiáng
Difficulty is like a spring. If you are weak, it will become stronger.

三分像人，七分像鬼　sān fēn xiàng rén, qī fēn xiàng guǐ
More like a devil than a man.

星	xīng (star)	【部首】日　【笔画】九画
	丨 フ 一 一 丿 一 一 丨 一	
	竖、横折、横、横、撇、横、横、竖、横	

甲骨文	金文	篆书	隶书	楷书	行书	简化字
甲骨文字形	金文字形	篆书字形	星	星	星	星
Oracle Bones	Bronze Script	Seal Script	Official Script	Regular Script	Semi-cursive Script	Simplified Character

　　"星"是形声字。"晶"是星的本字。甲骨文的"星"写作𤋮，在"晶"的字形𤋮(星群，众多发光天体)的基础上再加"生"𤯓(从无到有)，另造"曐"表示星群的"天生"现象。

　　金文的"星"写作𤯓，三个"日"并不是说有三个太阳，而是指三颗星星。古文中的"三"表示多数，表示天空中星星繁多的意思。距离地球最近的恒星是太阳。

到了夜晚，天空中会出(chū)现(xiàn)众多发光的星星。由于星星在夜空中明亮耀眼，现在常用来指代杰出的人物，如电影明星(影星)、歌星。

星(xīng)星(xing)

词或短语 Words & Phrases

足球明星	zúqiú míngxīng	soccer star
星期一	xīngqīyī	Monday
星期日	xīngqīrì	Sunday
北斗星	běidǒuxīng	the Big Dipper; the Plough

锦言妙语 Proverbs & Witticism

星星再小，也会发光 xīngxing zài xiǎo, yě huì fā guāng
Even a small star shines in the darkness.

星星之火，可以燎原 xīngxing zhī huǒ, ké yǐ liáo yuán
A single spark can start a prairie fire.

时　shí (time; hour)　【部首】日　【笔画】七画

丨 ㇇ 一 一 一 亅 丶
竖、横折、横、横、横、竖钩、点

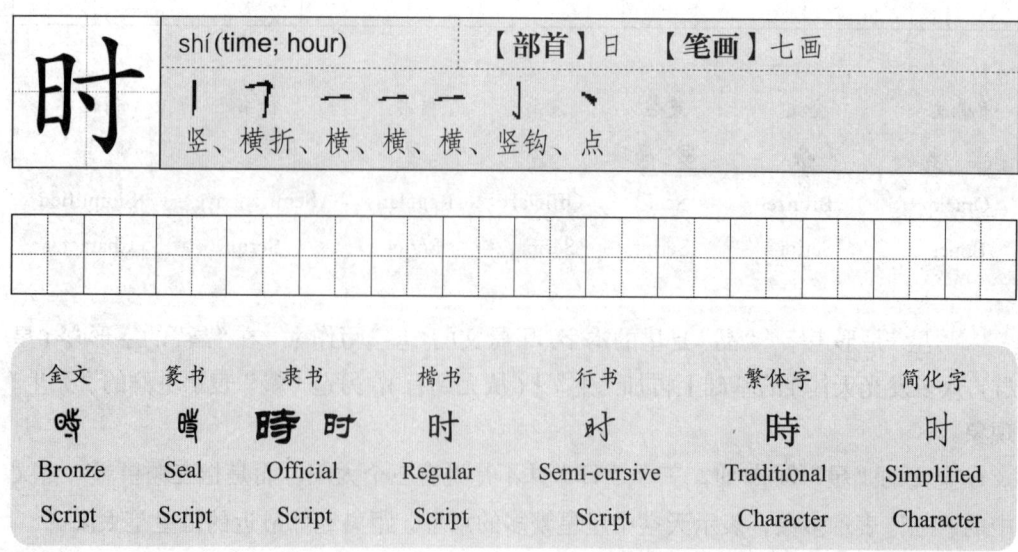

"时"是形声字。"时"本义指春(chūn)、夏(xià)、秋(qiū)、冬(dōng)四季，引申泛指时间，古代指时辰，现在指小时。

时(shí)辰(chén)

词或短语 Words & Phrases

时间	shíjiān	time
一个小时	yí gè xiǎoshí	an hour
时候	shíhou	(the duration of) time
时不我待	shíbùwǒdài	Time and tide wait for no man.

锦言妙语 Proverbs & Witticism

时间就是金钱 shíjiān jiù shì jīnqián
Time is money.

春争日，夏争时 chūn zhēng rì, xià zhēng shí
In spring every day counts; in summer every hour counts.

此一时，彼一时 cǐ yì shí, bǐ yì shí
The times are different, not comparable. ‖ This is one situation and that was another.

雪	xuě (snow)	【部首】雨 【笔画】十一画
	一 ノ フ 丨 丶 丶 丶 丶 フ 一 一	
	横、点、横撇/横钩、竖、点、点、点、点、横折、横、横	

甲骨文	金文	篆书	隶书	楷书	行书	简化字
Oracle Bones	Bronze Script	Seal Script	Official Script	Regular Script	Semi-cursive Script	Simplified Character

"雪"是会意字。甲骨文的"雪"写作 ，由 （白色羽毛）和 （雨点）组成，表示天空中纷纷扬扬像羽毛一样的白色物。

在篆书中，"雪"是一个形声字。上部仍为"雨"，表示字义，但下部演化成"彗"（huì，旧时读 suì），用来表示字音。因为"雪"是洁白的，所以人们常用其表示白色，或者高洁的人品。

哈(hā)尔(ěr)滨(bīn)雪(xuě)乡(xiāng)

词或短语　Words & Phrases

雪花　　　xuěhuā　　　　　　snowflake

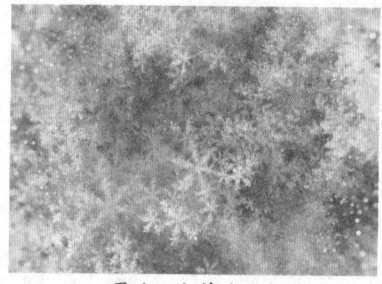

雪(xuě)花(huā)

雪白　　　xuěbái　　　　　　snow-white
下雪　　　xià xuě　　　　　　snowing
雪上加霜　xuěshàngjiāshuāng　one disaster after another; from bad to worse

锦言妙语　Proverbs & Witticism

各人自扫门前雪　gè rén zì sǎo mén qián xuě
Clear away the snow only in front of one's door — selfishness and lack of care for one another.

LESSON 2 Nature Worship • 第二课 自然崇拜

汽 qì (vapour; steam)　【部首】氵　【笔画】七画

丶丶丿一一乙
点、点、提、撇、横、横、横折弯钩

金文	篆书	隶书	楷书	行书	简化字
Bronze Script	Seal Script	Official Script	Regular Script	Semi-cursive Script	Simplified Character

"汽"是形声字。"汽"的篆书写作 ，由 （流水）和 （气）构成，意思是水的雾(wù)状(zhuàng)形态。

汽的简化字由"氵"(古文字的形体像流水，现在的形体像水滴）和"气"（云气）两部分构成。"气"(qì)兼表声。汽在物理学上指液体受热蒸(zhēng)发(fā)而变成的气体，又特指水蒸气。

蒸(zhēng)汽(qì)机(jī)车(chē)

气体从水中蒸发而出是水汽，气体被压进水中又成了汽水，如沈阳八王寺汽水。

词或短语　Words & Phrases

小汽车　　　xiǎo qìchē　　　car

小(xiǎo)汽(qì)车(chē)

吃 chī (eat or drink)　【部首】口　【笔画】六画

丨𠃍一丿一乙
竖、横折、横、撇、横、横折弯钩/横斜钩

金文	篆书	隶书	楷书	行书	简化字
		吃	吃	吃	吃
Bronze Script	Seal Script	Official Script	Regular Script	Semi-cursive Script	Simplified Character

"吃"是形声字。"口"为形,"乞"为声。"吃"本义指口吃,后表示吃东西的意思,也指喝、饮。

"吃"字图示

词或短语 Words & Phrases

吃早饭	chī zǎofàn	eat breakfast
吃米饭	chī mǐfàn	eat rice
吃面条	chī miàntiáo	eat noodles
吃饺子	chī jiǎozi	eat dumplings
吃喝玩乐	chīhē-wánlè	eat, drink, and be merry
吃苦耐劳	chīkǔ-nàiláo	be hardworking and able to bear hardships

锦言妙语 Proverbs & Witticism

吃得苦中苦,方为人上人 chī dé kǔ zhōng kǔ, fāng wéi rén shàng rén
He who can bear the bitterness of hardship can then be one above others.

吃人家的嘴软,拿人家的手短 chī rénjia de zuǐ ruǎn, ná rénjia de shǒu duǎn
A free man never asks for benefits or receives them.

吃苦在前,享乐在后 chīkǔ zài qián, xiǎnglè zài hòu
Be the first to bear hardships and the last to enjoy comforts.

LESSON 2 Nature Worship • 第二课 自然崇拜

伸 shēn (stretch; extend)　【部首】亻　【笔画】七画

丿丨丨𠃍一一丨
撇、竖、竖、横折、横、横、竖

金文	篆书	隶书	楷书	行书	简化字
Bronze Script	Seal Script	Official Script	Regular Script	Semi-cursive Script	Simplified Character

"伸"是形声兼会意字。"伸"的篆书写作𦨶，由亻(人)和申(申，展开)构成，意思是舒(shū)展(zhǎn)身体。从"人"(亻)，表示人体伸直；从"申"，申有舒展之义，申(shēn)兼表声。"伸"本义为展开、舒展。

伸 (shēn) 懒 (lǎn) 腰 (yāo)

词或短语 Words & Phrases

伸懒腰　　　shēn lǎn yāo　　　stretch oneself

锦言妙语 Proverbs & Witticism

大丈夫能屈能伸 dà zhàngfu néng qū néng shēn
A great man knows when to yield and when not — to be adaptable to circumstances.

衣来伸手，饭来张口 yī lái shēn shǒu, fàn lái zhāng kǒu
Have a living without doing any work.

伸手不见五指 shēn shǒu bú jiàn wǔ zhǐ
So dark that you can't see your hand in front of you.

二、注解 Notes

(一) 老子 (Lao Zi)

老子，姓李名耳，字伯阳，别名老聃 (dān)，楚国苦县人 (河南)。春秋时期著名思想家、教育家、哲学家、文学家和史学家，著有《道德经》(又称《老子》)，他是道家学派的始祖，与庄子并称"老庄"。在唐朝，老子被追认为李姓始祖，近代被列为世界百位历史文化名人之一。

老子做过周朝管理藏书的史官，阅读了大量的文献典籍，以博学多识而闻名天下，孔子曾向他问礼。春秋末年，天下大乱，老子欲弃官归隐，骑青牛西行，受人之请著《道德经》。老子以"道常无为而无不为"的"无为"思想解释人与自然，政治上主张无为而治，权术上讲究物极必反之理，修身上讲究不与人争的修持，其思想核心是朴素的辩证法观点，对中国哲学产生了深远影响。

道，是老子哲学思想的纽带。老子认为，人们对"道"并不是生而知之，而是后天逐步探索、认识，才能有所了解、感悟，因此"道"是可以阐述和解释的。但是，人们的探索是渐进的，认识是主观的、有限的，阐述和说解总是有局限的，与作为客观本体的"道"的玄妙幽深和丰富内涵还有相当大的距离，要想全面彻底地掌握"道"的真知，还需要一个长期不断的探索过程，所以说，"道可道，非常道"。同样，既然道本无名，道是由人们勉强命名的，所命之名只是仅就"道"的某一特征为理据，都不足以完全概括道的内涵、外延、情态和性状，所以说，"名可名，非常名"。

有关老子的话题研究不完、解释不尽，研究老子思想已成为一种国际性的文化现象。

(二) 孔子 (Confucius)

孔子 (公元前 551 年—公元前 479 年)，名丘，字仲尼，出生于山东曲阜。我国古代伟大的思想家、政治家、教育家，儒家学派创始人。

孔子的祖先本是贵族，家族因躲避政治祸乱，定居在鲁国 (今山东)。孔子三岁时，父亲去世，过着艰苦的生活。鲁国是一个礼仪之邦，孔子自幼受到周文化的熏陶，成年以后以好礼、知礼闻名。孔子在仕途上并不顺利。为了实现自己的理想和政治抱负，他曾同弟子们周游列国，奔走在许多国家之间，苦苦地和整个时代抗争，推行自己的德政思想，希望用他超时代的思想和智慧来影响春秋诸国的历史进程，但终未得到实权，无所作为，还曾险些遇害，所幸总有弟子追随。

孔子一生大部分时间从事教育，开中国历史上私人讲学的先河。相传孔子有三千名弟子，其中七十二人"通六艺"。孔子学说以"仁"为核心，贯穿于他的哲学、政治、教育、伦理、文化主张的诸多方面，即"一以贯之"。孔子思想以立身为出发点，而人能立身于世的首要条件就是具有"君子"人格，君子之魅力在于有仁爱之心，自重自律；表里如一，言行一致；积极进取，德才兼备；孜孜于学，注重实践；安贫乐道，谨守正义。可见，孔子伟大的人格感召力也凝聚于此。孔子的教育学说非常丰富，例如，他主张学思并重，学行统一；讲究因材施教，注重启发诱导；讲究有教无类，主张人人都有受教育的权利；强调身教胜于言教，注重人格精神的感化作用，等等。

孔子对中华文化产生了深远的影响，其言行思想主要记载于由弟子编撰的《论语》。孔夫子是人们对孔子的敬称，后世尊其为"至圣"(圣人中的圣人)、"万世师表"。

(三) 除夕 (Chinese New Year's Eve)

除夕又叫除夕夜、年三十、大年三十晚上，是农历年中最后一天的夜晚，即春节前一天的晚上。春节是中国四大传统节日之首，又称过年、过大年。除夕人们往往一夜不眠，叫守岁。除夕这一天，家里家外不但要打扫得干干净净，还要贴春联、贴年画、贴门神，人们都穿上新衣服。

年夜饭，又称年晚饭、团圆饭，特指年尾除夕(大年三十)全家人的大聚餐。除夕夜家家户户都要吃年夜饭，在外地工作、学习的家人，不论路途多么远，都会赶在除夕年夜饭之前回到家中和家人团聚。年夜饭对中国人来说是一年当中最重要的一顿晚餐，全家参与烹制，小孩子也不例外，其乐融融。家家户户都会摆上平日里少见的菜品，还得有几样寓意吉祥的菜品，桌上一般会有鱼(寓意年年有余)、有鸡(寓意吉祥如意)、有汤圆(寓意团团圆圆)等菜品，以求新年平安吉祥，饱含着人们对未来美好生活的期望和祝愿。年夜饭不仅菜品丰富，而且讲究很多。饭前先拜神祭祖，晚辈要给长辈磕头拜年，长辈给晚辈发红包(也叫压岁钱)。北方人除夕夜吃饺子，南方人习惯吃年糕，不管是吃饺子还是吃年糕，都要等到半夜十二点放过鞭炮后才开始吃。家家张灯结彩，互相祝福，祈盼新的一年风调雨顺、平安丰收，一年更比一年好。

年夜饭，吃的是期盼、祝福、喜悦，品的是亲情、甜甜蜜蜜、幸福美满，人们在美味佳肴中感受到的是家的味道。春节给人们带来的是对美好生活的追求和向往，展现了人们乐观、奋发向上的优良品格。

1949年12月23日，中华人民共和国中央人民政府规定每年春节放假三天。

(四) 时辰 (one of the 12 two-hour periods of the day)

时辰是中国传统计时单位，早在西周时 (公元前1046年—公元前771年) 就被使用。古人把一昼夜 (二十四小时) 平分为十二段，每一段称为一个时辰，每个时辰大致相当于现在的两小时。这十二个时辰分别以地支为名称，地支又称十二支，包括子 (zǐ)、丑 (chǒu)、寅 (yín)、卯 (mǎo)、辰 (chén)、巳 (sì)、午 (wǔ)、未 (wèi)、申 (shēn)、酉 (yǒu)、戌 (xū)、亥 (hài)。从夜间十一点算起，夜半十一点至一点是子时，夜一点至三点是丑时，中午十一点到一点是午时。

【子时】夜半，又名子夜、中夜，十二时辰的第一个时辰，23时至01时。

【丑时】鸡鸣，又名荒鸡，十二时辰的第二个时辰，01时至03时。

【寅时】平旦，又称黎明、早晨、日旦等，是夜与日的交替之际，03时至05时。

【卯时】日出，又名日始、破晓、旭日等，指太阳刚刚露脸、冉冉初升的那段时间，05时至07时。

【辰时】食时，又名早食等，是吃早饭的时间，07时至09时。

【巳时】隅 (yú) 中，又名日隅等，临近中午的时候称为隅中，09时至11时。

【午时】日中，又名日正、中午等，11时至13时。

【未时】日昳，又名日跌、日央等，太阳偏西为日昳，13时至15时。

【申时】晡时，又名日晡、夕食等，15时至17时。

【酉时】日入，又名日落、日沉、傍晚，意为太阳落山的时候，17时至19时。

【戌时】黄昏，又名日夕、日暮、日晚，此时太阳已落山，天将黑未黑，天地昏黄，万物朦胧，故称黄昏，19时至21时。

【亥时】人定，又名定昏，此时夜色已深，人们已经停止活动，安歇睡眠了，人定也就是人静，21时至23时。

三、反义词　Antonym

小—大

旦—夕

早—晚

明—暗

阳—阴

男—女

少—多

四、汉字的偏旁部首 The Structural Unit and Radical of Chinese Character

汉字数量很多，许多汉字都有共同的部首，部首是每个汉字的根本和灵魂，常用的部首有一百多个。

清代《康熙字典》收录了 47 035 个汉字和 214 个部首，其中有 7 个部首构成的汉字超出 1000 个，它们是：

"艹"字头 , grass (1902)

水（氵）, water (1595)

木 , tree (1369)

手（扌）, hand (1203)

口 , mouth (1146)

心（忄）, heart (1115)

虫 , insect (1067)

部首最初都是独体字。随着汉字的演变，有的独体字做部首时，形态上有所变化。例如"人"（人字头）、"亻"（单人旁）、"雨"（雨字头）、"力"部。

"人"（人字头）或"亻"（单人旁）

"人"字是个部首字，由"人"字组成的字大多与人的行为活动有关。带"人"（人字头）的字，"人"一般在字的上部，例如个、众、合、会、全等。

个	个人	gèrén	personal; individual
从	侍从	shìcóng	attendants
	跟从	gēncóng	follow
	顺从	shùncóng	obedience
众	群众	qúnzhòng	the masses
全	全体	quántǐ	all; entirety
会	集会	jíhuì	meeting; gathering
	一会儿	yíhuìr	a little while

	会议	huìyì	meeting
合	集合	jíhé	gather; assemble
舍	宿舍	sùshè	dormitory; hostel; lodging house
	舍弃	shěqì	give up; abandon
介	介绍	jièshào	introduce; recommend
	中介	zhōngjiè	intermediary agent
	介意	jièyì	care about; mind
企	企业	qǐyè	enterprise; firm; company
含	包含	bāohán	include; contain
今	今天	jīntiān	today
令	命令	mìnglìng	order; command
命	使命	shǐmìng	mission
仓	粮仓	liángcāng	grain barn
伞	雨伞	yǔsǎn	umbrella
余	剩余	shèngyú	remain; surplus
	余生	yúshēng	one's remaining years

"亻"（单人旁）是个部首，由"人"字演变而来，一般在字的左侧。例如休(xiū)，由"亻"（人）和"木"（树）构成，意思是人靠着树休息；再如，仁、他、体、住等。

仁	仁爱	rénài	kindheartedness
信	信心	xìnxīn	confidence
你	你们	nǐmen	you
您	您好	nínhǎo	hello(quite polite)
他	他们	tāmen	they; them
们	我们	wǒmen	we; us
休	休息	xiūxī	have a rest; take a rest
体	身体	shēntǐ	body
伸	伸懒腰	shēn lǎn yāo	stretch oneself; give a stretch
伙	伙伴	huǒbàn	partner; companion
什	什么	shénme	what
做	做人	zuò rén	behave
作	作业	zuòyè	school assignment
	作用	zuòyòng	role; function

化	文化	wénhuà	culture; civilization
	变化	biànhuà	change
伟	伟大	wěidà	greatness
住	住房	zhùfáng	housing
价	价格	jiàgé	price
任	责任	zérèn	duty; responsibility
	主任	zhǔrèn	director; chairman
借	借钱	jiè qián	borrow money
佃	佃农	diànnóng	tenant farmer
件	一件衬衫	yí jiàn chènshān	a shirt
依	依靠	yīkào	depend on; rely on
位	地位	dìwèi	position
俗	民俗	mínsú	folk-custom
但	但是	dànshì	but; however
例	例如	lìrú	such as; for example
使	使用	shǐyòng	use
停	停车	tíng chē	parking
便	方便	fāngbiàn	convenience
假	假期	jiàqī	vacation; holiday
傍	傍晚	bàngwǎn	at dusk; toward evening
舒	舒服	shūfu	comfortable
以	以前	yǐ qián	before; previously
	以后	yǐ hòu	afterwards; later
	以为	yǐwéi	believe; think
	所以	suóyǐ	so; therefore

"⻗"（"雨"字头）

"雨"部的字多与云、雨自然现象或气象情况有关，"雨"字头在上部，写作⻗，第二笔竖改为点，第三笔横折钩改为横钩。例如雪、霜、雹、雷等。

雪	下雪	xià xuě	snow; snowing
霜	霜冻	shuāngdòng	frost
零	零度	líng dù	zero; zero degree Celsius
雷	打雷	dǎ léi	thunder

雹	冰雹	bīngbáo	hail; hailstone
露	露水	lùshuǐ	dew
雾	雾霾	wùmái	smog; haze
霞	彩霞	cǎixiá	rosy clouds
震	地震	dìzhèn	earthquake
需	需要	xūyào	need; want
霉	青霉素	qīngméisù	penicillin
霸	霸道	bàdào	potent; bossy
	霸权	bàquán	hegemony; supremacy
	霸气	bàqì	aggressiveness

"力"部

"力"字是个部首字，由"力"字组成的字，大多都与力气、力量和行动有关。例如，助、勇、男、劳动、劣等。

办	办公室	bàngōngshì	office
	办法	bànfǎ	way; method
动	劳动	láodòng	labour
	动力	dònglì	power
	运动	yùndòng	exercise
劲	干劲	gànjìn	enthusiasm
加	增加	zēngjiā	add
助	帮助	bāngzhù	help; aid; assist
劝	劝说	quànshuō	persuade
励	鼓励	gǔlì	encourage
	勉励	miǎnlì	urge; encourage
功	成功	chénggōng	succeed; win
	功能	gōngnéng	function
	功夫	gōngfu	effort; kung fu
勇	勇敢	yǒnggǎn	brave
	勇气	yǒngqì	courage
勤	勤劳	qínláo	hard-working
	勤快	qínkuai	diligent
努	努力	nǔlì	strive; endeavor
势	势力	shìlì	force; power
	优势	yōushì	advantage

	劣势	lièshì	disadvantage
劣	恶劣	èliè	scurviness
	劣质品	lièzhìpǐn	products of inferior quality
劫	打劫	dǎjié	rob
务	任务	rènwù	task; mission; assignment

五、HSK 试题选做 Sample Questions of the New HSK

(一) 根据对话选择正确的图片 (Choose the Corresponding Pictures Based on the Dialogues)

1. A: 你什么时候来中国的？　　　　　　　　　　　　　　　(　　)
   B: 上周星期三来的。
2. A: 沈阳的冬天下雨吗？　　　　　　　　　　　　　　　　(　　)
   B: 沈阳的冬天不下雨，下雪，有时还下很大的雪。
3. A: 你喜欢什么运动？　　　　　　　　　　　　　　　　　(　　)
   B: 我喜欢骑自行车。
4. A: 最近这几天一直下雨。　　　　　　　　　　　　　　　(　　)
   B: 是啊，不过明天是晴天。
5. A: 你喜欢什么动物？　　　　　　　　　　　　　　　　　(　　)
   B: 我喜欢狗。

6. A: 这是我第一次在海边看日出。　　　　　　　　　　　　　　（　）
　　B: 我也是。

(二) 根据句子选择相应的图片 (Choose the Corresponding Pictures Based on the Sentences)

例如，大熊猫是世界上最珍贵的动物之一。　　　　　　　　　　　（ C ）
1. 很多人喜欢在吃完饭后马上吃水果，其实这样做对身体并不好，正确的做法是在饭后两个小时或饭前一个小时吃水果。　　　　　　　　　（　）
2. 闪电、打雷、下雨是地球上常见的自然现象，可是在水星上却不会有。（　）
3. 下象棋的人都挺聪明的。　　　　　　　　　　　　　　　　　（　）
4. 天气预报说，最近的天气都非常好，星期天我们一起去爬山吧！　（　）
5. 我喜欢运动，一直坚持晨跑。　　　　　　　　　　　　　　　（　）

六、朗读与书写练习　Reading and Writing Exercises

我们下一盘象棋吧。
一星期有五个工作日。
他每天日出而作，日落而息。
去年七月我们去了新加坡。
他们是在创造人间奇迹。
他是一个大老板。
劳动两个小时之后，我们在田头休息了一会儿。

老虎是兽中之王。
中国人民的生活已达到小康水平。
又下雨了！
青年人应该经风雨，见世面。
那是一个美丽的下午，蓝蓝的天空中飘着几朵白云。
只要人民团结一致，就能力挽狂澜。
天气真热！渴死我了！
这位老妇人靠乞讨生活。
电是一种重要的能源。
她申请的那几所大学都录取了她。
星期日我们去爬山吧。
战争使这个国家元气大伤。
科学家们在通宵达旦地工作。
这个问题不是一朝一夕能够圆满解决的。
太阳从东方升起。
又见到你了，太高兴了！
年轻人就像早晨七八点钟的太阳，希望寄托在你们身上。
一年三百六十五天。
只要人人都献出一点爱，世界将变成美好的明天。
A: 你叫什么名字？ B: 我叫白雪。
A: 你今年多大了？ B: 我三岁了。
她是个很有名气的大夫。
这本书上面写着我的名字。
台湾自古以来就是中国的领土。
中国人口众多，地大物博。
把地夯实。
只有各学校的学生尖子才能通过HSK5级考试。
我们都很年轻，难免会犯错误。
他将为自己的劣迹付出代价。
只有因材施教，才能多出人才。
他为病所困多年。
我困了，想睡觉。
他的勇气感动了所有的人。
只要大家行动起来，事情就好办了。
小孩儿在马路上玩耍是很危险的。

她们姐妹俩长得太像了。
才学习一年,她的汉语说得挺像样子了。
鲜艳的五星红旗高高飘扬在北京天安门广场。
昨晚天上布满了星星。
人们常说时间就是金钱,然而时间却比金钱更贵重——时间就是生命。
发言的时候你怎么想就怎么说。
天在下雪。
天上飘着雪花。
这孩子被宠坏了,吃不得苦。

[第三课]
LESSON 3

五行
The Five Elements

道生一，一生二，二生三，三生万物。

——老子

From Tao comes the oneness of being; From oneness comes the duality of Yin and Yang; From duality comes the equilibrium of Yin and Yang; From equilibrium come all things under heaven.

— Lao Zi

一、读写基本汉字 Read and Write Basic Chinese Characters

象形字
Pictographic Characters

火	huǒ (fire)	【部首】火　【笔画】四画
	丶ノノ乀 点、撇、撇、捺	

甲骨文	金文	篆书	隶书	楷书	行书	简化字
Oracle Bones	Bronze Script	Seal Script	Official Script	Regular Script	Semi-cursive Script	Simplified Character

"火"是象形字。甲骨文的"火"写作 ，形似火焰(yàn)升腾。《说文解字》："火，毁也。"火可以烧毁很多东西。"火"本义是指物体燃(rán)烧(shāo)时产生的光焰。在上下结构的汉字中作偏旁时，"火"被写成四点底"灬"。

五行之中，火代表南方属性，火光熊熊，气势向上。

中医指人身出现阳性、热性一类现象即为上火、内火。现在，"火"还被用作动词，表示脾气不好，如发火、火暴脾气；也表示紧急，如火速、十万火急、心急火燎。

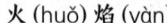

火(huǒ)焰(yàn)

北京猿人用火图

词或短语　Words & Phrases

火车站　　　huǒchēzhàn　　　railway station

LESSON 3 The Five Elements • 第三课 五行

火 (huǒ) 车 (chē) 站 (zhàn)

火光	huǒguāng	flare; blaze
上火	shàng huǒ	get inflamed
发火	fā huǒ	get angry
十万火急	shíwànhuǒjí	most urgent

锦言妙语 Proverbs & Witticism

火车跑得快，全靠车头带 huǒchē pǎo de kuài, quán kào chētóu dài
Trains run fast all because of the engine.

不到火候不揭锅 bú dào huǒhou bù jiē guō
Not to lift the pot cover until the food is properly cooked — very patient.

火趁风威，风助火势 huǒ chèn fēng wēi, fēng zhù huǒshì
As the wind fanned the fire, the fire grew in the might of the wind.

白 bái (white; brightness) 【部首】白 【笔画】五画

ノ 丨 𠃍 一 一
撇、竖、横折、横、横

甲骨文	金文	篆书	隶书	楷书	行书	简化字
Oracle Bones	Bronze Script	Seal Script	Official Script	Regular Script	Semi-cursive Script	Simplified Character

"白"是象形字。一种解(jiě)释(shì)认为,"白"形似一粒白米;另一种解释认为"白"像初升的太阳。白本义是白色,如雪白、白云。

甲骨文的"白"像燃(rán)烧(shāo)的蜡烛,形似烛光,中心部分是烛芯。蜡烛燃烧给人带来光明,所以"白"的本义是光亮或明亮,如白天;引申表示清楚,如明白、清白、不白之冤。

蜡(là)烛(zhú)

词或短语 Words & Phrases

白天	báitiān	daytime
白雪	báixuě	white snow
白颜色	bái yánsè	white
明白	míngbai	understand
清白	qīngbái	innocency
白酒	báijiǔ	alcohol; liquor
蓝天白云	lántiān báiyún	blue sky and white cloud
白手起家	báishǒuqǐjiā	build up from nothing

锦言妙语 Proverbs & Witticism

白日做梦,痴心妄想 báirìzuòmèng, chīxīnwàngxiǎng
An idiot's daydream.

瞎子点灯——白费蜡 xiāzi diǎn dēng——bái fèi là
As useless as a blind man lighting a candle. ‖ It is like lighting a lamp for a blind man — absolutely useless.

小葱拌豆腐——一清二白 xiǎocōng bàn dòufu—— yì qīng èr bái
Spring onions mixed with beancurd — very green and very white. (The onions are of an azure green, while the beancurd is white. Used on anything which is entirely lucid.)

LESSON 3　The Five Elements • 第三课　五行

愁一愁，白了头；笑一笑，十年少 chóu yi chóu, bái le tóu; xiào yi xiào, shí nián shào
You'll get ten years younger when you keep smiling while you may have gray hairs once in worries.

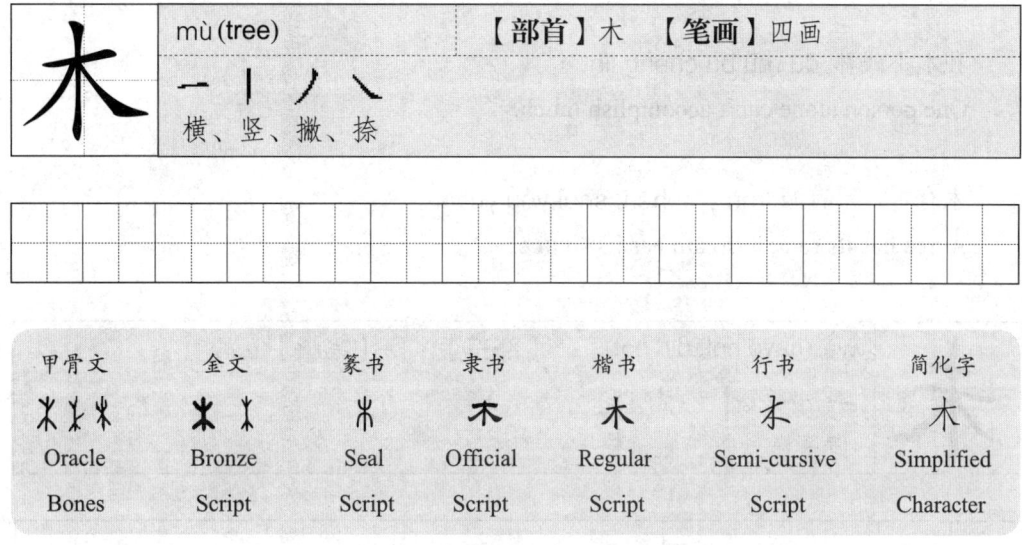

"木"是象形字。甲骨文的"木"写作 ✳ ✳ ✳，如同树(shù)的形状，上有枝 ⍋，下有根 ⍎。树在上古时称为木，后来才称为树。"木"本义指树木，后引申指木头、木料。

树(shù) 木(mù)

词或短语　Words & Phrases

木材　　　　mùcái　　　wood; timber

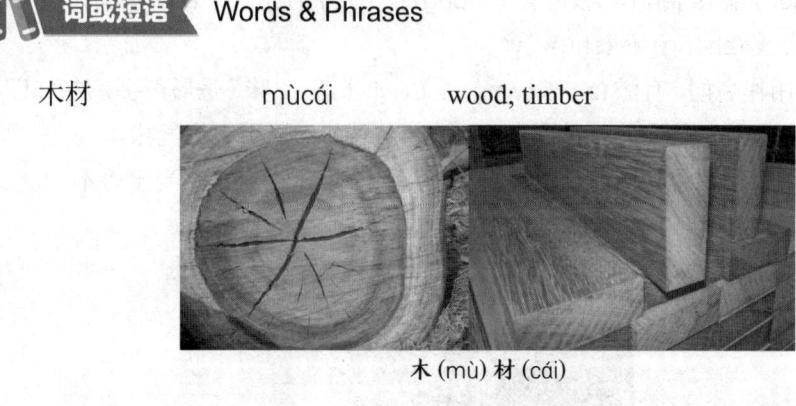

木(mù) 材(cái)

积木　　　　jīmù　　　building block; toy bricks

锦言妙语 Proverbs & Witticism

板上钉钉——十拿九稳 bǎn shàng dìng dīng——shínájiǔwěn
To put a nail into a board — to be sure to succeed.

独木不成林 dú mù bù chéng lín
One person alone can't accomplish much.

木有本，水有源 mù yǒu běn, shuǐ yǒu yuán
A tree has its root; a stream has its source.

未　wèi (have not; did not)　【部首】木　【笔画】五画
一、一、丨、丿、㇏
横、横、竖、撇、捺

甲骨文	金文	篆书	隶书	楷书	行书	简化字
Oracle Bones	Bronze Script	Seal Script	Official Script	Regular Script	Semi-cursive Script	Simplified Character

　　"未"是象形字。甲骨文的"未"写作，由（木或树）和（枝叶）构成，形体像树木茂(mào)盛(shèng)、枝叶重(chóng)叠(dié)的样子，表示繁茂。此时果树上的果实还没有成(chéng)熟(shú)。

　　现在，"未"用作名词，有滋(zī)味(wèi)之义，如味道。"味"是形声字，从"口"、从"未"，未兼表声，表示舌头尝到的味道，甜味、苦味，又引申指气味。

　　另外，"未"字常用作副词，意思是没有、不曾，表示否定，相当于"不"。

未(wèi)熟(shú)的(de)果(guǒ)子(zi)

LESSON 3 The Five Elements • 第三课 五行

词或短语 Words & Phrases

未成年	wèichéngnián	under age
未必	wèibì	may not; not sure
未婚	wèihūn	unmarried
未来	wèilái	future
未老先衰	wèilǎoxiānshuāi	prematurely senile
闻所未闻	wénsuǒwèiwén	never heard of before

锦言妙语 Proverbs & Witticism

古今中外，前所未有 gǔjīn-zhōngwài, qiánsuǒwèiyǒu
It was unprecedented, either in China or abroad, in ancient or modern society.

兵马未到，粮草先行 bīngmǎ wèi dào, liángcǎo xiān xíng
Food and fodder should go before troops and horses — proper preparation should be made in advance.

愚者暗于成事，智者见于未萌 yú zhě àn yú chéng shì, zhì zhě jiànyú wèi méng
Fools are blind to what already exists whereas the wise perceive what is yet to come.

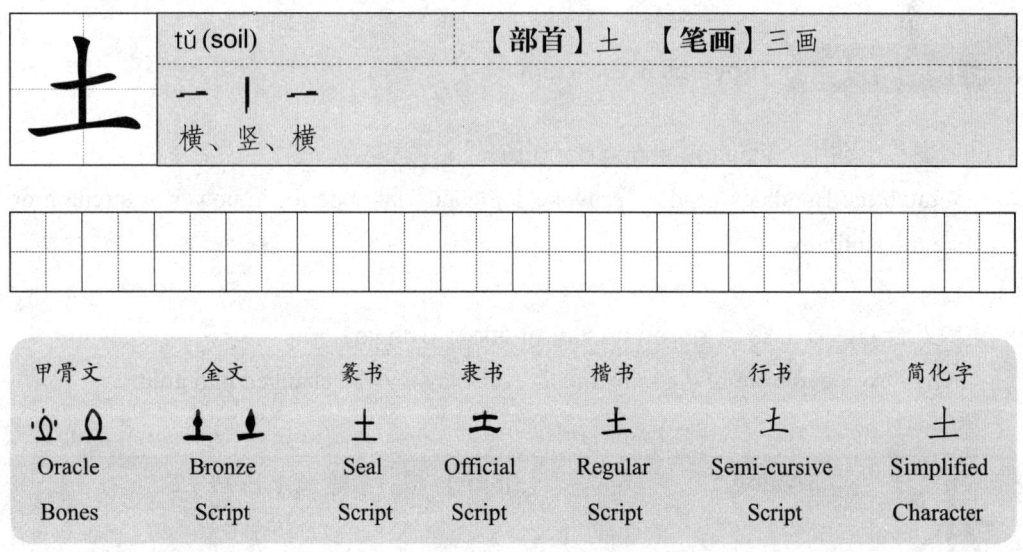

"土"是象形字。甲骨文的"土"写作 ⚲ ，表示泥土，下面的 ▬ 表示土地，上面

- 085 -

的 ◊ 表示土堆 (duī)。《说文解字》："土，地之吐生物者也。"土的上下两横表示在地面之下、泥土之中，中间的一竖像植物破土而出。

"土"本义指土地、泥土、土壤，由土地引申为家乡、乡土、故土、国土、领土，又引申为本地的、地方的。土地是人类的生存之本，古人对土地的感情极为深厚。

土 (tǔ) 地 (dì)

词或短语　Words & Phrases

土地	tǔdì	land; soil
沙土	shātǔ	sandy soil
土壤	tǔrǎng	soil
故土	gùtǔ	homeland; native land
国土	guótǔ	territory
土特产	tǔtèchǎn	local and special products
土生土长	tǔshēng-tǔzhǎng	born and brought up on one's native soil

锦言妙语　Proverbs & Witticism

太岁头上动土　tàisuì tóu shàng dòng tǔ

Scratch the Buddha's head — provoke somebody far superior in power or strength or provoke the almighty.

二人合心，黄土变金　èr rén hé xīn, huángtǔ biàn jīn

When two people are of the same mind, even clay may be changed into gold.

LESSON 3 The Five Elements • 第三课 五行

甲骨文	金文	篆书	隶书	楷书	行书	简化字
水	水	水	水	水	水	水
Oracle Bones	Bronze Script	Seal Script	Official Script	Regular Script	Semi-cursive Script	Simplified Character

"水"是象形字。古文字的"水"形似一条弯曲的河 (hé) 流 (liú)，文字中的几个点表示水滴或浪花。"水"本义指河流、水流，又泛指江 (jiāng)、河、湖 (hú)、海 (hǎi)、地下水等。水也指一种无色无味的透明液体，被称为生命之源。

五行中，水代表北方的属性。

黄 (huáng) 河 (hé) 壶 (hú) 口 (kǒu) 瀑 (pù) 布 (bù)

词或短语 Words & Phrases

水滴　　　shuǐdī　　　　　　water drops

水 (shuǐ) 滴 (dī)

山水画　　shānshuǐhuà　　　landscape painting

山 (shān) 水 (shuǐ) 画 (huà)

水果　　　　shuǐguǒ　　　　　　fruit

水 (shuǐ) 果 (guǒ)

汗水	hànshuǐ	sweat
水平	shuǐpíng	level; standard; horizontal
白开水	báikāishuǐ	plain boiled water
水到渠成	shuǐdàoqúchéng	When water flows, a channel is formed.
上善若水	shàngshànruòshuǐ	The highest excellence is like that of water.

锦言妙语　Proverbs & Witticism

水火不相容　shuǐ huǒ bù xiāng róng
Be incompatible like water and fire.

水往低处流，人往高处走　shuǐ wǎng dī chù liú, rén wǎng gāo chù zǒu
Water always flows from a higher to a lower level, but everyone has an ambition to rise higher up in society.

桂林山水甲天下　Guilin shānshuǐ jiǎ tiānxià
Guìlín's scenery is the best in the world.

泉　quán (water spring)　　【部首】水　【笔画】九画

丿 丨 ㄱ 一 一 亅 ㄱ 丿 乀
撇、竖、横折、横、横、竖钩、横撇/横钩、撇、捺

甲骨文	金文	篆书	隶书	楷书	行书	简化字
Oracle Bones	Bronze Script	Seal Script	Official Script	Regular Script	Semi-cursive Script	Simplified Character

"泉"是象形字。甲骨文的"泉"写作🝙、🝚,形似泉水从泉眼(yǎn)中流出。《说文解字》:"泉,水源。""泉"本义指水的源(yuán)头(tóu),后泛指地下水。

山(shān)泉(quán)

词或短语 Words & Phrases

温泉	wēnquán	thermal spring; spa
甘泉	gānquán	sweet spring
矿泉水	kuàngquánshuǐ	mineral water

锦言妙语 Proverbs & Witticism

生活是创作的源泉 shēnghuó shì chuàngzuò de yuánquán
Life reality is the source of literary creation.

知识好像地下泉水,掘得越深越清澈
zhīshi hǎoxiàng dìxià quánshuǐ, juéde yuè shēn yuè qīngchè
Knowledge is like the spring water underground, the deeper you dig, the clearer the water is.

川	chuān (river; stream) 丿丨丨 撇、竖、竖	【部首】丿	【笔画】三画

甲骨文	金文	篆书	隶书	楷书	行书	简化字
𝕴𝕴𝕴	川	巛	川	川	川	川
Oracle Bones	Bronze Script	Seal Script	Official Script	Regular Script	Semi-cursive Script	Simplified Character

"川"是象形字。甲骨文的"川"写作𝕴,金文的"川"简化为𝕴,皆形似河水流动。"川"本义指河流、水道。

在造字时代,水流的源头叫"泉";石壁上飞溅的山泉叫"水";众多小河汇集成的水流叫"川";众多川流汇成的大川叫"河",最大的河叫"江",如黄河、长江。

现在,"川"字经常作为四川省的简称。四川的三大特色是美食、美景、美女,漂亮的"川妹子"就是指四川姑娘。

川 (chuān) 流 (liú)

词或短语　Words & Phrases

冰 (bīng) 川 (chuān)

冰川	bīng chuān	glacier
山川	shānchuān	mountains and rivers
川菜	chuāncài	Sichuan cuisine
川剧	chuānjù	Sichuan opera
名山大川	míngshān-dàchuān	well-known mountains and rivers
川流不息	chuānliúbùxī	The stream never stops flowing.
百川归海	bǎichuānguīhǎi	All rivers flow into the sea.

锦言妙语　Proverbs & Witticism

海纳百川,有容乃大 hǎinàbǎichuān, yǒuróngnǎidà
The ocean is vast because it is fed by hundreds of rivers. || A man should be as inclusive as the vast ocean which admits hundreds of rivers.

积土成山,积水成川 jītǔchéngshān, jīshuǐchéngchuān
Heaped-up earth becomes a mountain, and accumulated water becomes a river.

防民之口，甚于防川 fáng mín zhī kǒu, shèn yú fáng chuān
Blocking the speech of the people is more harmful than blocking a river.

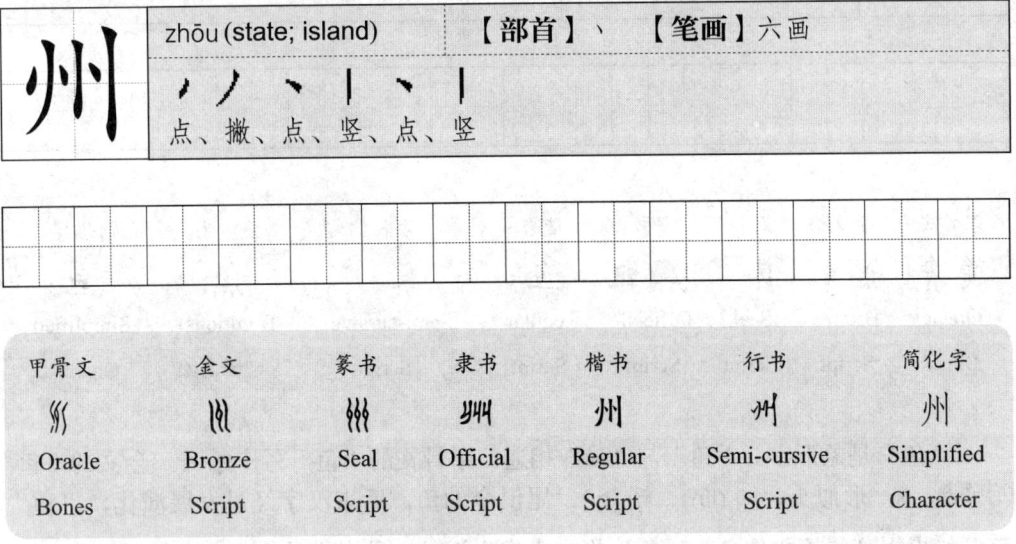

"州"是象形字。甲骨文的"州"写作⽔，形似一条河流，中间的小椭圆表示一小块陆地，形似可以居住生活的小岛 (dǎo)，这一小块地势较高的水中陆地叫"州"。"州"是"洲"的古字。"州"本义指水中的一块陆地。

据说上古时经常发生水灾，人们就迁到地势高的地方居住，这个高地也称为州。相传大禹把这种高地划分成九个部分，称为九州。汉代以后，"州"指一种地方行政区域，有的沿用至今，如扬州、苏州、杭州、广州、福州、贵州、兰州等。

词或短语　Words & Phrases

州官	zhōuguān	district magistrate
神州大地	shénzhōudàdì	the Wonderful Land of China

锦言妙语　Proverbs & Witticism

只许州官放火，不许百姓点灯 zhǐ xǔ zhōuguān fàng huǒ, bù xǔ bǎixìng diǎn dēng

The magistrates are free to burn down houses, while the common people are forbidden even to light lamps — the privileged are legally permitted to do whatever they like, while the underprivileged are prohibited from their means of livelihood.

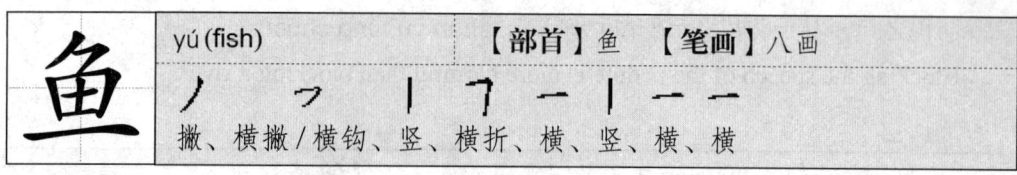

甲骨文	金文	篆书	隶书	楷书	行书	繁体字	简化字
Oracle Bones	Bronze Script	Seal Script	Official Script	Regular Script	Semi-cursive Script	Traditional Character	Simplified Character

"鱼"是象形字。"鱼"与"渔"相通。甲骨文的"鱼"写作🐟、🐟，金文的"鱼"写作🐟、🐟，形似头、鳞(lín)、鳍(qí)、尾俱全的鱼。后来汉字经过发展演化，"鱼"字开始慢慢变得不再像鱼。"鱼"指在水中生活的一种脊椎动物。

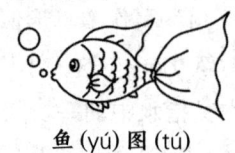

鱼(yú)图(tú)

词或短语 Words & Phrases

三文鱼　　　　　sānwényú　　　　　salmon

三(sān)文(wén)鱼(yú)

打(捕)鱼　　　　dǎ(bǔ)yú　　　　　catch fish

锦言妙语 Proverbs & Witticism

水至清则无鱼　shuǐ zhì qīng zé wú yú
Fish do not come when water is too clear.

鱼与熊掌，不可兼得　yú yǔ xióngzhǎng, bù kě jiān dé

LESSON 3　The Five Elements • 第三课　五行

You cannot have your cake and eat it too.

浑水好摸鱼　hún shuǐ hǎo mō yú
It is good fishing in troubled waters.

网	wǎng (net; netlike thing)	【部首】冂　【笔画】六画
	丨 冂 丿 丶 丿 丶 竖、横折钩、撇、点、撇、点	

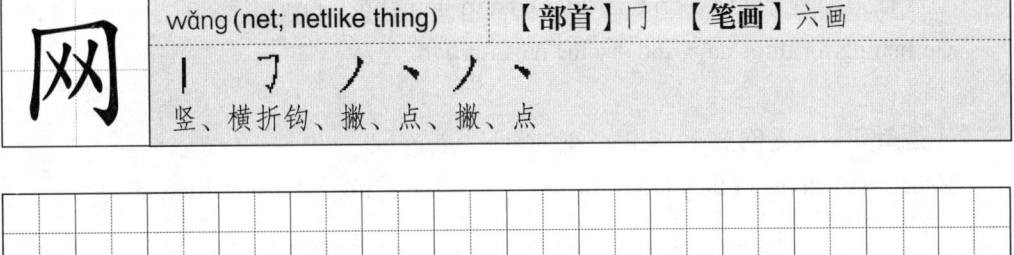

"网"是象形字。甲骨文的"网"写作 ⺳、⺳，像用绳(shéng)线(xiàn)结成的一张网，用来捕鸟、兽、鱼。⺳像两根木桩‖之间绳线交(jiāo)织(zhī)，⺳则简化了格状的绳线。"网"本义指一种用绳线编(biān)织成的捕(bǔ)鱼、鳖、鸟、兽的工(gōng)具(jù)。

鱼(yú)网(wǎng)

　Words & Phrases

捕鱼　　　bǔ yú　　　fishing

捕(bǔ)鱼(yú)

| 法网 | fǎwǎng | the net of justice |
| 上网 | shàng wǎng | surfing the Internet |

锦言妙语 Proverbs & Witticism

三天打鱼，两天晒网 sān tiān dǎ yú, liǎng tiān shài wǎng
Go fishing for three days and dry the nets for two.

不是鱼死，就是网破 bú shì yú sǐ, jiù shì wǎng pò
Either the fish die or they break the net — to wage a life-and-death struggle.

一网打不尽河里的鱼 yì wǎng dǎ bú jìn hé lǐ de yú
You cannot catch all the fish in the river in one haul — you can't achieve everything at one stroke.

指事字
Self-explanatory Characters

一	yī (one; oneness)	【部首】一　【笔画】一画
	横	

甲骨文	金文	篆书	隶书	楷书	行书	简化字
一	一	一	一	一	一	一
Oracle Bones	Bronze Script	Seal Script	Official Script	Regular Script	Semi-cursive Script	Simplified Character

"一"是指事字，用一横画表示抽象的数目一。"一"代表最为简单的起源，也代表最为丰富的混沌整体。老子认为"道生一，一生二，二生三，三生万物"，就是说，太初混沌的存在整体是"一"；然后由太初混沌的"一"，分出天地"二"极；

天地二极之间，又生出人这第"三"部分；天地人三者，衍化出宇宙万物。天、地、人，总体代表万物之源。

词或短语　Words & Phrases

一块钱	yī kuài qián	one yuan
第一	dìyī	first
一般	yìbān	ordinary; common
一定	yídìng	certainly; must be; by all means
统一	tǒngyī	unify
万一	wànyī	in case
一起	yìqǐ	together
一共	yígòng	altogether; in all
一直	yì zhí	all the time; always
一边	yì biān	at the same time
一心一意	yìxīn-yíyì	undivided attention
一举两得	yìjǔliǎngdé	kill two birds with one stone

锦言妙语　Proverbs & Witticism

一年之计在于春　yì nián zhī jì zài yú chūn
Spring is the best time to do the year's work.

一日之计在于晨　yí rì zhī jì zài yú chén
Morning hours is the best time of the day to work.

一花独放不是春，百花齐放春满园
yì huā dú fàng bú shì chūn, bǎihuāqífàng chūn mǎn yuán
Spring does not arrive with the blossoming of a single flower. || When one hundred flowers blossom, spring permeates the orchard.

二	èr (two)	【部首】一　【笔画】二画
	一一 横、横	

甲骨文	金文	篆书	隶书	楷书	行书	简化字
二	二	二	二	二	二	二
Oracle Bones	Bronze Script	Seal Script	Official Script	Regular Script	Semi-cursive Script	Simplified Character

"二"是指事字，一加一之和。古文的"二"字，由两条长度相等且不相 (xiāng) 交 (jiāo) 的短线表示。老子认为，二表示天地"二"极，上面的一横代表天，下面的一横代表地。

词或短语 Words & Phrases

星期二	xīngqī'èr	Tuesday
合二为一	hé'èrwéiyī	become one; combined
略知一二	lüèzhīyī'èr	know a little about
独一无二	dúyīwú'èr	alone
说一不二	shuōyībú'èr	stand by one's word

锦言妙语 Proverbs & Witticism

二虎相争，必有一伤 èr hǔ xiāng zhēng, bì yǒu yì shāng
When two tigers fight, one is sure to lose.

一山不容二虎 yì shān bù róng èr hǔ
Two tigers can't share the same mountain.

三	sān (three)	【部首】一 【笔画】三画
	———	
	横、横、横	

甲骨文	金文	篆书	隶书	楷书	行书	简化字
☰	三	三	三	三	三	三
Oracle Bones	Bronze Script	Seal Script	Official Script	Regular Script	Semi-cursive Script	Simplified Character

"三"是指事字,由三横组成。老子认为,"道生一,一生二,二生三,三生万物"。就是说,混沌太初的存在整体是"一";然后由太初混沌的"一",分出天地"二"极;天地二极之间,又生出人这第"三"部分;天、地、人三者,衍化出宇宙万物。"三"的上下两横代表天地,中间的一横代表人。《说文解字》:"三,天地人之道也"。

词或短语 Words & Phrases

三年级	sān nián jí	grade three
三心二意	sānxīn-èryì	half-hearted
三思而行	sānsī'érxíng	Look before you leap.
三长两短	sāncháng-liǎngduǎn	unexpected misfortune especially death
举一反三	jǔyī-fǎnsān	draw inferences about other cases from one instance

锦言妙语 Proverbs & Witticism

三个和尚没水吃 sān gè héshang méi shuǐ chī
Everyone's business is nobody's business.

三个臭皮匠,顶个诸葛亮 sān gè chòu píjiang dǐng gè Zhūgě Liàng
Two heads are better than one. ‖ Three cobblers with their wits combined equal Zhuge Liang the master mind — the wisdom of the masses exceeds that of the wisest individual.

一日不见,如隔三秋 yí rì bú jiàn, rú gé sān qiū
One day away from a dear one seems as long as three years.

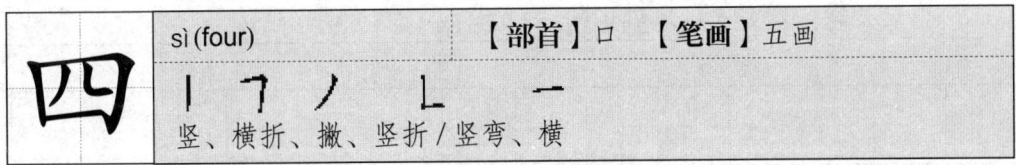

sì (four) 　【部首】囗　【笔画】五画

四　丨 ㇆ 丿 ㄴ 一
竖、横折、撇、竖折/竖弯、横

甲骨文	金文	篆书	隶书	楷书	行书	简化字
Oracle Bones	Bronze Script	Seal Script	Official Script	Regular Script	Semi-cursive Script	Simplified Character

"四"是特殊指事字。甲骨文的"四"写作☰,表示其为"二"的两倍。金文的"四"承续甲骨文字形。将金文的☰竖写,就成了川,将川与二(二,表示四是二的倍数)合写,就成了皿。

词或短语 Words & Phrases

四季	sìjì	the four seasons
四面八方	sìmiàn-bāfāng	all directions
四通八达	sìtōng-bādá	extend in all directions
低三下四	dīsān-xiàsì	degrading; lowly

锦言妙语 Proverbs & Witticism

四海之内皆兄弟 sì hǎi zhī nèi jiē xiōngdi
Within the four seas, all men are brothers.

四肢发达,头脑简单 sìzhī fādá, tóunǎo jiǎndān
Have well-developed limbs but a moronic head.

百 bǎi (hundred) 【部首】白 【笔画】六画

一ノ丨フ一一
横、撇、竖、横折、横、横

甲骨文	金文	篆书	隶书	楷书	行书	繁体字	简化字
Oracle Bones	Bronze Script	Seal Script	Official Script	Regular Script	Semi-cursive Script	Traditional Character	Simplified Character

甲骨文的"百"写作⊖，在"白"（⊖）字上加一横画 ——，为指事符号，以区别于"白"字，而仍以"白"字为声，表示述说不尽。"百"字本义指代数字，十个十是一百。后来，"百"常用来形容众多，如老百姓，指的是广大人民。

中 (zhōng) 国 (guó) 百 (bǎi) 家 (jiā) 姓 (xìng) 举 (jǔ) 例 (lì)

词或短语 Words & Phrases

百家姓	bǎijiāxìng	the Book of Family Names
百科全书	bǎikēquánshū	encyclopedia
百货商店	bǎihuò shāngdiàn	department store
数以百计	shùyǐbǎijì	count by the hundreds
百思不解	bǎisībùjiě	incomprehensible

锦言妙语 Proverbs & Witticism

三百六十行，行行出状元 sān bǎi liù shí háng, hángháng chū zhuàngyuan
One may distinguish himself in all trades and professions.

百闻不如一见 bǎi wén bù rú yí jiàn
It is better to see once than hear a hundred times. ‖ Seeing is believing.

知己知彼，百战百胜 zhī jǐ zhī bǐ, bǎi zhàn bǎi shèng
To know one's own strength and the enemy's is the sure way to victory.

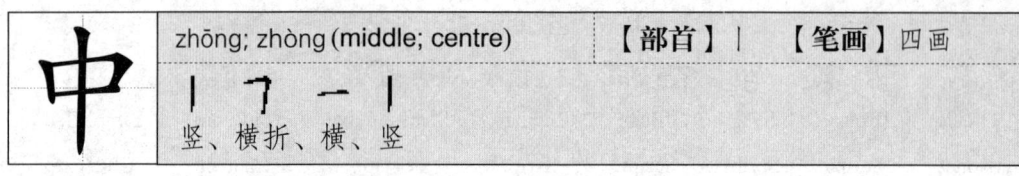

甲骨文	金文	篆书	隶书	楷书	行书	简化字
Oracle Bones	Bronze Script	Seal Script	Official Script	Regular Script	Semi-cursive Script	Simplified Character

"中"是指事字。古文字的"中"形似一面旗子，旗杆竖立中间，飘(piāo)带(dài)迎风招展。一个竖"丨"直接穿过口(wéi，古"围"字)中心，表明中间、中央的位置。"中"本义为氏族社会的徽(huī)帜(zhì)正好插在栅栏的正中央。

"中"又读zhòng，用作动词，表示正对上、正好合上，如百发百中、猜中、中意、正中(zhòng)靶(bǎ)心(xīn)。

靶(bǎ)心(xīn)

词或短语 Words & Phrases

中国	Zhōngguó	China
中文	zhōngwén	Chinese
中午	zhōngwǔ	noon
中间	zhōngjiān	middle; intermediate
在研究中	zài yánjiū zhōng	under study
看中	kànzhòng	feel satisfied with
猜中	cāizhòng	guess correctly
中意	zhòngyì	love
目中无人	mùzhōngwúrén	be overweening

锦言妙语 Proverbs & Witticism

中华人民共和国 Zhōnghuárénmíngònghéguó

LESSON 3 The Five Elements • 第三课　五行

The People's Republic of China (PRC)

家中不和邻里欺 jiā zhōng bù hé línlǐ qī
If the family is disunited, the neighbors will take advantage of the rift.

炉中添炭，火上浇油 lú zhōng tiān tàn, huǒshàngjiāoyóu
It was as if coals were heaped upon a fire and oil was poured upon the flames.

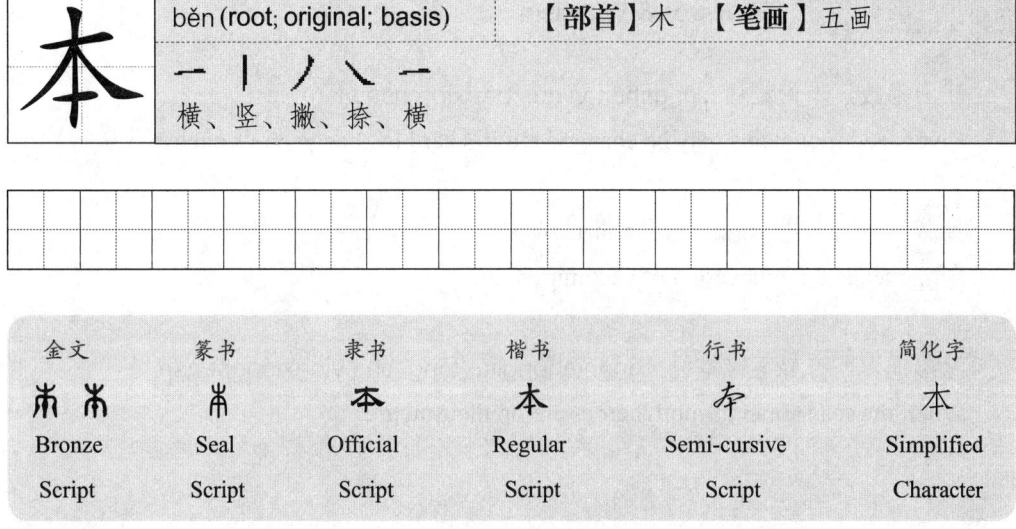

"本"是指事字。金文的"本"写作朩、朩，篆书的"本"写作朩，在"木"字中标明树根的位置所在。《说文解字》："本，木下为本。""本"本义指树木的根或茎干，树木需要它们吸(xī)收(shōu)和输(shū)送(sòng)水分及营养，后来"本"泛指草木的根(gēn)茎(jīng)，引申为根本、主体、原来、原始等意义。

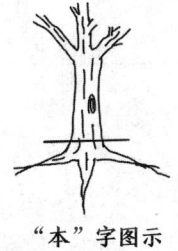

"本"字图示

词或短语　Words & Phrases

本来	běnlái	original
基本	jīběn	basic; fundamental

- 101 -

课本	kèběn	textbook
笔记本	bǐjìběn	notebook
本钱	běnqián	capital
本年	běn nián	current year
本人	běn rén	self; in person
本领	běnlǐng	ability
本地	běn dì	native place

锦言妙语 Proverbs & Witticism

江山易改，本性难移 jiāngshān yì gǎi, běnxìng nán yí
Rivers and mountains may be changed but it's hard to change one's nature.

勤劳为致富之本 qínláo wéi zhìfù zhī běn
Diligence is the foundation of becoming rich.

沧海横流，方显英雄本色 cānghǎihéngliú, fāng xiǎn yīngxióngběnsè
When the seas are in turmoil, heroes are on their mettle.

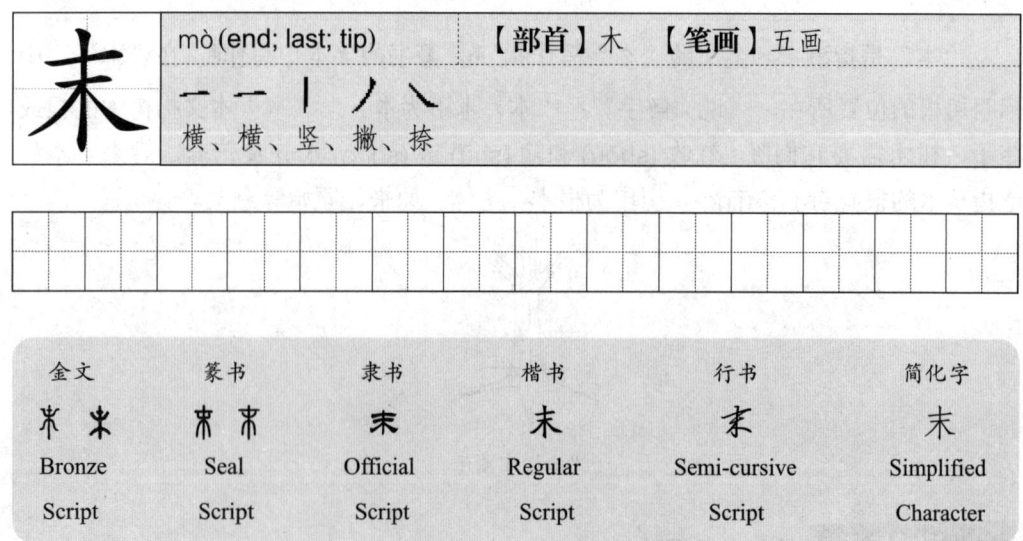

末 mò (end; last; tip) 【部首】木 【笔画】五画
一 一 丨 丿 乀
横、横、竖、撇、捺

金文	篆书	隶书	楷书	行书	简化字
Bronze Script	Seal Script	Official Script	Regular Script	Semi-cursive Script	Simplified Character

"末"是指事字。金文的"末"写作木，其中，木(木)代表树，树上端加"一"指示部位。《说文解字》："末，木上为末。"树的顶部叫末。"末"本义指树梢(shāo)，

泛指事物的尾部、顶 (dǐng) 端 (duān)、末端、末梢。

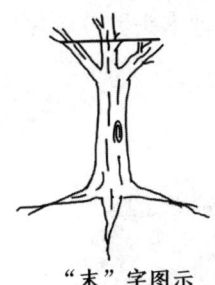

"末"字图示

词或短语 Words & Phrases

周末愉快	zhōumò yúkuài	have a nice weekend
期末考试	qīmò kǎoshì	final exam
本末倒置	běnmòdàozhì	Take the branch for the root; put the cart before the horse.

锦言妙语 Proverbs & Witticism

合抱之木，生于毫末 hé bào zhī mù, shēng yú háo mò
A huge tree grows from a tiny seedling.

物有本末，事有始终 wù yǒu běn mò, shì yǒu shǐ zhōng
There is a proper sequence of foundation and end-results.

片	piàn (sth. thin and flat; slice)	【部首】片　【笔画】四画
	ノ丨一𠃍 撇、竖、横、横折	

金文	篆书	隶书	楷书	行书	简化字
片 片	片 片	片	片	片	片
Bronze Script	Seal Script	Official Script	Regular Script	Semi-cursive Script	Simplified Character

"片"是指事字。"片"的字形为古文字木(米)的右半部分片,表示由树木劈(pī)裂(liè)而成的木片。"片"本义指把木头劈分成片,泛指片状的东西,用作名词,如照片。

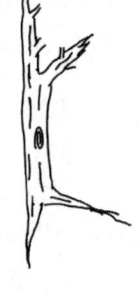

"片"字图示

 **Words & Phrases**

羊肉片　　　　yángròu piàn　　　　lamb slice

羊(yáng) 肉(ròu) 片(piàn)

动画片　　　　dònghuàpiàn　　　　animated cartoon film
照片　　　　　zhàopiàn　　　　　　photo; photograph

 Proverbs & Witticism

请稍等片刻　qǐng shāo děng piànkè
Wait a moment, please.

拨亮一盏灯,映红一大片　bōliàng yì zhǎn dēng, yìnghóng yí dà piàn
Once a lamp is lit, a great expanse is made bright.

片云足以遮全日　piàn yún zúyǐ zhē quán rì
One cloud is enough to eclipse all the sun.

LESSON 3　The Five Elements • 第三课　五行

会意字
Associative Compound Characters

| 伙 | huǒ (partner; group) | 【部首】亻 | 【笔画】六画 |

ノ 丨 丶 ノ ノ 乀
撇、竖、点、撇、撇、捺

金文	篆书	隶书	楷书	行书	简化字
𧘪	夥	伙	伙	伙	伙
Bronze Script	Seal Script	Official Script	Regular Script	Semi-cursive Script	Simplified Character

"伙"是会意字。从"亻"(人)、从"火"，火(huǒ)兼表声。"火"是中国古代兵制伙食单位，军营炊(chuī)煮(zhǔ)造(zào)饭，十人共用一火，古时同火的人称为"火伴"，又写作"伙伴"。"伙"本义是伙伴。现在，"伙"也用作动词，指结为伙伴或同伙，如合伙、入伙、搭伙、散伙。

词或短语　Words & Phrases

伙伴	huǒbàn	partner
同伙	tónghuǒ	work in partnership
伙夫	huǒfū	mess cook
伙食	huǒshí	food
大家伙	dàjiāhuo	big guys
合伙	héhuǒ	form a partnership
拉帮结伙	lābāng-jiéhuǒ	gang up

锦言妙语　Proverbs & Witticism

三个一群，五个一伙　sān gè yì qún, wǔ gè yì huǒ
In small group; in twos and threes.

- 105 -

当面叫哥哥，背后摸家伙 dāng miàn jiào gēge, bèi hòu mō jiāhuo
Honey on one's lips and murder in one's heart.

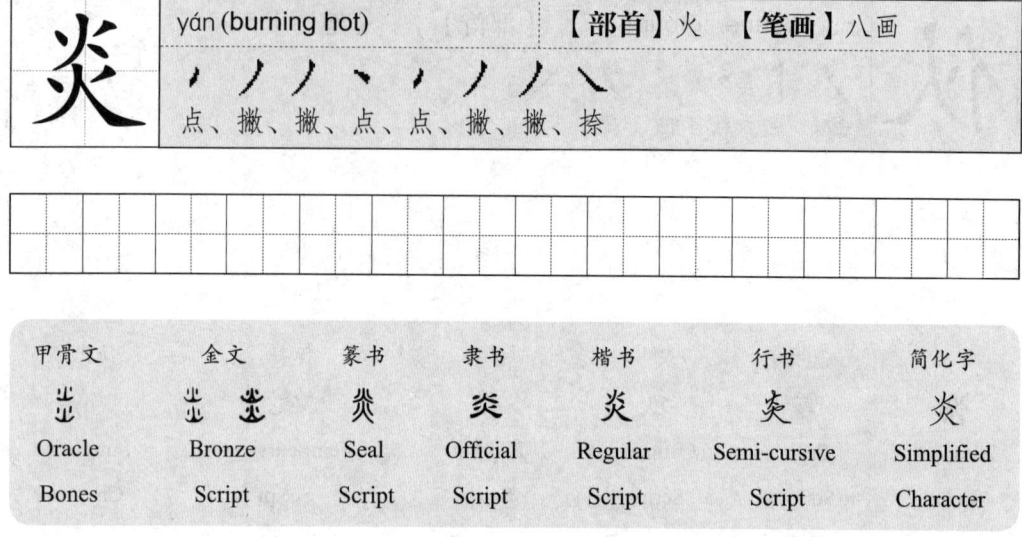

"炎"是会意字。金文的"炎"写作 ，由 (火堆)和 (火堆)构成，像两把火，表示火势很大，燃烧得很旺盛，火光冲天。"炎"本义指火光上升，引申指天气炎热(rè)。相传炎帝是中国上古部落首领，炎黄子孙指的就是中华民族。

词或短语 Words & Phrases

炎热	yánrè	burning hot
炎症	yánzhèng	inflammation
发炎	fāyán	inflammation
肺炎	fèiyán	pneumonia
炎黄子孙	yánhuángzǐsūn	Chinese descendants

锦言妙语 Proverbs & Witticism

烈日炎炎，遍地似火 lièrì yányán, biàn dì sì huǒ
The inexhaustible sun seems to enforce his cumulative, innumerable fires upon every inch of ground.

LESSON 3　The Five Elements • 第三课　五行

金文	篆书	隶书	楷书	行书	繁体字	简化字
㓕	㓕	滅灭	灭	灭	滅	灭
Bronze Script	Seal Script	Official Script	Regular Script	Semi-cursive Script	Traditional Character	Simplified Character

　　"灭"是会意字。简化字"灭"，从"一"、从"火"，上下组合而成，表示把火压住。"灭"本义指将火熄(xī)灭。

灭 (miè) 火 (huǒ)

词或短语　Words & Phrases

灭火　　　miè huǒ　　　　　　　　put out a fire
灭亡　　　mièwáng　　　　　　　　die out; be destroyed

恐 (kǒng) 龙 (lóng)

消灭	xiāomiè	wipe out
灭绝	mièjué	die out; extinction
灭火器	mièhuǒqì	fire extinguisher
灭顶之灾	mièdǐngzhīzāi	a great calamity

锦言妙语 Proverbs & Witticism

飞蛾扑火，自取灭亡 fēi é pū huǒ, zì qǔ miè wáng
When the moth flies around the flame, it burns itself to death.

长他人之志气，灭自己之威风 zhǎng tārén zhī zhìqì, miè zìjǐ zhī wēifēng
Boost other people's morale and reduce our own courage.

灶 zào (brick kitchen range)　【部首】火　【笔画】七画
丶ノノ丶一丨一
点、撇、撇、点、横、竖、横

金文	篆书	隶书	楷书	行书	简化字
灶	灶	灶	灶	灶	灶
Bronze Script	Seal Script	Official Script	Regular Script	Semi-cursive Script	Simplified Character

"灶"是会意字。"灶"由"火"和"土"两部分组成，"土"代表有洞(dòng)窟(kū)的土台，指"烧火煮饭的土台"。"灶"本义指炉灶，厨(chú)房(fáng)里烧火做饭的设备。

灶(zào)台(tái)

LESSON 3 The Five Elements • 第三课 五行

词或短语 Words & Phrases

炉灶　　　　　lúzào　　　　　　　cooking stove

炉 (lú) 灶 (zào)

煤气灶　　　　méiqìzào　　　　　gas cooker

锦言妙语 Proverbs & Witticism

先到灶头先得食 xiān dào zào tóu xiān dé shí
The early bird catches the worms. ‖ Those who are first at the fire will get their dinner first.

另起炉灶重开张 lìng qǐ lúzào chóng kāizhāng
Set up another household. ‖ Start something all over again, not just making minor changes here and there.

黑	hēi (black)	【部首】黑　【笔画】十二画
	丨 乛 丶 丿 一 丨 一 一 丶 丶 丶 丶	
	竖、横折、点、撇、横、竖、横、横、点、点、点、点	

甲骨文	金文	篆书	隶书	楷书	行书	简化字
Oracle Bones	Bronze Script	Seal Script	Official Script	Regular Script	Semi-cursive Script	Simplified Character

甲骨文的"黑"写作 ，形似一个 (人) 的脸 ，表示脸上有烟灰之类的污点。古人烧火烹煮时头部经常靠近火堆以便吹火，因此脸上、身上容易沾上黑色的烟灰。

黑在金文中是会意字，上部是"窗"(chuāng)的古文，即"囱"(cōng)字，下部是"火"，上下两部分合起来表示在屋子里生火做饭，烟通过烟囱冒了出去，烟囱积满黑灰。"黑"本义指炉火将烟囱熏黑了，即黑色。黑与白相对。

土 (tǔ) 灶 (zào)

词或短语　Words & Phrases

黑板　　　　hēibǎn　　　　　blackboard

黑 (hēi) 板 (bǎn)

黑色	hēisè	black
乌黑	wūhēi	pitch-black; jet-black
黑暗	hēi'àn	darkness
天黑	tiānhēi	get dark
黑夜	hēiyè	night

锦言妙语　Proverbs & Witticism

天下乌鸦一般黑　tiānxià wūyā yì bān hēi
Crows are black all over the world.

不管黑猫白猫，能捉老鼠的就是好猫　bù guǎn hēimāo báimāo, néng zhuō lǎoshǔ de jiù shì hǎo māo
A black plum is as sweet as a white. || Never mind whether she is a black cat or a white cat; if she catches rats, she is a good cat.

有白必有黑，有甜就有苦　yǒu bái bì yǒu hēi, yǒu tián jiù yǒu kǔ
Every white has its black, and every sweet has its bitter.

mò (inkstick; Chinese ink) 【部首】黑 【笔画】十五画

丨 フ 丶 丿 一 丨 一 一 丶 丶 丶 丶 一 丨 一
竖、横折、点、撇、横、竖、横、横、点、点、点、点、横、竖、横

金文	篆书	隶书	楷书	行书	简化字
Bronze Script	Seal Script	Official Script	Regular Script	Semi-cursive Script	Simplified Character

"墨"是会意字，由"黑"和"土"会意，表示墨是用黑土制成的。"墨"本义指用毛笔书写时用的黑色颜料，借助砚，加水研磨，可以产生墨汁。由于墨汁是黑色的，现在"墨"字也指黑色。

笔、墨、纸、砚是中国传统的书写和绘画工具，统称为"文房四宝"。

墨 (mò) 和砚 (yàn)

词或短语 Words & Phrases

墨汁	mòzhī	ink
墨水	mòshuǐ	prepared Chinese ink
墨镜	mòjìng	sunglasses

锦言妙语 Proverbs & Witticism

近朱者赤，近墨者黑 jìn zhū zhě chì, jìn mò zhě hēi
He who handles vermilion will be reddened, and he who touches ink will be blackened.

树 shù (tree)

【部首】木　【笔画】九画

一 丨 丿 丶 ㇇ 丶 一 亅 丶
横、竖、撇、点、横撇/横钩、点、横、竖钩、点

甲骨文	金文	篆书	隶书	楷书	行书	繁体字	简化字
Oracle Bones	Bronze Script	Seal Script	Official Script	Regular Script	Semi-cursive Script	Traditional Character	Simplified Character

"树"是会意字。甲骨文的"树"写作，由（木）、（豆，容器）及（手）构成，表示手持树苗将其栽种在盆子里。篆书形体像一棵树，从"木"，从"尌"，"尌"是树的本字，形似用手植树，"尌"(shù)兼表声。简体字的"树"从"木"、从"又"、从"寸"，表示双手（又、寸）植树（木）。"树"本义指栽树，转指树木。

树 (shù) 苗 (miáo)

词或短语　Words & Phrases

树木	shùmù	trees
树根	shùgēn	tree root
十年树木	shí nián shù mù	It takes ten years to grow a tree.
百年树人	bǎi nián shù rén	It takes a hundred years to educate the people.

锦言妙语　Proverbs & Witticism

树大招风，名高招忌 shù dà zhāo fēng, míng gāo zhāo jì
After honor and status, follow envy and hate. ‖ Detraction pursues the great.

树有根，水有源 shù yǒu gēn, shuǐ yǒu yuán
Every tree has its roots and every river has its source—everything has its origin.

LESSON 3　The Five Elements • 第三课　五行

前人栽树，后人乘凉 qián rén zāi shù, hòu rén chéng liáng
One generation plants the trees under whose shade another generation rests — profiting by the labor of one's forefathers.

林	lín (forest)	【部首】木　【笔画】八画
	一丨丿丶一丨丿㇏ 横、竖、撇、点、横、竖、撇、捺	

甲骨文	金文	篆书	隶书	楷书	行书	简化字
Oracle Bones	Bronze Script	Seal Script	Official Script	Regular Script	Semi-cursive Script	Simplified Character

"林"是会意字。甲骨文的"林"写作 ⅩⅩ，金文的"林"写作 ⅩⅩ，像两棵并排在一起的树，表示树木多。"林"本义指树林。简化字的"林"由两个"木"字构成，表示树木连成片，指成片的竹、树，引申为汇集在一起的事物或人。"林"用作形容词，意为众多。

树 (shù) 林 (lín)

 Words & Phrases

香蕉林　　　xiāngjiāo lín　　　banana plantation

香 (xiāng) 蕉 (jiāo) 林 (lín)

园林	yuánlín	park; gardens
林业	línyè	forestry
植树造林	zhí shù zào lín	afforestation; forest planting

锦言妙语　Proverbs & Witticism

独木不成林　dú mù bù chéng lín
One tree does not make a forest.

农林牧副渔　nóng lín mù fù yú
Farming, forestry, animal husbandry, side-line production and fishery.

森　sēn (full of trees; gloomy)　【部首】木　【笔画】十二画
一丨丿乀一丨丿乀一丨丿乀
横、竖、撇、捺、横、竖、撇、点、横、竖、撇、捺

甲骨文	金文	篆书	隶书	楷书	行书	简化字
森	森	森	森	森	森	森
Oracle Bones	Bronze Script	Seal Script	Official Script	Regular Script	Semi-cursive Script	Simplified Character

　　"森"是会意字。甲骨文的"森"写作🌳，比"林"多一"木"，表示"森"为"大林"。简化字的"森"由三个"木"构成，表示树木很多的样子。"森"本义指树木多而密。

　　因为树木多了便会显得阴暗，"森"后来也引申为阴沉、幽暗的环境，如阴森的走廊。

森 (sēn) 林 (lín)

LESSON 3 The Five Elements • 第三课 五行

词或短语 Words & Phrases

森林	sēnlín	forest
阴森森	yīnsēnsēn	spooky; gloomy

锦言妙语 Proverbs & Witticism

只见树木，不见森林 zhǐ jiàn shùmù, bú jiàn sēnlín
See the minute details but miss the major issue.

焚 fén (burn)   【部首】火   【笔画】十二画

一丨丿丶一丨丿丶丶丿丿㇏
横、竖、撇、点、横、竖、撇、点、点、撇、撇、捺

甲骨文	金文	篆书	隶书	楷书	行书	简化字
Oracle Bones	Bronze Script	Seal Script	Official Script	Regular Script	Semi-cursive Script	Simplified Character

"焚"是会意字。甲骨文的"焚"写作 ，由 ❦❦（林或野草）和 ⌒（火）构成，形似火烧树林，表示为狩(shòu)猎(liè)或开(kāi)垦(kěn)荒地而引火烧林、烧荒。甲骨文的"焚"也可写作 ❦，由 ❦❦（树林）、❦（火把）及 ❦（手）构成，进一步明确手持火把、人为烧荒、烧林的含义。"焚"本义指用火烧林木或草，泛指烧。

林 (lín) 火 (huǒ)

词或短语 Words & Phrases

焚毁	fénhuǐ	destroy by fire

| 玩火自焚 | wánhuǒzìfén | Somebody who plays with fire will get burnt. |
| 心急如焚 | xīnjírúfén | be burning with anxiety |

锦言妙语　Proverbs & Witticism

玩火者必自焚　wán huǒ zhě bì zì fén
He who plays with fire will get himself burnt.

焚屋取暖者，仅得一时温暖　fén wū qú nuǎn zhě, jǐn dé yì shí wēnnuǎn
He that burns his house warms himself for once.

dōng (east)　　【部首】一　【笔画】五画
一㇇亅ノ丶
横、撇折、竖钩、撇、点

甲骨文	金文	小篆	隶书	楷书	行书	繁体字	简化字
Oracle Bones	Bronze Script	Seal Script	東 Official Script	东 Regular Script	东 Semi-cursive Script	東 Traditional Character	东 Simplified Character

　　"东"是会意字。繁体"東"简化为"东"。从"日"(太阳)、从"木"(树木)，表示太阳升起的方向。"东"本义指东方，即太阳升起的方位，与"西"相对。
　　由于古代主人的位子在东，宾客的位子在西，东字引申为主人，如东家、房东、股东、做东。
　　按"五行"来分，东方属于木；按"四时"来分，东为春。

日 (rì) 出 (chū) 东 (dōng) 方 (fāng)

词或短语　Words & Phrases

东方　　　　dōngfāng　　　　the Orient; east

房东	fángdōng	landlord
做东	zuòdōng	play the host
东山再起	dōngshānzàiqǐ	return to power

锦言妙语 Proverbs & Witticism

今日爱东，明日爱西 jīnrì ài dōng, míngrì ài xī
Drift east today, west tomorrow — inconsistent.

寿比南山，福如东海 shòu bǐ nánshān, fú rú dōnghǎi
May your age be as Mountain Tai and your happiness as the Eastern Sea! || May your fortune be as boundless as the East Sea and your life last long like the South Mountain!

孩提时代学到的东西，到老死也不会忘记
háití shídài xué dào de dōngxi, dào lǎo sǐ yě bú huì wàngjì
What is learned in the cradle is carried to the grave.

休 xiū (rest; cease; stop)   【部首】亻   【笔画】六画

丿 丨 一 丨 丿 乀
撇、竖、横、竖、撇、捺

甲骨文	金文	篆书	隶书	楷书	行书	简化字
Oracle Bones	Bronze Script	Seal Script	Official Script	Regular Script	Semi-cursive Script	Simplified Character

"休"是会意字。甲骨文的"休"写作 ，像一个人（ ）站在大树（ ）的枝叶之下，表示古人在野外劳作时，选(xuǎn)择(zé)在大树下歇(xiē)息(xī)。简化字的"休"由"亻"(人)和"木"(树)左(zuǒ)右(yòu)两部分构成，像人背靠大树歇息。"休"本义指歇息，引申指休(xiū)假(jià)。

休(xiū) 息(xi)

词或短语 Words & Phrases

休息	xiūxi	take a rest
休眠	xiūmián	hibernation; winter sleep
休假	xiūjià	have a holiday
休学	xiūxué	suspension of schooling
退休	tuìxiū	retire
休养生息	xiūyǎngshēngxī	rehabilitate

锦言妙语 Proverbs & Witticism

人无笑脸休开店 rén wú xiàoliǎn xiū kāi diàn
A man having not a pleasant face should not open a shop.

一不做，二不休 yì bú zuò, èr bù xiū
Carry the thing through, whatever the consequences — be determined to go the whole hog.

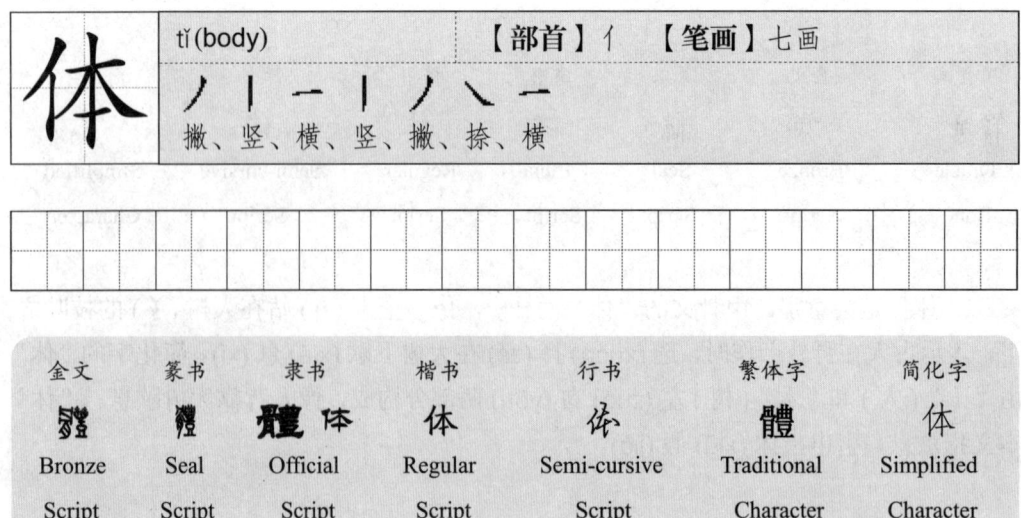

LESSON 3 The Five Elements • 第三课 五行

"体"的简化字是会意字,从"亻"(人)、从"本",表示身(shēn)体(tǐ)是人之本。"体"本义指身躯。

词或短语 Words & Phrases

体温	tǐwēn	body temperature
体育运动	tǐyù yùndòng	physical exercise; sports
体重	tǐzhòng	body weight
体验	tǐyàn	experience
液体	yètǐ	liquid
体力活	tǐlìhuó	physical work
体弱多病	tǐ ruò duō bìng	in poor health and frequently ill

锦言妙语 Proverbs & Witticism

顾大局，识大体 gù dà jú, shí dà tǐ
Take the overall situation into account and have the cardinal principles in mind.

身体是革命的本钱 shēntǐ shì gémìng de běnqián
The body is the capital of revolution.

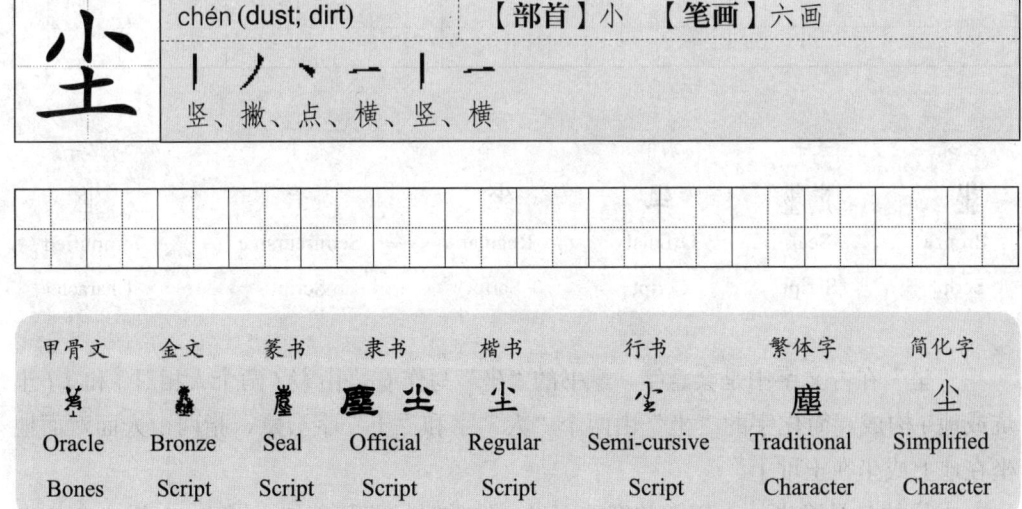

甲骨文的"尘"写作🦌，由🦌(鹿)和 ⊥ (土)构成,意指鹿群奔(bēn)跑(pǎo),

后面扬起尘土。简化字的"尘"是会意字，上部为"小"，下部为"土"，意指微尘，即尘土。"尘"本义指飞扬的细土、尘土。

飞(fēi) 奔(bēn) 的(de) 鹿(lù) 群(qún)

词或短语　Words & Phrases

尘土	chéntǔ	dust
灰尘	huīchén	dust; ash
一尘不染	yìchénbùrǎn	stainless
望尘莫及	wàngchénmòjí	too far behind to catch up with
尘土飞扬	chéntǔ fēiyáng	raising a cloud of dust

坐　zuò (sit; kneel; be seated)　【部首】土　【笔画】七画

丿、丶、丿、丶、一、丨、一
撇、点、撇、点、横、竖、横

金文	篆书	隶书	楷书	行书	简化字
坐	坐	坐	坐	坐	坐
Bronze Script	Seal Script	Official Script	Regular Script	Semi-cursive Script	Simplified Character

　　"坐"在古文字中是会意字，篆书的"坐"写作坐，由 人人 (两个人相对) 和 土 (土炕或地) 构成。简化字的"坐"由两个"人"字和"土"字会意，指两个人面对面地坐在地上或坐在土堆上。

　　古代的坐是跪坐，人们常常席地而坐，坐的时候双膝着地，臀(tún)部(bù)压在脚跟上。坐是古人休息的一种方式。

　　"坐"还有乘坐之义，如乘坐火车、乘坐飞机。

LESSON 3 The Five Elements • 第三课 五行

席 (xí) 地 (dì) 而 (ér) 坐 (zuò)

词或短语 Words & Phrases

坐井观天 zuòjǐngguāntiān
Sit in a well and look at the sky — a limited outlook, have a very narrow view.

坐 (zuò) 井 (jǐng) 观 (guān) 天 (tiān)

坐火车	zuò huǒchē	by train
乘坐飞机	chéngzuò fēijī	by plane
请坐	qǐng zuò	have a seat, please
坐吃山空	zuòchīshānkōng	use up one's resources without working

锦言妙语 Proverbs & Witticism

行不更名，坐不改姓 xíng bù gèng míng, zuò bù gǎi xìng
I do not change my name when traveling.

坐山观虎斗 zuò shān guān hǔ dòu
Sit on top of the mountain to watch the tigers fighting — which in safety while others fight, then reap the spoils when both sides are exhausted.

站没站相，坐没坐相 zhàn méi zhàn xiàng, zuò méi zuò xiàng
Not to know how to stand or sit properly.

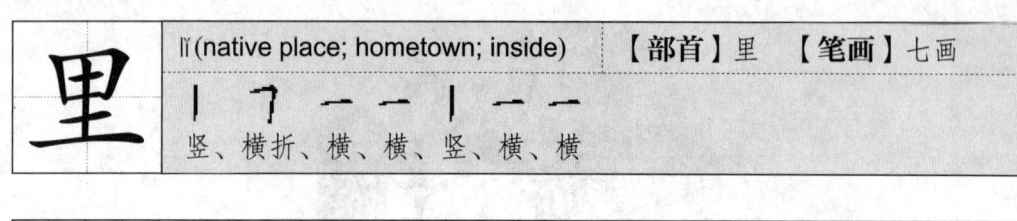

金文的"里"写作 ▣，由 ▣（田，农作物）和 ▣（土地、土墙或房子）构成，表示人们赖以生存的田地、农作物和房子。古人主要通过农业劳动获得食物，有田有土地才能生存，在田地丰饶的地方，一般也是人群聚居的地方。《说文解字》："里，居也。"

简化字的"里"是会意字，由"田"和"土"两部分构成，合起来表示有了田地种庄(zhuāng)稼(jia)，就可以定居了。"里"本义指古代居民居住的地方，如荣归故里，引申指街(jiē)坊(fang)邻(lín)居(jū)，如邻里之间。

现在，"里"常用来指代内部，与"外"相对。"里"也是长度单位，1里等于500米，即1/2公里。

词或短语 Words & Phrases

心里	xīnlǐ	in the heart
手里	shǒu lǐ	in the hand
表里如一	biǎolǐrúyī	be the same outside and inside
笑里藏刀	xiàolǐcángdāo	hide a dagger behind a smile
回归故里	huíguī gùlǐ	return to hometown

锦言妙语 Proverbs & Witticism

千里之行，始于足下 qiān lǐ zhī xíng, shǐ yú zú xià
A thousand-li journey begins by taking the first step.

离题十万八千里 lí tí shíwàn bāqiān lǐ
Miles away from the subject; completely off the point.

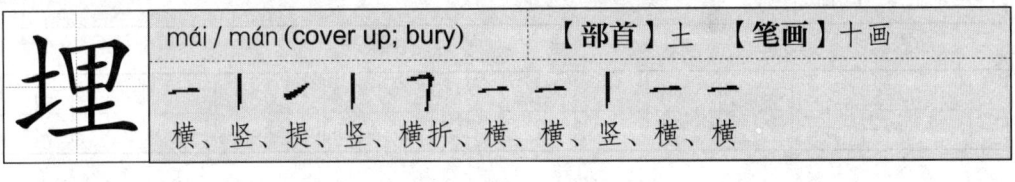

甲骨文	金文	篆书	隶书	楷书	行书	简化字
Oracle Bones	Bronze Script	Seal Script	Official Script	Regular Script	Semi-cursive Script	Simplified Character

甲骨文的"埋"写作⊗、⊕、☰、⊞，字形多样化，像牛、羊、鹿、犬等各种动物被抛 (pāo) 在土坑∪里。古人挖土坑将生病死亡的牛、羊、鹿、犬等家 (jiā) 畜 (chù) 埋入土中，土葬 (zàng)，以祭奉地神，祈福众畜平安。

"埋"字在甲骨文中是个会意字，从"土"（泥土）、从"里"（里面），表示把东西放入坑里用土盖上。现在，"埋"的常用义是隐 (yǐn) 藏 (cáng)，使其显露不出来，如她的才能被埋没了。此外，"埋"还可读 mán，埋怨，意思是因事情不如意而对人或事物表示不满。

词或短语 Words & Phrases

埋藏	máicáng	hide; bury
埋怨	mányuàn	complain of
埋头苦干	máitóukǔgàn	quietly put one's shoulder to the wheel
埋没人才	máimò réncái	to stifle real talents

锦言妙语 Proverbs & Witticism

自己无能，埋怨刀钝 zìjǐ wúnéng, mányuàn dāo dùn
A bad workman quarrels with his tools.

金 jīn (metal; gold)

【部首】金　【笔画】八画

ノ 𠃋 一 一 丨 丶 ノ 一
撇、捺、横、横、竖、点、撇、横

金文	篆书	隶书	楷书	行书	简化字
Bronze Script	Seal Script	Official Script	Regular Script	Semi-cursive Script	Simplified Character

"金"是会意字。"金"的下部是土，"土"字周围的点表示藏 (cáng) 在地下的金属矿物，上边倒扣的三角表示盖 (gài) 子。"金"本义指青铜和黄铜等金属，也作为金属的统称，后多用于表示黄金。

由于黄金抗腐 (fǔ) 蚀 (shí)、稀有，自古以来人们都将其用于制作珍贵的饰 (shì) 品 (pǐn)。金在古代又作为货币使用，所以金也指钱，如金钱。"金"是部首字，从"金"(钅) 取义的字多与金属有关，如钢、铁、银、铜、铅、铝。

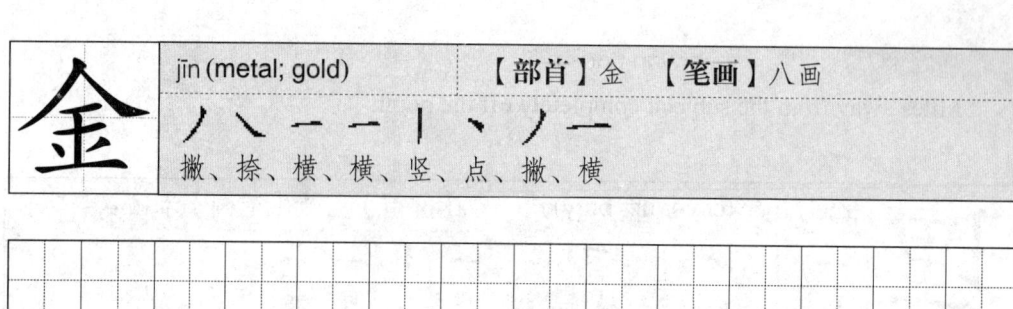

淘 (táo) 金 (jīn)　　　金 (jīn) 币 (bì)

词或短语 Words & Phrases

黄金　　huángjīn　　gold

黄 (huáng) 金 (jīn)

LESSON 3 The Five Elements • 第三课 五行

金碗   jīnwǎn   the golden bowl

金 (jīn) 碗 (wǎn)

金属   jīnshǔ   metal
合金   héjīn   alloy
金牌   jīnpái
gold medal — the highest prize awarded to the winner in a contest
金融   jīnróng   finance; banking
挥金如土   huījīnrútǔ   spend money like dirt/water; blow money

锦言妙语 Proverbs & Witticism

一寸光阴一寸金，寸金难买寸光阴

yí cùn guāngyīn yí cùn jīn, cùnjīn nán mǎi cùn guāngyīn

An inch of time is as valuable as an inch of gold, but an inch of gold cannot buy an inch of time.

金无足赤，人无完人 jīn wú zú chì, rén wú wán rén

There are spots on the sun. ‖ Each of us has his imperfections.

真金不怕火炼 zhēn jīn bú pà huǒ liàn

Pure gold does not fear the furnace; truth fears not the flames of slander and injustice.

泵 bèng (pump)   【部首】水 【笔画】九画

一 丿 丨 乛 一 亅 ㇇ 丿 ㇏
横、撇、竖、横折、横、竖钩、横撇 / 横钩、撇、捺

- 125 -

金文	篆书	隶书	楷书	行书	简化字
Bronze Script	Seal Script	Official Script	Regular Script	Semi-cursive Script	Simplified Character

"泵"是会意字，从"石"（像山崖下有块石头）、从"水"（像流水飞溅出水花），合起来表示水冲击石头。现用作英语 pump 的译音字，表示一种能吸 (xī) 入 (rù) 或排 (pái) 出 (chū) 液体或气体的装置或机械，按照用途可分为水泵、油泵等。

词或短语 Words & Phrases

水泵	shuǐbèng	water pump
油泵	yóubèng	oil pump
气泵	qìbèng	air pump

渔 yú (fishing; catch fish)　【部首】氵　【笔画】十一画

点、点、提、撇、横撇/横钩、竖、横折、横、竖、横、横

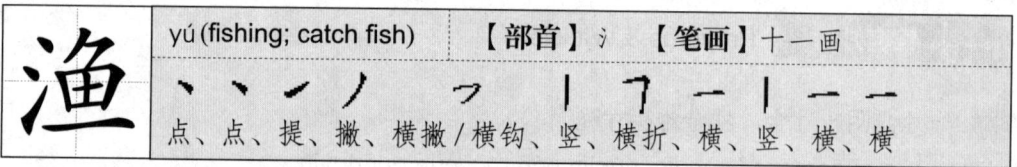

甲骨文	金文	篆书	隶书	楷书	行书	繁体字	简化字
Oracle Bones	Bronze Script	Seal Script	Official Script	Regular Script	Semi-cursive Script	Traditional Character	Simplified Character

"渔"是会意字。甲骨文的"渔"写作 ，表示将"河中之鱼"变成"岸上之鱼"，即捕 (bǔ) 鱼。甲骨文的"渔"也可写作 ，由 （鱼）和 （水）构成，表示从水中捕鱼。甲骨文的"渔"还可写作 ，表示一手执竿 （手 + 钓竿 ）钓 (diào) 鱼 。有的甲骨文的"渔"写作 ，表示两手撒网 捕鱼 ，即用渔网捕鱼。

金文的"渔"写作 ，由 （水）和 （鱼）及 （双手）构成，强调徒 (tú) 手 (shǒu) 捕 (bǔ) 鱼的形象。

隶书的"渔"写作 ，"漁"逐渐演变成"渔"，从"氵"、从"鱼"。"渔"

本义指捕鱼，如授人以鱼，不如授人以渔。

渔 (yú) 翁 (wēng) 图 (tú)

词或短语　Words & Phrases

渔网	yúwǎng	fishing net
渔夫	yúfū	fisherman
渔翁得利	yúwēngdélì	The third party gets the profit.

锦言妙语　Proverbs & Witticism

授人以鱼，不如授人以渔　shòu rén yǐ yú, bù rú shòu rén yǐ yú
Give people fish and you feed them for a day. Teach them how to fish and you feed them for a lifetime.

鹬蚌相争，渔翁得利　yù bàng xiāng zhēng, yú wēng dé lì
When the snipe and the clam grapple, it is the fisherman who profits.

宜农则农，宜林则林，宜牧则牧，宜渔则渔
yí nóng zé nóng, yí lín zé lín, yí mù zé mù, yí yú zé yú
Farming, forestry, animal husbandries, and fishery should be developed in respective areas suitable for them.

鲁	lǔ (stupid; crude and rash)	【部首】鱼　【笔画】十二画
	ノ　ク　丨　フ　一　丨　一　丨　フ　一　一	
	撇、横撇／横钩、竖、横折、横、竖、横、横、竖、横折、横、横	

甲骨文	金文	篆书	隶书	楷书	行书	简化字
Oracle Bones	Bronze Script	Seal Script	Official Script	Regular Script	Semi-cursive Script	Simplified Character

在甲骨文和金文中，"鲁"是会意字。甲骨文的"鲁"写作 ，由 （鱼）和 （口）构成，表示吃鱼，也表示食物味道美或吃到了美味的食物。"鲁"本义为美好。吃带骨刺的鱼是很危(wēi)险(xiǎn)的，有的人大口吃鱼，会被鱼刺扎(zhā)到，由此产生鲁莽(mǎng)的含义，如他的性格有些鲁莽。

鱼在水里游，自由自在，所以"鲁"字也可引申为任性、率直。鲁是今中国山东省的简称。

词或短语　Words & Phrases

鲁莽　　　　lúmǎng　　　crude and rash
粗鲁　　　　cūlǔ　　　　rude

锦言妙语　Proverbs & Witticism

鲁班门前弄大斧　Lǔ Bān mén qián nòng dà fǔ
Axe in front of the gate of Lu Ban, the Great Carpenter – to overestimate oneself.

鲁莽一时，悔之一世　lúmǎng yì shí, huǐ zhī yí shì
To do sth. rash will make one repent forever.

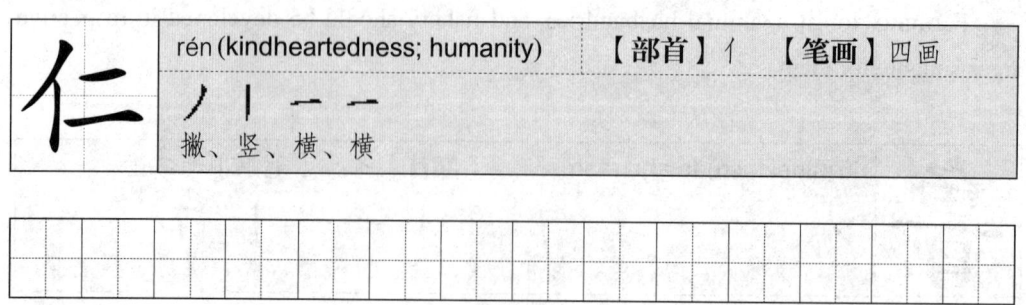

甲骨文	金文	篆书	隶书	楷书	行书	简化字
⺅=	⺅=	仁 仁	仁	仁	仁	仁
Oracle Bones	Bronze Script	Seal Script	Official Script	Regular Script	Semi-cursive Script	Simplified Character

甲骨文的"仁"写作⺅=，由⺅(人，表示君或民) 和 =（表示等同或一样）构成，表示人人平等，即君民平等、相亲相爱。

"仁"是会意字，由"亻"和"二"两部分左右组合而成，表示爱自己和他人，即同时爱"二人"。"仁"本义指待人友善、友爱和仁爱，表明人与人之间要和谐相处。仁爱是中国儒家思想的核心，经典的表述为"仁者爱人"。儒家学派创始人孔子出生于鲁国（今山东曲阜）。

另外，果核中最里面的部分称为"仁"，如杏仁、核桃仁。

孔 (kǒng) 子 (zǐ) 讲 (jiǎng) 学 (xué) 图 (tú)

词或短语 Words & Phrases

仁爱	rén'ài	kindheartedness
仁义	rényì	kindheartedness and justice
果仁	guǒrén	kernel; nutlet
一视同仁	yíshìtóngrén	treat equally without discrimination

锦言妙语 Proverbs & Witticism

仁者见仁，智者见智 rénzhě jiàn rén, zhìzhě jiàn zhì
Different men have different opinions on the same questions.

仁者乐山，智者乐水 rénzhě lè shān, zhìzhě lè shuǐ
A true man loves the mountains, and a wise man loves the sea.

仁者无敌 rénzhě wú dí
No one can challenge the benignant man.

原	yuán (source of water; original)	【部首】厂 【笔画】十画
	一ノノ丨フ一一亅ノ丶	
	横、撇、撇、竖、横折、横、横、竖钩、撇、点	

金文	篆书	隶书	楷书	行书	简化字
	原	原	原	原	原
Bronze Script	Seal Script	Official Script	Regular Script	Semi-cursive Script	Simplified Character

"泉"是"原"的本字。《说文解字》："原，水泉本也。""原"指的就是山泉。

"原"是会意字。金文的"原"写作，字形的上方是一个"厂"字，代表陡峭的山崖，表示洁净的泉水从山间石头下流淌出来。"原"本义是水源，现在常用作形容词，意思是原始的、最初的、开始的，如原来、原本、本来。

水 (shuǐ) 源 (yuán)

 Words & Phrases

草原　　cǎoyuán　　　　grassland

草 (cǎo) 原 (yuán)

原始	yuánshǐ	original; first-hand; primary
原配	yuánpèi	first wife (husband)
原料	yuánliào	raw material
原因	yuányīn	reason; cause
原谅	yuánliàng	forgive
原原本本	yuányuánběnběn	from beginning to end

Pictophonetic Characters

橡 xiàng (oak tree; acorn; rubber tree) 　【部首】木　【笔画】十五画

一丨ノ丶ノ ⺈ 丨𠃍一ノ亅ノノ㇏
横、竖、撇、点、撇、横撇/横钩、竖、横折、横、撇、弯钩、撇、撇、撇、捺

金文	篆书	隶书	楷书	行书	简化字
橡	橡	橡	橡	橡	橡
Bronze Script	Seal Script	Official Script	Regular Script	Semi-cursive Script	Simplified Character

"橡"是形声字。"木"为形，表意，其古文字形体像一棵树，表示"橡"是一种树木。"象"(xiàng)为声。"橡"本义指橡树。橡子，是栎(lì)树(shù)的果实。"橡"又指橡胶树。

橡 (xiàng) 子 (zi)

词或短语 Words & Phrases

橡树	xiàngshù	oak

橡子	xiàngzi	acorn
橡皮	xiàngpí	rubber; eraser
橡胶	xiàngjiāo	rubber

柏 bǎi (cypress) 【部首】木 【笔画】九画

一丨ノ丶ノ丨フ一一
横、竖、撇、点、撇、竖、横折、横、横

金文	篆书	隶书	楷书	行书	简化字
柏	柏柏	柏	柏	柏	柏
Bronze Script	Seal Script	Official Script	Regular Script	Semi-cursive Script	Simplified Character

　　"柏"是形声字。"柏"本义指一种常绿乔木。从"木",其形似树;白(bái)为声,白有赞美、显扬之义。柏树为常绿乔木,苍劲挺拔、耐寒、耐旱、耐贫瘠,有显扬夸赞之义。柏树多用于建筑、制作家具,其籽、根、叶和树皮可入药。

柏(bǎi)树(shù)

 Words & Phrases

松柏　　　　sōngbǎi　　　　pine and cypress

坦 tǎn (flat; open-hearted) 【部首】土 【笔画】八画

一丨㇀丨フ一一一
横、竖、提、竖、横折、横、横、横

金文	篆书	隶书	楷书	行书	简化字
(Bronze Script)	坦 (Seal Script)	坦 (Official Script)	坦 (Regular Script)	坦 (Semi-cursive Script)	坦 (Simplified Character)

"坦"是形声字。金文的"坦"写作 ，由 (土，土堆)和 (旦，光明)构成。"土"为形，表意，古文字形体像地面上有堆土，表示与地面或泥土有关；"旦"(dàn)为声，"旦"形似太阳初升，寓意光明、灿烂，表示平坦的大地一片光明。"坦"本义指地面很平，引申指内心平静、为人直(zhí)爽(shuǎng)。

词或短语 Words & Phrases

坦率　　tǎnshuài　　　　frank
坦诚　　tǎnchéng　　　　frank and sincere; be honest

锦言妙语 Proverbs & Witticism

坦白从宽，抗拒从严 tǎnbái cóng kuān, kàngjù cóng yán
Anyone who comes clean gets treated with leniency, and anyone who holds back the truth gets treated harshly.

君子坦荡荡 jūnzǐ tǎndàngdàng
A gentleman is open and magnanimous.

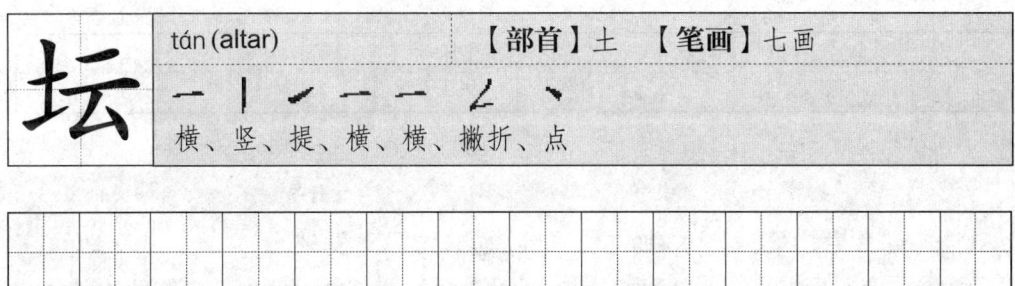

坛 tán (altar)　　【部首】土　【笔画】七画
一丨㇀一一㇜丶
横、竖、提、横、横、撇折、点

金文	篆书	隶书	楷书	行书	繁体字	简化字
壇	壇	壇 坛	坛	坛	壇	坛
Bronze Script	Seal Script	Official Script	Regular Script	Semi-cursive Script	Traditional Character	Simplified Character

"坛"是形声兼会意字。篆书的"坛"写作壇,由土(土)和亶(亶,塔形粮仓)构成。从"土",表示坛用土垒成;亶(dàn)表声,兼表意,"亶"有粮多之义。简化字的"坛"从"土"、从"云",表示土台高或建在高处。"坛"本义指中国古代为祭(jì)祀(sì)、盟(méng)誓(shì)或誓师等重大活动而筑的高台。

天(tiān)坛(tán)
the Temple of Heaven:
an Imperial Sacrificial Altar in Beijing

词或短语 Words & Phrases

天坛	Tiāntán	the Temple of Heaven (in Beijing)
体坛	tǐtán	the sporting world; sports circles
酒坛子	jiǔtánzi	a jar of wine

地 dì (land; earth) 　【部首】土　【笔画】六画

一　丨　㇀　㇇　丨　乚
横、竖、提、横折钩、竖、竖弯钩

金文	篆书	隶书	楷书	行书	简化字
地	墬 埊	地	地	地	地
Bronze Script	Seal Script	Official Script	Regular Script	Semi-cursive Script	Simplified Character

"地"是形声兼会意字。篆书的"地"可写作 墬，由 ⛰(山)、≋(水)及 土 (土，表示田园)构成，表示由山、水、田园构成的广阔空间，即大地。地，从"土"，表示地面、土地；从"也"，"也"是古"蛇"字，上古时地面草木丛生，蛇虫随处可见。"地"本义指大地、地面，特指用来耕(gēng)种(zhòng)的土地，与"天"相对。

词或短语 Words & Phrases

地铁　　　　　dìtiě　　　　　　　metro; subway

地(dì)铁(tiě)

土地　　　　　tǔdì　　　　　　　land; soil
地方　　　　　dìfang　　　　　　place
地点　　　　　dìdiǎn　　　　　　place
地图　　　　　dìtú　　　　　　　map
地位　　　　　dìwèi　　　　　　status; position
社会地位　　　shèhuì dìwèi　　　social position; social status
出人头地　　　chūréntóudì　　　　make a rise in life; stand out

锦言妙语 Proverbs & Witticism

天时不如地利，地利不如人和 tiān shí bù rú dì lì, dì lì bù rú rén hé
The time isn't as important as the terrain, but the terrain isn't as important as unity with the people.

万丈高楼平地起 wàn zhàng gāo lóu píng dì qǐ
High buildings rise from the ground. || Great oaks from little acorns grow.

置之死地而后生 zhì zhī sǐ dì ér hòu shēng
Put the troops in danger of death and they will live.

- 135 -

城	chéng (city wall; town)	【部首】土　【笔画】九画
	一丨一ノ一ノフ乀ノ丶	
	横、竖、提、横、撇、横折钩、斜钩、撇、点	

金文	篆书	隶书	楷书	行书	简化字
	城城	城	城	城	城
Bronze Script	Seal Script	Official Script	Regular Script	Semi-cursive Script	Simplified Character

"城"是形声兼会意字。金文的"城"写作 ，左边像城墙，右边像一把兵器，有用武器保卫城池的意思。"成"(chéng)表声。篆书的"城"从"土"、从"成"，表示城用土筑成，具有军事防御用途。"城"本义指城墙，由城墙引申为被城墙围护的地方，即城邑(yì)。

西(xī)安(ān)城(chéng)墙(qiáng)

词或短语　Words & Phrases

长城　　　　　Chángchéng　　　　　the Great Wall

万(wàn)里(lǐ)长(cháng)城(chéng)

城市　　　　　chéngshì　　　　　　city
城里人　　　　chénglǐrén　　　　　city dwellers; townspeople
众志成城　　　zhòngzhìchéngchéng　Unity is strength.

LESSON 3 The Five Elements • 第三课 五行

锦言妙语 Proverbs & Witticism

城门失火，殃及池鱼 chéng mén shī huǒ, yāng jí chí yú
A fire on the city gate brings disaster to the fish in the moat – in a disturbance innocent bystanders get into trouble.

攻城为下，攻心为上 gōng chéng wéi xià, gōng xīn wéi shàng
It is better to win the hearts of the people than to capture the city.

"冲"是形声字。甲骨文的"冲"写作 , 由 (河川)和 (中)构成，意思是在河的中央被激流冲击，相关词如冲洗、冲茶、冲突、缓冲。

"冲"从"水"( )，现在写成" "；"中"(zhōng)表声，表示水域中的水涌动。"冲"本义指水涌动。读作冲(chòng)，引申为朝、向、对，如大家冲她鼓掌；又引申为气味浓、猛烈、浓烈，如这香烟太冲。

激(jī)流(liú)冲(chōng)击(jī)

 Words & Phrases

冲浪	chōng làng	surfing

冲 (chōng) 浪 (làng)

冲茶	chōng chá	make tea
冲突	chōngtū	conflict
冲动	chōngdòng	impulse; impulsion

 Proverbs & Witticism

大水冲了龙王庙，一家人不认一家人

dà shuǐ chōng le lóngwángmiào, yì jiā rén bú rèn yì jiā rén

The flood dashes against the Temple of the Dragon King. Conflicts arise between the people on one's own side.

霾 mái (smog; haze) 　【部首】雨　【笔画】二十二画

一丶㇇丨丶丶丶丶ノ丶丶ノ亅ノノ丨㇇一一丨一一
横、点、横撇/横钩、竖、点、点、点、点、撇、点、点、撇、弯钩、撇、撇、竖、横折、横、横、竖、横、横

甲骨文	金文	篆书	隶书	楷书	行书	简化字
霾	霾	霾霾	霾	霾	霾	霾
Oracle Bones	Bronze Script	Seal Script	Official Script	Regular Script	Semi-cursive Script	Simplified Character

"霾"是形声字。甲骨文的"霾"写作 霾 ，由 (雨) 和 (动物) 构成，表示天上落下沙尘，埋没地上的家畜。"雨"为形表意，表示空中混浊，如烟雨蒙蒙；貍表意，表示沙尘从天而降。"霾"本义指大风扬起沙尘，使空中一片混 (hún) 浊 (zhuó)。

古"貍"同"埋","埋"指放入坑中盖满泥土,表示霾使空中布满烟尘。现实中的霾是指空气污染,如雾霾,是指因空气中飘浮着大量烟、尘等微粒而形成的混浊现象。

沙 (shā) 尘 (chén) 暴 (bào)

 Words & Phrases

雾霾　　　　　　wùmái　　　　　　　　smog; pea soup fog

雾 (wù) 霾 (mái)

阴霾　　　　　　yīnmái　　　　　　　　haze

二、注解　Notes

(一) 五行 (The Five Elements)

五行是中国古代的一种物质观,是古人认识世界的基本方式,广泛用于历法、哲学、命理、中医学和占卜等方面。该学说认为,大自然由五种要素构成,一曰水,二曰火,三曰木,四曰金,五曰土。水代表浸润,火代表破灭,木代表生长,金代表聚敛,土代表融合。

"行",呈现的是一种自然的"运行",是遵循本身之为,是一种规则而持续的运动,是一种自然的作为。阴阳五行并不神秘,这是古人对现实生活的概括和总结。早晨一觉醒来,太阳升起,一片光明;傍晚,夕阳西下,天色渐暗,黑夜来临。日复一日,年复一年。对白天、黑夜两种相反现象的概括,体现了古人朴素的唯物认识。

阴阳是宇宙的基本法则，宇宙间一切事物都由阴阳相互作用而产生。阴阳代表事物的对立关系，如天地、日月、男女、正负、上下等，是以自然哲学的思想方式归纳出的概念，反映矛盾双方的对立、统一、消长、互根。

后人根据对五行的认识，又创造出五行相生相克理论。相生是指两类属性不同的事物之间存在相互帮助、相互促进的关系，如木生火，火生土，土生金，金生水，水生木。木能燃烧产生火；火燃烧后会留下灰烬，产生土；金属矿藏大多埋在地下，所以说土生金；用金属制作的工具更容易挖井得到水；植物生长需要水，所以说水生木。相克则与相生相反，克是"战胜"的意思。五行相克是说五行中的一行战胜另一行，如木克土，土克水，水克火，火克金，金克木。植物种子埋在土里，条件允许时会生根发芽钻出地面，意味着木战胜了土；堆土可阻挡水流，土战胜了水；大水可熄灭火焰，水战胜了火；烈火可熔化金属，火战胜了金；金属可制成锋利的刀具削砍树木，金战胜了木。五行相生相克是古人在现实生活、生产中获得的直观经验，既不神秘，又不唯心。

中国古代哲学家用五行理论来说明宇宙万物的形成及其相互关系，描述事物的运动形式以及转化关系。自然界各种事物和现象的发展、变化，都是这五种不同的条件不断运动和相互作用的结果。这五种要素用于许多传统领域解释广泛的现象，从内脏到宇宙，从药性到政治制度。阴阳五行与部分现实事物的对应关系如表3-1所示。

表3-1 阴阳五行与部分现实事物的对应关系

五行	阳	阴	方位	五色	五脏	五官	五味	五志	五候	五体
木	甲	乙	东	青	肝	目	酸	怒	风	筋
火	丙	丁	南	红	心	舌	苦	喜	热	脉
土	戊	己	中	黄	脾	口	甘	思	湿	肉
金	庚	辛	西	白	肺	鼻	辛	悲	燥	皮
水	壬	癸	北	黑	肾	耳	咸	恐	寒	骨

五行学说是中国传统文化的核心，是中国古代劳动人民独创的，其哲学思想对科学事业的发展有重大的促进作用。自古以来，中国先贤把五行理论巧妙地运用于医学领域，以五行辩证的生克关系来认识、解释生理现象，尽力适应人体内部自然规律以养生，努力掌握人体运行机制以防病、治病，取得了丰富的经验和成果。

(二) 山水画 (Mountains-and-Waters Painting)

中国山水画简称"山水画"，产生于东晋（公元317—420年）时期，唐代是山水画发展的鼎盛时期，五代时期、宋代、元代、明代和清代，都出现了许多有名的画家。山水画主要描绘山川自然风景，如在宋代画家笔下，高山为最大的主题。山水画表现了丰富多彩的自然美，体现了中国古代人民的自然观与社会审美意识。道家追求的是自然无为、天人合一的精神境界，所以，道家的绘画作品都是以水墨表现为主，以色为辅，人物形象在广阔的自然界中被画得很小。

早期山水画的形成源于人们对于自己赖以生存的自然之热爱，在耕作闲暇之时自娱自乐，不经意间用树枝或石块在岩石和土地上描绘出简单的自然景观，从中体会自然美景带来的视觉享受。到了秦汉时期，山水画逐渐走向规范化，趋向具体写实，把山川树木一丝不苟地画入纸绢之上并带进居室，加以装裱，挂在厅堂之中，既装饰了居室又陶冶了性情。寄情于物、怡悦自我、陶冶性情，从山水画创作中获得快意。这种进步的绘画思想伴随着华夏儿女直至今天。

松(sōng)崖(yá)访(fǎng)友(yǒu)图(tú)

(三) 四川 (Szechwan)

四川简称"川"或"蜀"，省会成都，位于中国大陆西南腹地，是中国西部门户，大熊猫的故乡。四川物产丰富、山清水秀，自古就有"天府之国"之美誉。

四川历史悠久，文化灿烂，自然风光秀美，拥有九寨沟、黄龙、都江堰、青城山、乐山大佛、峨眉山、三星堆、武侯祠、杜甫草堂等名胜旅游景区。

在商周时期，四川地区建立了以古蜀族为中心的蜀国。公元前316年，秦国兼并了蜀国，设立了蜀郡。公元221年，刘备称帝，国号"汉"，史称"蜀汉"，首都设在成都。

第二次国内革命战争时期，中国工农红军一、二、四方面军先后长征进入四川。红四方面军于1932年12月至1935年4月，以今四川省通江县为中心，建立了川陕革命根据地，人口达700万人，是当时全国第二大革命根据地。1949年12月27日，中国人民解放军进驻成都。1952年，中华人民共和国中央人民政府撤销川东、川西、川南、川北行署区，恢复四川省称谓。

四川菜简称川菜，作为中国四大菜系之一，川菜在中国烹饪史上占有重要地位，享有"食在中国，味在四川"的美誉。川菜讲究在"味"上下功夫，以味的多、广、厚著称。它取材广泛，口味清鲜醇浓并重，以善用麻辣著称，烹调方法别具一格，地方风味浓郁。四川火锅享誉海内外。

(四) 长城 (The Great Wall)

长城，又称万里长城，是中国古代的军事防御工事。长城从西周时期(公元前

1046 年—公元前 771 年）开始修建，发生在首都镐 (hào) 京 (jīng)（今陕西西安）的著名典故"烽火戏诸侯"就源于此。

　　春秋战国时期，列国争霸，互相防守。当时，诸侯国为保护自己的安全，曾在边界筑墙作为防御工事。秦始皇灭六国统一中国后，为阻挡北方游牧民族的入侵，将这些墙 (qiáng) 垣 (yuán) 连接和修缮成为一个整体，开始有了万里长城的名称。现在人们所说的长城一般是指明长城。明长城总长度为 8851.8 千米，秦汉及早期长城超过 1 万千米，长城总长超过 2.1 万千米。

　　1961 年 3 月 4 日，长城被国务院公布为第一批全国重点文物保护单位。1987 年 12 月，长城被列为世界文化遗产。

　　"不到长城非好汉。"古今中外，凡到过长城的人无不惊叹它的磅礴气势、宏伟规模。它融汇了古人的智慧、坚毅、意志。长城是稀世珍宝，也是艺术非凡的文物古迹，它象征着中华民族坚不可摧、永存于世的伟大意志和力量，是中华民族的骄傲，也是整个世界的骄傲。

长 (cháng) 城 (chéng)

三、反义词　Antonym

　　白—黑
　　本—末
　　炎热—寒冷
　　东—西
　　买—卖
　　里—外
　　天—地

四、汉字的偏旁部首　The Structural Unit and Radical of Chinese Character

"氵"(三点水)或"冫"(两点水)

"氵"是一个部首,由"水"字演变而来。"氵"部的字多与河流、水、液体有关。例如江、河、海、港、湾、冰、冷(lěng)等。

河　　黄河　　　　Huáng Hé　　　　the Yellow River

黄(huáng)河(hé)

江　　长江　　　　Cháng Jiāng　　　the Yangtze River

长(cháng)江(jiāng)

港　　香港　　　　Xiānggǎng　　　　Hong Kong

香(xiāng)港(gǎng)维(wéi)多(duō)利(lì)亚(yà)港(gǎng)

湾　　台湾　　　　Táiwān　　　　　Taiwan

台(tái)湾(wān)日(rì)月(yuè)潭(tán)

冰	冰雕	bīngdiāo	ice sculpture
	北冰洋	Běibīng Yáng	the Arctic Ocean
	冰箱	bīngxiāng	refrigerator
凉	凉爽	liángshuǎng	nice and cool
净	干净	gānjìng	clean
湖	湖泊	húpō	lake
海	海洋	hǎiyáng	seas and oceans
	上海	Shànghǎi	Shanghai
洋	太平洋	Tàipíng Yáng	the Pacific Ocean
漂	漂亮	piàoliang	pretty; beautiful
渴	渴望	kěwàng	desire; be eager for
汉	汉语	hànyǔ	Chinese; Mandarin
汗	汗水	hànshuǐ	sweat
沈	沈阳	Shěnyáng	Shenyang
洗	洗澡	xǐzǎo	take a bath
	洗衣机	xǐyījī	washing machine
沙	沙漠	shāmò	desert
游	游泳	yóuyǒng	swimming
	旅游	lǚyóu	take a trip; travelling
池	游泳池	yóuyǒngchí	swimming pool
汽	小汽车	xiǎo qìchē	car
	汽油	qìyóu	gasoline
演	表演	biǎoyǎn	performance; show
没	没问题	méiwèntí	out of question; no problem
	没关系	méiguānxi	It doesn't matter; never mind
沉	沉没	chénmò	sink
汁	果汁	guǒzhī	fruit juice
治	治病	zhì bìng	treat an illness
洪	洪水	hóngshuǐ	flood
清	清楚	qīngchu	clear; understand
污	空气污染	kōngqì wūrǎn	air pollution
汤	汤圆	tāngyuán	sweet dumplings
沐	沐浴	mùyù	have a bath; take a shower
浅	肤浅	fūqiǎn	superficial
法	法规	fǎguī	laws and regulations

泪	泪水	lèishuǐ	tear; teardrop
注	注意	zhùyì	attention; notice
淡	淡水	dànshuǐ	fresh water
沸	沸水	fèishuǐ	boiling water
温	温暖	wēnnuǎn	warm
浇	浇花	jiāohuā	water the flowers
酒	白酒	báijiǔ	liquor
涨	涨价	zhǎngjià	rise in price
活	活鱼	huó yú	live fish
流	河流	héliú	river
满	满意	mǎnyì	satisfaction
源	源源不断	yuányuánbúduàn	a steady flow of
冲	冲茶	chōng chá	make tea
决	决定	juédìng	decide; make up one's mind
减	减少	jiǎnshǎo	reduce; decrease
况	情况	qíngkuàng	condition; status; situation

"火"字旁和"灬"（四点底）

火部的字多和火有关。火字旁一般在字的左边。例如，烟、烧、炒等。"灬"（四点底）是由火字演变而来的，一般在字的下部。例如点、热等。

烟	香烟	xiāngyān	cigarette
灯	台灯	táidēng	desk lamp

台 (tái) 灯 (dēng)

炮	大炮	dà pào	cannon

大 (dà) 炮 (pào)

炒	炒菜	chǎo cài	a fried dish

炒 (chǎo) 菜 (cài)

羔	羊羔	yánggāo	lamb

羊 (yáng) 羔 (gāo)

烧	烧烤	shāokǎo	barbecue
	发烧	fā shāo	have a fever
	焚烧	fén shāo	incineration
	燃烧	ránshāo	burn
点	点燃	diǎnrán	set fire to; light
热	热情	rèqíng	enthusiasm; warmth
	炎热	yánrè	burning hot
	燥热	zàorè	hot and dry
蒸	蒸馒头	zhēng mántou	steamed bun; steamed bread
	蒸汽机	zhēngqìjī	steam engine
煮	煮鸡蛋	zhǔ jīdàn	boiled egg
熟	成熟	chéngshú	mature
	熟悉	shúxī	be familiar with
灶	炉灶	lúzào	cooking range
煤	煤炭	méitàn	coal
焰	火焰	huǒyàn	flame
灰	灰烬	huījìn	ash; ember
炕	土炕	tǔkàng	heatable adobe sleeping platform
烛	蜡烛	làzhú	candle
炼	锻炼	duànliàn	have a physical exercise

炬	火炬	huǒjù	torch
爆	爆炸	bàozhà	explode; blast; bomb
烦	烦恼	fánnǎo	annoyance; trouble
灿	灿烂的笑容	cànlàn de xiàoróng	bright smile; big smile
照	照片	zhàopiàn	photograph; picture
	照顾	zhàogù	look after
然	当然	dāngrán	of course; certainly
	然后	ránhòu	then; after that
	虽然	suīrán	although

"土"（提土旁）

随着汉字的演变，"土"字用作部首时，形体上有一点变化，变为"土"。提土旁一般在字的左边。提土旁的字多和泥土、地域或地形有关。例如，地 (dì) 由"土"和"也"构成，指大地。再如，场、块、塔、城、堡、墙等。

场	飞机场	fēijīchǎng	airport

飞 (fēi) 机 (jī) 场 (chǎng)

块	一块面包	yí kuài miànbāo	a piece of bread

面 (miàn) 包 (bāo)

塔	大雁塔	dàyàn tǎ	Greater Wild Goose Pagoda

大 (dà) 雁 (yàn) 塔 (tǎ)

基	基本	jīběn	basic; fundamental
城	城市	chéngshì	city
墙	城墙	chéngqiáng	city wall
	墙壁	qiángbì	wall
堆	土堆	tǔduī	hill; mound
堡	城堡	chéngbǎo	castle
址	地址	dìzhǐ	address
幸	幸运	xìngyùn	lucky; good luck
在	现在	xiànzài	now; at present
	正在	zhèngzài	in process of
坏	累坏了	lèihuàile	exhausted
去	过去	guòqù	in the past; pass by
寺	寺庙	sìmiào	temple
垃	垃圾	lājī	rubbish; waste
地	地铁	dìtiě	metro; subway
	地图	dìtú	map
	坟地	féndì	graveyard; cemetery
均	平均	píngjūn	on average
坑	挖坑	wā kēng	digging a pit
坐	坐火车	zuò huǒchē	by train
坦	平坦	píngtǎn	flat; smooth
堤	堤坝	dībà	dam
坡	山坡	shānpō	hillside; mountain slope
墅	别墅	biéshù	villa; cottage; country house
境	环境	huánjìng	environment; surroundings
埋	埋葬	máizàng	bury
培	培育	péiyù	cultivate; foster
填	填空	tiánkòng	gap filling; fill in the blanks
塑	塑料	sùliào	plastic
型	发型	fàxíng	hair style
增	增加	zēngjiā	increase; add

"木"字旁

"木"部的字多和树木、木材有关。例如，森、林。木表示一棵树，三棵树在一起表示很多树木，很多树木在一起就形成森林。松树、杨柳、桃树等。

LESSON 3 The Five Elements • 第三课 五行

梨	梨树	líshù	pear

梨 (lí) 树 (shù)

松	松树	sōngshù	pine

松 (sōng) 树 (shù)

桃	桃子	táozi	peach

桃 (táo) 子 (zi)

柿	柿子	shìzi	persimmon

柿 (shì) 子 (zi)

李	李子树	lǐzishù	plum

李 (lǐ) 子 (zi) 树 (shù)

杏	杏树	xìngshù	apricot

- 149 -

银杏树　　　　yínxìngshù　　　　ginkgo

银 (yín) 杏 (xìng) 树 (shù)
（中国的国树）

橘　　橘子树　　júzǐshù　　　　orange

橘 (jú) 子 (zi) 树 (shù)

核　　核桃　　hétao　　　　walnut

核 (hé) 桃 (táo)

枸　　枸杞　　gǒu qǐ　　　　medlar

枸 (gǒu) 杞 (qǐ)

樱　　樱桃树　　yīngtáoshù　　　　cherry

樱 (yīng) 桃 (táo) 树 (shù)

LESSON 3　The Five Elements • 第三课　五行

| 杨 | 杨树 | yángshù | poplar |

杨 (yáng) 树 (shù)

| 柳 | 柳树 | liǔshù | willow |

柳 (liǔ) 树 (shù)

梅	梅花	méihuā	wintersweet; plum blossom
柏	柏树	bǎishù	cypress
枫	枫树	fēngshù	maple
橡	橡树	xiàngshù	oak
根	根据	gēnjù	on the basis of; in line with
	树根	shùgēn	tree root
椅	椅子	yǐzi	chair
桌	桌子	zhuōzi	table
村	农村	nóngcūn	countryside; village
植	植物	zhíwù	plant
枯	枯萎	kūwěi	die away; withered
林	森林	sēnlín	forest; woods
栽	栽树	zāishù	plant trees
枝	树枝	shùzhī	tree branch
栖	栖息	qīxī	inhabit
机	司机	sījī	driver
	飞机场	fēijīchǎng	airport
	机会	jīhuì	opportunity
	机械	jīxiè	machinery
杯	杯子	bēizi	cup; glass
校	学校	xuéxiào	school
检	检查	jiǎnchá	examine; check up

样	一样	yíyàng	the same; equally
	榜样	bǎngyàng	example
构	构造	gòuzào	structure
	结构	jiégòu	structure
相	相貌	xiàngmào	appearance; facial features
栅	栅栏	zhàlán	fence; barrier
架	书架	shūjià	bookrack; bookshelf
桥	大桥	dàqiáo	bridge
	桥梁	qiáoliáng	bridge
格	人格	réngé	human dignity
权	权力	quánlì	power
极	北极	běijí	the Arctic Pole
楼	教学楼	jiàoxuélóu	teaching building

五、HSK 试题选做 Sample Questions of the New HSK

(一) 根据对话选择正确的图片 (Choose the Corresponding Pictures Based on the Dialogues)

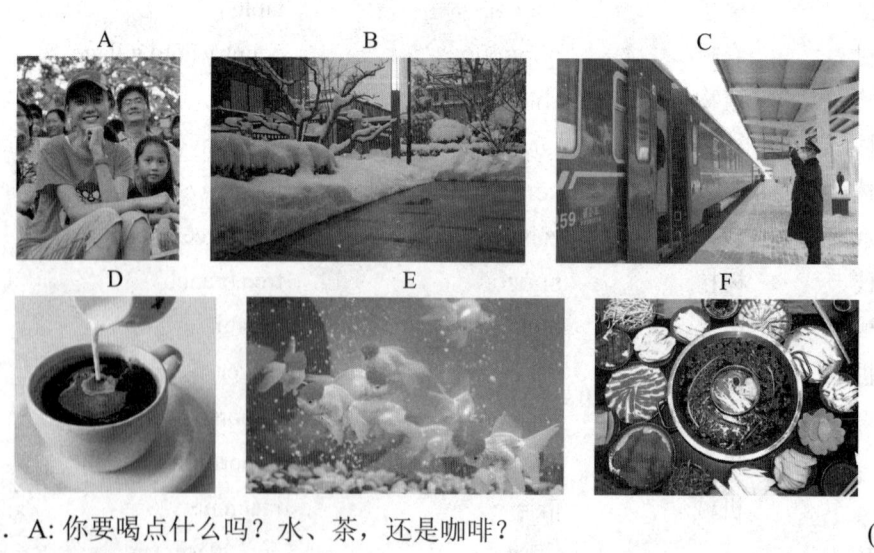

1. A: 你要喝点什么吗？水、茶，还是咖啡？ ( )
   B: 来杯咖啡吧，谢谢！
2. A: 你家养了这么多鱼，真漂亮。 ( )

B: 是啊，我很喜欢鱼。
3. A: 沈阳的冬天很冷吗？ （　　）
   B: 有点儿冷，但不算太冷。
4. A: 今天别去食堂了，我请客，咱们去吃火锅。 （　　）
   B: 太好了！我最爱吃火锅了。
5. A: 能不能帮我拍张照片？ （　　）
   B: 好的。笑一笑。
6. A: 火车来了！ （　　）
   B: 上车吧，一路顺风。

(二) 选词填空 (Choose the Corresponding Words Based on the Sentences)

A. 老百姓　　B. 白色　　C. 热　　D. 休息　　E. 地铁　　F. 水资源

例如：我们一般早上八点上班，中午（ D ）两个小时。

1. 大熊猫头大而圆，身体肥胖，尾巴很短，眼睛周围及四肢都是黑色，其余部分为（　　）。
2. 我喜欢春天和秋天，不冷也不（　　）。
3. 这部电影反映了旧社会中国（　　）的真实生活。
4. 中国（　　）比较缺乏，近年来随着经济的发展，用水量的增加，这种情况更加严重了。
5. 我经常选择坐（　　）和公共汽车上下班，一般不开车。

六、朗读与书写练习　Reading and Writing Exercises

日本是一个多火山的国家。
不努力学习，就想做科学家，真是白日做梦。
她是一位土生土长的中国画家。
都说"桂林山水甲天下"，到桂林一看，果然名不虚传。
我真想喝杯水。
水是生命的源泉，人类的一切生命活动都离不开水。
泉水从岩石中渗出。
鱼离不开水，水是鱼的天然生活环境。
我从小就喜欢捕鱼捞虾，至今乐此不疲。

对于孩子来说，生活就是一所学校，一花一树、一草一木都可以成为研究、探索的对象。

百闻不如一见，你最好亲自去看一看。

中国人民勤劳勇敢、珍重友谊、热爱和平。

我对中国传统文化很感兴趣，比如书法、剪纸和茶艺。

台湾岛是中国最大的岛屿。

老师送给了我一本书。

你相信世界末日吗？

一到周末，我除了睡大觉，什么都不干。

这场大火烧掉了许多珍贵的照片。

他是一个好伙伴。

这种炎热的天气真让人受不了。

植树造林，绿化祖国。

沈阳的东边有座棋盘山森林公园。

太阳从东方升起，在西方落下。

喝杯咖啡，休息一会儿。

他们整天工作，只在中午休息一个小时。

今天下雪了，路很滑，我不开车了，还是坐地铁去学校吧。

她荣归故里。

他的价值谁都埋没不了。

她一向视金钱如粪土。

美名胜过金钱。

我把事情的经过原原本本地说了一遍，大家都明白了。

哎呀，原来如此。

我们最好坦诚相见。

地铁站就在我家门前马路对面。

教室后面的墙上挂着一张中国地图。

现在，城市人口和乡村人口几乎一样多。

乡村变化太大了，我们逐渐缩小了城乡差别。

一场大雨把马路冲洗得干干净净。

医生建议我们在雾霾天少运动。

第四课
LESSON 4

目见耳闻
What Is Seen and Heard

口之于味也，有同嗜焉；
耳之于声也，有同听焉；
目之于色也，有同美焉。

——孟子

People share similar standards in determining if a taste is agreeable to the mouth, a sound to the ears, and a sight to the eyes.

—Mencius

一、读写基本汉字　Read and Write Basic Chinese Characters

象形字
Pictographic Characters

口	kǒu (mouth)	【部首】口　【笔画】三画
	丨 𠃍 一　竖、横折、横	

甲骨文	金文	篆书	隶书	楷书	行书	简化字
Oracle Bones	Bronze Script	Seal Script	Official Script	Regular Script	Semi-cursive Script	Simplified Character

　　"口"是象形字。甲骨文的"口"形似人或动物张开的嘴(zuǐ)巴(ba)，金文和篆书也是如此。"口"本义指人的口腔器官，即人的嘴。

　　嘴是人用来吃饭、说话、呼吸的器官。口还可用作量词，如一口人、一口井。

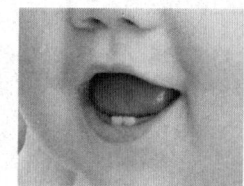

嘴(zuǐ)巴(ba)

词或短语　Words & Phrases

一家三口人	yì jiā sān kǒu rén	three family members in one family
人口	rénkǒu	population
口才	kǒucái	eloquence
口音	kǒuyīn	accent
门口	ménkǒu	gateway; doorway

LESSON 4 What Is Seen and Heard • 第四课　目见耳闻

出口	chūkǒu	exit
入口	rùkǒu	entrance
口口相传	kǒukǒuxiāngchuán	pass on by word of mouth
口是心非	kǒushìxīnfēi	duplicity; say yes and mean no

锦言妙语　Proverbs & Witticism

一口吃不成个胖子　yì kǒu chī bù chéng gè pàngzi
No one grows fat in one mouthful — nothing can be accomplished at one single stroke.

口若悬河，成事无多　kǒuruòxuánhé, chéng shì wú duō
Doers are not always talkers, nor are talkers doers.

病从口入，祸从口出　bìngcóngkǒurù, huòcóngkǒuchū
Diseases enter by the mouth, and misfortunes issue from it. ‖ A closed mouth catches no flies.

耍嘴皮子　shuǎ zuǐpízi
Show off one's eloquence; talk glibly.

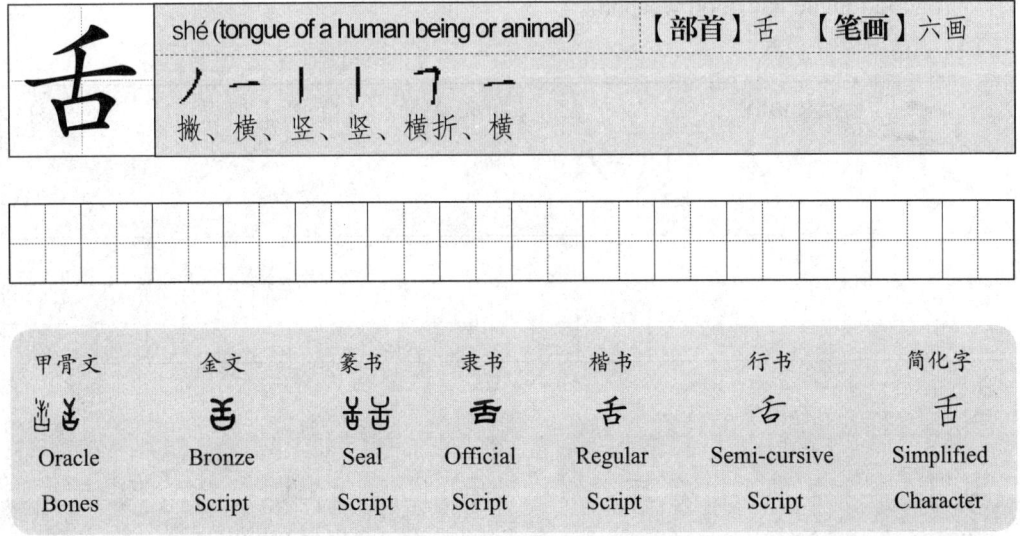

"舌"是象形字。甲骨文的"舌"写作 ，由 （蛇信子）和 （口）构成，字形像蛇张开口伸出舌头的样子。《说文解字》："舌，在口中，用以言说、辨味之器官。""舌"本义是舌头，口腔内的味(wèi)觉(jué)器官，现在还指代言语，如诸葛亮舌战群儒。

- 157 -

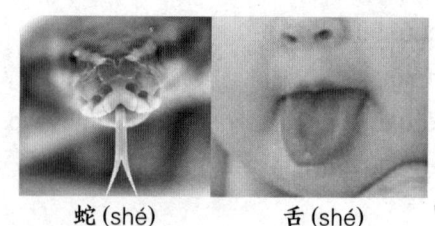

蛇(shé)　　　舌(shé)

词或短语　Words & Phrases

舌头	shétou	tongue
舌尖	shéjiān	tongue tip
七嘴八舌	qīzuǐ-bāshé	all sorts of gossip
鹦鹉学舌	yīngwǔxuéshé	imitate mechanically

锦言妙语　Proverbs & Witticism

舌头底下压死人　shétou dǐ xia yā sǐ rén
Criticism should be feared.

会说话的舌头是一件精良的武器　huì shuōhuà de shétou shì yí jiàn jīngliáng de wǔqì
A good tongue is a good weapon.

牙	yá (tooth)	【部首】牙　【笔画】四画
	一 ㇄ 亅 丿	
	横、撇折、竖钩、撇	

金文	篆书	隶书	楷书	行书	简化字
与 与	月	牙	牙	牙	牙
Bronze Script	Seal Script	Official Script	Regular Script	Semi-cursive Script	Simplified Character

"牙"是象形字。金文的"牙"写作 与、与，形似上下交错的牙齿。"牙"本义指大齿、臼 (jiù) 齿 (chǐ)、牙齿，特 (tè) 别 (bié) 指象牙。

LESSON 4 What Is Seen and Heard • 第四课 目见耳闻

象 (xiàng) 牙 (yá)

词或短语 Words & Phrases

牙齿	yáchǐ	tooth
门牙	ményá	front tooth
牙疼	yá téng	have a toothache
牙医	yáyī	dentist
刷牙	shuā yá	brush one's teeth

锦言妙语 Proverbs & Witticism

以牙还牙，以眼还眼 yǐ yá huán yá, yǐ yǎn hái yǎn
An eye for an eye and a tooth for a tooth. ‖ Return blow for blow.

狗嘴里吐不出象牙 gǒuzuǐ lǐ tǔ bù chū xiàngyá
No ivory will come from a dog's mouth. ‖ What can you expect from a hog but a grunt?

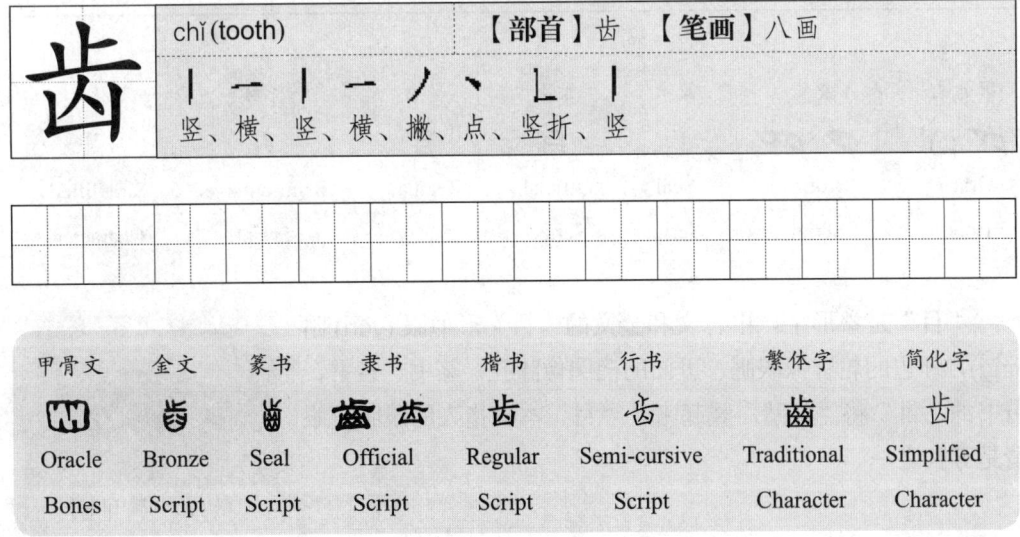

"齿"是象形字。甲骨文的"齿"写作 ，形似张口露出牙齿，以及上下相对的门牙。《说文解字》："齿，口腔中用来咬断骨头、嚼(jiáo)食(shí)的器官。"繁体"齒"后简化为"齿"，本义指牙齿，泛指牙齿。

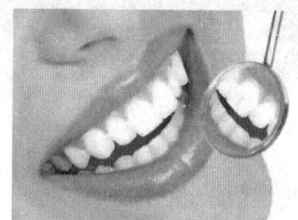

牙(yá)齿(chǐ)

词或短语 Words & Phrases

牙齿	yáchǐ	tooth
齿轮	chǐlún	gear wheel
口齿伶俐	kóuchǐlínglì	a good talker
咬牙切齿	yǎoyá-qièchǐ	gnash

目	mù (eye)	【部首】目　【笔画】五画
	丨 𠃍 一 一 一 竖、横折、横、横、横	

甲骨文	金文	篆书	隶书	楷书	行书	简化字
Oracle Bones	Bronze Script	Seal Script	Official Script	Regular Script	Semi-cursive Script	Simplified Character

"目"是象形字。甲骨文和金文的"目"形似眼(yǎn)睛(jing)，外边的轮廓像眼眶，里面的椭圆像瞳孔。篆书、隶书、楷书的"目"将"眼睛"竖起来。"目"本义指人的眼睛。眼睛是五官之一。

眼(yǎn)睛(jing)

LESSON 4 What Is Seen and Heard • 第四课 目见耳闻

词或短语 Words & Phrases

目光	mùguāng	brightness of the eye; vision; sight
目标	mùbiāo	target; goal
目的	mùdì	objective; purpose; aim; target
目前	mùqián	now; at present
目录	mùlù	catalogue; table of contents; list
节目	jiémù	program
目的地	mùdìdì	destination
目击者	mùjīzhě	eye witness
一目了然	yímùliǎorán	be clear at a glance

锦言妙语 Proverbs & Witticism

目不侧视，耳不旁听 mù bú cè shì, ěr bù páng tīng
To be deaf and blind to everything going on around – to concentrate on.

不识庐山真面目，只缘身在此山中
bù shí Lú Shān zhēn miàn mù, zhǐ yuán shēn zài cǐ shān zhōng
You fail to see the real face of Mount Lushan, only because you live in the mountains.

眉 méi (eyebrow)   【部首】目   【笔画】九画

フ 丨 一 ノ 丨 フ 一 一 一
横折、竖、横、撇、竖、横折、横、横、横

甲骨文	金文	篆书	隶书	楷书	行书	简化字
Oracle Bones	Bronze Script	Seal Script	Official Script	Regular Script	Semi-cursive Script	Simplified Character

"眉"是象形字。甲骨文的"眉"可写作 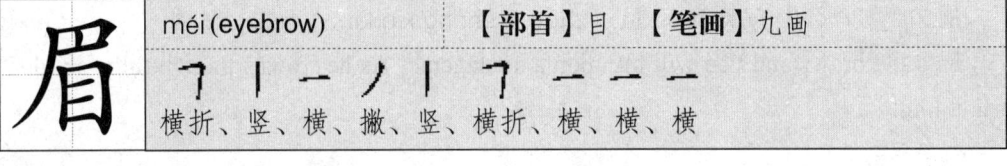，在眼睛 上方画一道曲线 ，

表示长在眼睛上方可伸展、可皱缩(suō)的毛发。金文的"眉"基本延续甲骨文的字形。"眉"本义指长在人眼睛上方的眉毛。

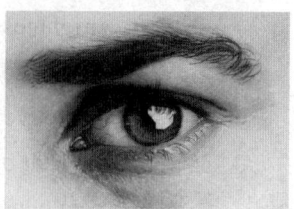

眉(méi)毛(mao)

词或短语　Words & Phrases

眉毛	méimao	eyebrow
眉开眼笑	méikāi-yǎnxiào	joyful; smile from ear to ear; be all smiles
眉清目秀	méiqīng-mùxiù	bright eyes and graceful eyebrows; handsome
火烧眉毛	huǒshāoméimao	the most urgent situation

锦言妙语　Proverbs & Witticism

眉毛胡子一把抓　méimao húzǐ yì bǎ zhuā

Try to grasp the eyebrows and beard all at once — try to attend to big and small matters all at once.

眉头一皱，计上心来　méitóu yí zhòu, jì shàng xīn lái

Knit the brows and you will hit upon a stratagem. ‖ As he frowns thoughtfully, an idea strikes him.

柳眉倒竖，杏眼圆睁　liǔméi dào shù, xìngyǎn yuán zhēng

Her eyebrows shot up and her eyes were round with rage.

自　　zì (oneself)　　【部首】自　【笔画】六画

丿丨㇆一一一
撇、竖、横折、横、横、横

LESSON 4 What Is Seen and Heard • 第四课 目见耳闻

甲骨文	金文	篆书	隶书	楷书	行书	简化字
ᕼ	自	自	自	自	自	自
Oracle Bones	Bronze Script	Seal Script	Official Script	Regular Script	Semi-cursive Script	Simplified Character

"自"是象形字。"自"是"鼻"(bí)的本字。甲骨文的"自"写作 ᕼ，形似一个大鼻子，有鼻梁、鼻翼，鼻孔在下面，中间的两横或一横用来表示鼻纹。"自"本义指鼻子。人们说到自己时，常常会用手指指自己的鼻子，由此产生"自己"的含义。

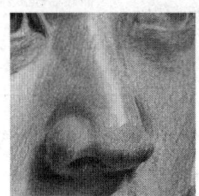

鼻(bí)子(zi)

词或短语 Words & Phrases

自己	zìjǐ	oneself
亲自	qīnzì	in person
自大	zìdà	arrogancy
自私	zìsī	selfishness; selfish
自立	zìlì	self-reliance; earn one's own living
自学	zìxué	self-study
自行车	zìxíngchē	bicycle; bike
自愿参加	zìyuàn cānjiā	voluntary participation
自言自语	zìyán-zìyǔ	think aloud
自作聪明	zìzuòcōngmíng	be wise in one's own conceit

锦言妙语 Proverbs & Witticism

自力更生，奋发图强 zìlìgèngshēng, fènfātúqiáng
Self-reliance and hard struggle.

天不言自高，地不言自厚 tiān bù yán zì gāo, dì bù yán zì hòu
Heaven does not speak from the high, and the earth does not speak from the thick.

自以为了不起 zì yǐwéi liǎobùqǐ
Think oneself terrific.

知人者智，自知者明 zhī rén zhě zhì, zì zhī zhě míng
He who knows other is learned, and he who knows himself is wise.

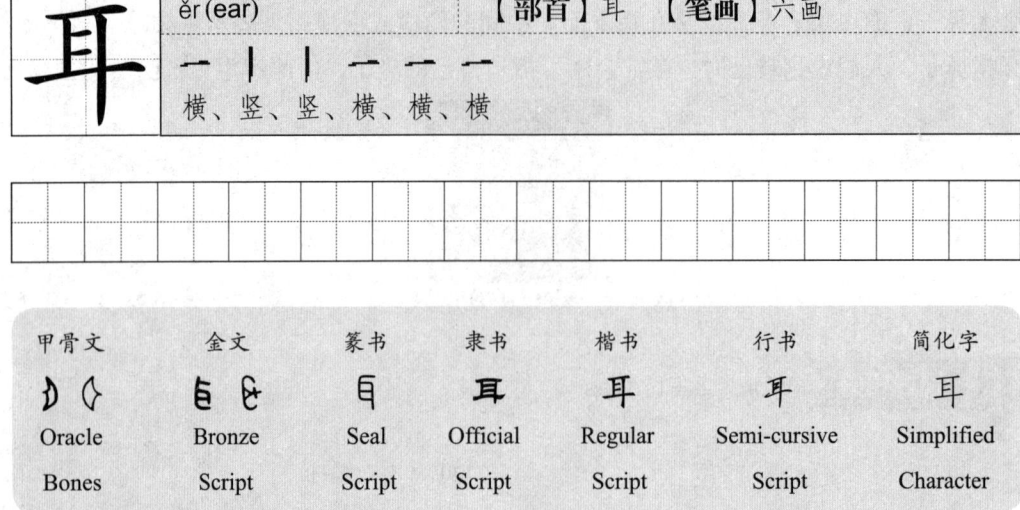

"耳"是象形字。"耳"是"取"的本字。甲骨文和金文的"耳"都与耳朵的形状十分相像。"耳"本义指耳朵，引申指形状与耳朵相似的东西或事物。

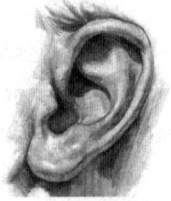

耳 (ěr) 朵 (duo)

词或短语　Words & Phrases

耳朵	ěrduo	ear
木耳	mùěr	black fungus

木 (mù) 耳 (ěr)

LESSON 4 What Is Seen and Heard • 第四课 目见耳闻

耳机	ěrjī	ear phone
耳聋	ěr lóng	deaf
洗耳恭听	xǐ'ěrgōngtīng	listen with respectful attention
耳闻目睹	ěrwén-mùdǔ	what one sees and hears
耳聪目明	ěrcōng-mùmíng	able to hear and see well; have sharp ears and eyes
耳目一新	ěrmùyìxīn	find everything fresh and new
隔墙有耳	géqiángyǒu'ěr	somebody may be listening on the other side of the wall

锦言妙语 Proverbs & Witticism

耳听为虚，眼见为实 ěr tīng wéi xū, yǎn jiàn wéi shí
Hearing can be vague, but seeing is definite.

墙有缝，壁有耳 qiáng yǒu féng, bì yǒu ěr
Walls have ears, there may even be cracks in them. || Walls have ears, we may be under close watch.

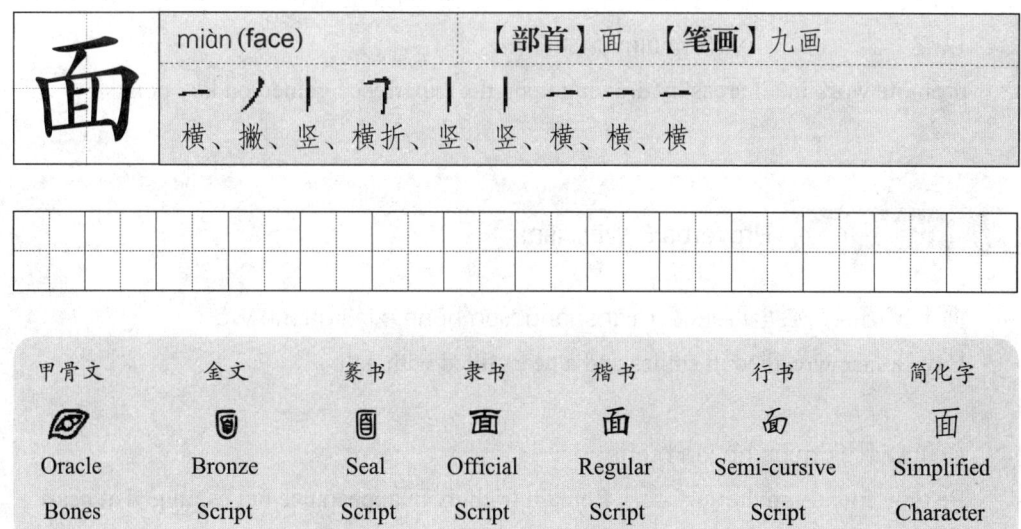

"面"是象形字。甲骨文的"面"写作 ，里面是甲骨文的"目"字，好像眼睛的形状，外面的 像一张脸的轮廓，即脸(liǎn)庞(páng)，表示人的脸上长有眼睛，所以古人也将"脸"称为"面目"，如面目一新、面目全非。"面"本义指脸。

"面"现在常指各种物体的表面或表层，如地面、水面、桌面。此外，"面"也有"当面、面对、面向"的意思。例如，我们最好当面谈谈。

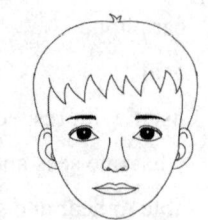

面 (miàn) 部 (bù) 简 (jiǎn) 画 (huà)

词或短语　Words & Phrases

脸面	liǎnmiàn	face
体面	tǐmiàn	dignity; propriety
前面	qiánmiàn	front; previous
后面	hòumiàn	behind
面对面	miànduìmiàn	face to face
面包	miànbāo	bread
面条	miàntiáo	noodle
丢面子	diū miànzi	lose face
爱面子	ài miànzi	be sensitive about one's reputation
以点带面	yǐdiǎndàimiàn	

promote work in all areas by drawing upon the experience gained on key points

锦言妙语　Proverbs & Witticism

面上笑呵呵，心里毒蛇窝 miànshàng xiào hēhē, xīnlǐ dúshé wō
Have a face wreathed in smiles and a heart filled with gall.

面和心不和 miàn hé xīn bù hé
Be only friends on the surface. || Remain friendly in appearance but estranged at heart.

死要面子活受罪 sǐ yào miànzi huó shòu zuì
Keep up appearance to cover up one's predicament

矮子面前莫论侏儒 ǎizi miànqián mò lùn zhūrú
One doesn't talk about midgets in front of dwarfs.

首	shǒu (head)	【部首】首　【笔画】九画
	丶ノ一ノ丨㇕一一一	
	点、撇、横、撇、竖、横折、横、横、横	

甲骨文	金文	篆书	隶书	楷书	行书	简化字
Oracle Bones	Bronze Script	Seal Script	Official Script	Regular Script	Semi-cursive Script	Simplified Character

"首"是象形字。甲骨文"首"字写作 ᗡ、ᗡ，形似一个头(tóu)，有发、有眼、有嘴，但不是很像人类的头，更像动物的头。"首"本义指头。

头是人体最上面的部位，首领是集体中权力最大、地位最高的人。在现代汉语中，"首"常常引申为在众人当中地位最高或权力最大的人，如首领、元首、首脑；又引申为第一、首要、最重要的、首创；此外，"首"还可用作量词，如一首诗、三首歌曲。

词或短语 Words & Phrases

中国的首都	Zhōngguó de shǒudū	the capital of China
首领	shóulǐng	leader; head
首相	shǒuxiàng	premier; prime minister
首席	shǒuxí	chief
首创	shǒuchuàng	initiate
首先	shǒuxiān	firstly
首尾相顾	shóuwěixiānggù	the beginning and end correspond (with each other)

锦言妙语 Proverbs & Witticism

横眉冷对千夫指，俯首甘为孺子牛　héng méi lěng duì qiān fū zhǐ, fǔ shǒu gān wéi rúzǐniú

Fierce-browed, I coolly defy a thousand pointing fingers; head-bowed, like a willing ox I serve the children.

人生在世的首要大事是保持灵魂的高尚
rénshēng zài shì de shǒuyào dàshì shì bǎochí línghún de gāoshàng
The principal thing in this world is to keep one's soul noble.

熟读唐诗三百首，不会作诗也会吟 shú dú tángshī sān bǎi shǒu, bú huì zuò shī yě huì yín
When one learns 300 poems of the Tang Dynasty by heart, one is sure to be able to write poetry.

心	xīn (heart)	【部首】心　【笔画】四画
	､ 乚 ､ ､	
	点、斜钩、点、点	

甲骨文	金文	篆书	隶书	楷书	行书	简化字
Oracle Bones	Bronze Script	Seal Script	Official Script	Regular Script	Semi-cursive Script	Simplified Character

　　"心"是象形字。心的甲骨文、金文、篆书写法形如人的心脏(zàng)。"心"本义指心脏。心脏位于身体的中央，为全身供血、供氧，所以心也引申为中心、核心、中央。

　　古中医认为"心主神明"，产生思(sī)维(wéi)和感情也是心的功能，所以常将心理活动用"心"来表示，如心思、心意、伤心、担心、心不在焉等。

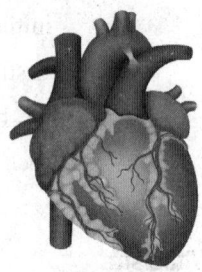

心 (xīn) 脏 (zàng)

词或短语　Words & Phrases

心情　　　xīnqíng　　　　　mood; temper

小心	xiǎoxīn	be careful; take care
小心眼儿	xiǎo xīnyǎnr	a narrow mind
担心	dānxīn	worry
放心	fàngxīn	rest one's heart
耐心	nàixīn	patience
伤心	shāngxīn	sad; heart-broken
信心	xìnxīn	confidence
心明眼亮	xīnmíng-yǎnliàng	be able to see everything clearly and corectly
心满意足	xīnmǎn-yìzú	be perfectly satisfied
心事重重	xīnshì chóngchóng	be preoccupied by some troubles
心地善良	xīndì shànliáng	kind hearted

锦言妙语 Proverbs & Witticism

心有灵犀一点通 xīn yǒu líng xī yì diǎn tōng
The hearts which beat in union are linked.

心静自然凉 xīn jìng zìrán liáng
So long as one keeps calm, one doesn't feel the heat too much.

知人知面不知心 zhī rén zhī miàn bù zhī xīn
It is impossible to judge a man's heart from his face.

相识满天下，知心能几人 xiāngshí mǎn tiānxià, zhīxīn néng jǐ rén
One's acquaintances may fill the world, but one's real friends may be few.

耍心眼儿 shuǎ xīnyǎnr
Exercise one's wits for personal gain; pull a smart trick.

页	yè (head; page)	【部首】页　【笔画】六画
	一 丿 丨 𠃌 丿 丶 横、撇、竖、横折、撇、点	

甲骨文	金文	篆书	隶书	楷书	行书	繁体字	简化字
𦣻	𦣻	頁	頁	页	页	頁	页
Oracle Bones	Bronze Script	Seal Script	Official Script	Regular Script	Semi-cursive Script	Traditional Character	Simplified Character

"页"是象形字。甲骨文的"页"写作𦣻，由 𦣻 (首或头) 和 𠘧 (人) 构成，像一个头部很大的人，形象生动地展现一个人跪坐在地上，夸张地显露他的头部。《说文解字》："页，头也。""页"本义指人头，也表示书页的意思。

词或短语 Words & Phrases

页数	yèshù	number of pages
页码	yèmǎ	pagination; page number

须 xū (facial hair; must; have to)　　【部首】彡　【笔画】九画

丿 丿 丿 一 丿 丨 𠃍 丿 丶
撇、撇、撇、横、撇、竖、横折、撇、点

甲骨文	金文	篆书	隶书	楷书	行书	繁体字	简化字
須	須	須	須	须	须	須	须
Oracle Bones	Bronze Script	Seal Script	Official Script	Regular Script	Semi-cursive Script	Traditional Character	Simplified Character

"须"是象形字。甲骨文的"须"字写作須，由 𠀉 (人)、𠀃 (下巴) 及 彡 (彡，表示毛发) 构成，表示长在下巴上的毛发。金文的"须"写作須，像人脸上长着许多胡子。《说文解字》："须，面毛也。""须"本义指胡须、胡子，又指像胡须的东西。

"须"后假借为"必须"，如"男大须婚，女大须嫁，古今常理"。

LESSON 4 What Is Seen and Heard • 第四课 目见耳闻

胡 (hú) 须 (xū)

词或短语 Words & Phrases

胡须	húxū	beard; moustache
必须	bìxū	must; have to; be obliged to

锦言妙语 Proverbs & Witticism

树老根须多，人老见识多 shù lǎo gēnxū duō, rén lǎo jiànshi duō
Old trees have more roots, and men that live longest see most.

要学惊人艺，须下苦功夫 yào xué jīngrén yì, xū xià kǔ gōngfu
One has to make painstaking efforts to master a skill.

室雅何须大，花香不在多 shì yǎ hé xū dà, huā xiāng bú zài duō
A cleanly chamber wouldn't lay claim to largeness, the fragrant flowers are careless of their number.

而   ér (and; but)   【部首】而   【笔画】六画

一ノ｜フ｜｜
横、撇、竖、横折钩、竖、竖

甲骨文	金文	篆书	隶书	楷书	行书	简化字
Oracle Bones	Bronze Script	Seal Script	Official Script	Regular Script	Semi-cursive Script	Simplified Character

- 171 -

"而"是象形字。甲骨文的"而"写作 ，形似下巴上的胡须飘(piāo)拂(fú)。金文的"而"写作 ，形似像人的胡须分为内外两层，外层代表两腮的胡子，内层代表嘴巴下方的胡子。"而"本义指胡须。

现代汉语中，"而"常用作虚词，表示转折、递进和反问，如然而、聪明而勇敢。

胡(hú)须(xū)

词或短语 Words & Phrases

而且	érqiě	and; not only...but also...
然而	rán'ér	however
三十而立	sānshí'érlì	a man should be independent at the age of thirty

锦言妙语 Proverbs & Witticism

温故而知新 wēn gù ér zhī xīn
Gain new insights through restudying old material. || Gain new knowledge by reviewing old.

勿以恶小而为之，勿以善小而不为 wù yǐ è xiǎo ér wéi zhī, wù yǐ shàn xiǎo ér bù wéi
Do not fail to do good even if it's small, and do not engage in evil even if it's small.

刚而不怒，满而不溢 gāng ér bú nù, mǎn ér bú yì
Strong without rage, and full without overflowing.

长	cháng; zhǎng (long; elder)	【部首】长 【笔画】四画
	ノ 一 ㄴ ㄟ 撇、横、竖提、捺	

甲骨文	金文	篆书	隶书	楷书	行书	繁体字	简化字
Oracle Bones	Bronze Script	Seal Script	Official Script	Regular Script	Semi-cursive Script	Traditional Character	Simplified Character

"长"是象形字。甲骨文的"长"形似一位头发很长 (cháng)、拄着拐杖的老人。"长"本义指两点间的距离大、长度大，也指时间久远、长久。此外，它用作名词，意思是长 (cháng) 处、优点。

"长"也读 zhǎng，意思是长大、成长。例如，人只有长 (zhǎng) 大了，才能比较客观地认识到自己的长 (cháng) 处和短处。"长"引申指年长 (zhǎng)，又指领导人，如首长、校 (xiào) 长 (zhǎng)、部长。

年 (nián) 长 (zhǎng) 的 (de)

词或短语　Words & Phrases

长江	Cháng Jiāng	Yangtze River
长城	Chángchéng	the Great Wall
擅长	shàncháng	be good at
校长	xiàozhǎng	headmaster; schoolmaster; rector
夜长梦多	yècháng-mèngduō	a long delay may cause trouble
说长道短	shuōcháng-dàoduǎn	gossip

锦言妙语　Proverbs & Witticism

尺有所短，寸有所长　chǐ yǒu suǒ duǎn, cùn yǒu suǒ cháng
Everyone has his shortcomings and merits.

张家长，李家短　zhāngjiā cháng, lǐjiā duǎn
Gossip about this or that family. || The virtues of the Zhang's and the defects of the Li's.

以己之长，攻人之短 yǐ jǐ zhī cháng, gōng rén zhī duǎn
Compare one's strong points with someone else's weak points.

岁月教人长智慧 suìyuè jiāo rén zhǎng zhìhuì
Years bring wisdom.

欠	qiàn (yawn; owe; not enough)	【部首】欠 【笔画】四画
	ノ ㇇ ノ ㇏	
	撇、横撇/横钩、撇、捺	

甲骨文	金文	篆书	隶书	楷书	行书	简化字
Oracle Bones	Bronze Script	Seal Script	Official Script	Regular Script	Semi-cursive Script	Simplified Character

　　"欠"是象形字。甲骨文的"欠"字写作　，形似一个人　张大嘴巴　，好像正在打哈欠。"欠"本义指张大嘴，打哈欠。打哈欠会导致气不足，现在"欠"多引申为减少、短少、不足，如欠款、欠债、欠条、欠缺、欠安。

打 (dǎ) 哈 (hā) 欠 (qian)

词或短语　Words & Phrases

打哈欠	dǎ hāqian	yawn
欠条	qiàntiáo	a bill signed in acknowledgement of debt
欠款	qiànkuǎn	debt
身体欠佳	shēntǐ qiàn jiā	in poor health

LESSON 4 What Is Seen and Heard • 第四课 目见耳闻

锦言妙语 Proverbs & Witticism

欠债要清，许愿要还 qiàn zhài yào qīng, xǔ yuàn yào huán
Pay what you owe and fulfil what you promise.

万事俱备，只欠东风 wànshìjùbèi, zhǐ qiàn dōngfēng
Everything is ready, then all we need is an east wind – all is ready except what is crucial. (origin: A story in *The Romance of the Three Kingdoms*. Zhou Yu planned to attack Cao Cao with fire. Though all was ready, he could not start the attack for the east wind was not blowing.)

指事字
Self-explanatory Characters

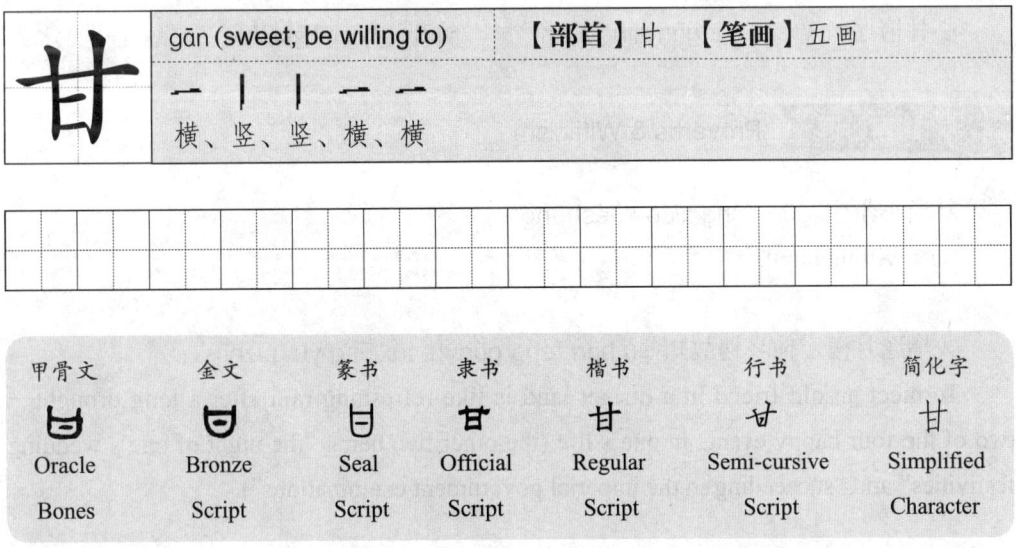

"甘"是指事字。"甘"是"甜"的本字，古代"甘""甜"通用。甲骨文的"甘"写作🄱，在"口"中加一横作为指事符号，表示口腔、舌头体验到舒(shū)服(fu)、美妙的味(wèi)道。

"甘"本义指食物的味道好，特指味甜，又引申为美好。"甘"和"苦"相对。

此外，"甘"也有情愿、乐意的意思，如现代汉语中经常用到的"心甘情愿""甘心付出"。

甘 (gǎn) 蔗 (zhe)

词或短语 Words & Phrases

甘蔗	gānzhe	sugarcane
甘泉	gānquán	sweet spring water
甘甜	gāntián	sweet
同甘共苦	tónggān-gòngkǔ	share the joys and sorrows with somebody
苦尽甘来	kǔjìn-gānlái	after suffering comes happiness
心甘情愿	xīngān-qíngyuàn	willingly and gladly

锦言妙语 Proverbs & Witticism

甘当小学生 gān dāng xiǎo xuéshēng
Be a willing pupil.

久旱逢甘雨，他乡遇故知 jiǔ hàn féng gānyǔ, tāxiāng yù gùzhī
To meet an old friend in a distant land is like refreshing rain after a long drought—two of the four happy events in one's life (the other two being "the night of one's wedding festivities" and "succeeding in the imperial government examinations").

曰	yuē (say)	【部首】曰　【笔画】四画
	丨 𠃍 一 一　竖、横折、横、横	

LESSON 4 What Is Seen and Heard • 第四课 目见耳闻

甲骨文	金文	篆书	隶书	楷书	行书	简化字
ᗜ	ᗜ	ᴗ	曰	曰	曰	曰
Oracle Bones	Bronze Script	Seal Script	Official Script	Regular Script	Semi-cursive Script	Simplified Character

　　"曰"是指事字。甲骨文的"曰"写作ᗜ、ᗜ，下面的ᗜ(口)表示人的嘴巴；上面的一个横画表示从人口中说出的话，也是一个指事符号。

　　篆书的"曰"写作ᴗ，横画从中间转弯向上，形象生动地描绘了人说话时不断从口中哈出的气或口中发出的声音。"曰"本义指说，如子曰，就是孔子说；引申为称为，如金木水火土名曰五行。

锦言妙语 Proverbs & Witticism

　　孟子曰："尽信书，则不如无书。" Mèngzǐ yuē: "jìn xìn shū, zé bù rú wú shū."
Mencius said: "To believe everything in books is worse than to have no books at all."

　　故曰，教学相长也 gù yuē, jiào xué xiāng zhǎng yě
So, we say, teaching others is teaching yourself.

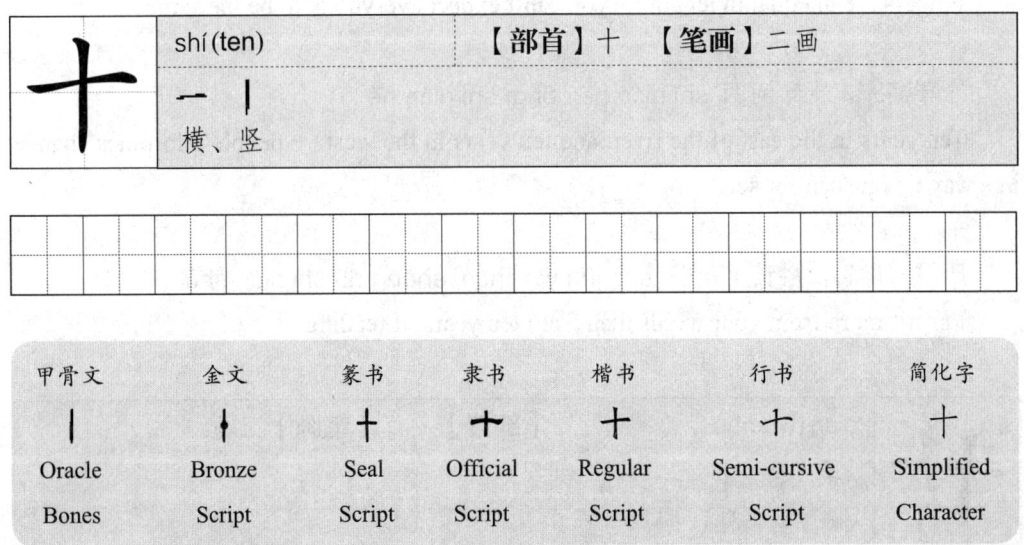

甲骨文	金文	篆书	隶书	楷书	行书	简化字
ǀ	╂	十	十	十	十	十
Oracle Bones	Bronze Script	Seal Script	Official Script	Regular Script	Semi-cursive Script	Simplified Character

　　"十"是指事字。甲骨文的"十"写作ǀ，金文的"十"将其中间加宽，逐渐演变成一个圆点●作为指事符号，有"结绳计数"之义，后中间圆点逐渐演变为一横，

写作"十"。"十"本义指数字十,也指十指,后来引申为多、最、极、完全。

双 (shuāng) 掌 (zhǎng) 合 (hé) 十 (shí)

词或短语　Words & Phrases

合十	héshí	put the palms together
十分	shífēn	completely; very
十指连心	shízhǐliánxīn	The nerves of the fingertips are linked with the heart.
十全十美	shíquán-shíměi	perfect; the peak of perfection
十万火急	shíwànhuǒjí	most urgent

锦言妙语　Proverbs & Witticism

十个指头有长短　shí gè zhǐtou yǒu cháng duǎn
Fingers are unequal in length — you can't expect everybody to be the same.

十年河东,十年河西　shí nián hé dōng, shí nián hé xī
Ten years in the east of the river, and ten years in the west — people's fortunes change in a way no one can for see.

听君一席话,胜读十年书　tīng jūn yì xí huà, shèng dú shí nián shū
I profit more from your words than from ten years of reading.

廿	niàn (twenty) 一丨丨一 横、竖、竖、横	【部首】一　【笔画】四画

LESSON 4 What Is Seen and Heard • 第四课 目见耳闻

甲骨文	金文	篆书	隶书	楷书	行书	简化字
廿	廿	廿	廿	廿	廿	廿
Oracle Bones	Bronze Script	Seal Script	Official Script	Regular Script	Semi-cursive Script	Simplified Character

"廿"是指事字。《说文解字》："廿，二十并也。"甲骨文的"廿"，是两个"十"字连在一起，"十"在甲骨文中常写作一竖"丨"，所以"廿"就用两个竖画相连来表示。金文的"廿"在两条竖画上各加一个点儿，篆书的"廿"将两点连成横线。"廿"本义指数字二十。"念(niàn)"是数目字"廿"的大写。

旬　xún (a period of ten days; a period of ten years)　【部首】勹　【笔画】六画

丿　㇆　丨　𠃍　一　一
撇、横折钩、竖、横折、横、横

甲骨文	金文	篆书	隶书	楷书	行书	简化字
Oracle Bones	Bronze Script	Seal Script	Official Script	Regular Script	Semi-cursive Script	Simplified Character

"旬"是指事字。甲骨文的"旬"写作 ，形似一个圆圈，并在圆圈的一端加一划，作为指事符号。古人计日，十天为一个循环，因此甲骨文的 就表示一个循环。金文的"旬"字加上一个日，表示每天周而复始。"旬"本义指每十天为一旬。一个月分上、中、下三旬。后来，又将十年作为一旬来表示人的年龄，如八旬老母，指八十岁的老母亲。

词或短语　Words & Phrases

上旬	shàngxún	the first ten days of a month
年过八旬	nián guò bā xún	over 80 years old

- 179 -

上

shàng (upper; top)　　【部首】一　【笔画】三画

丨 一 一
竖、横、横

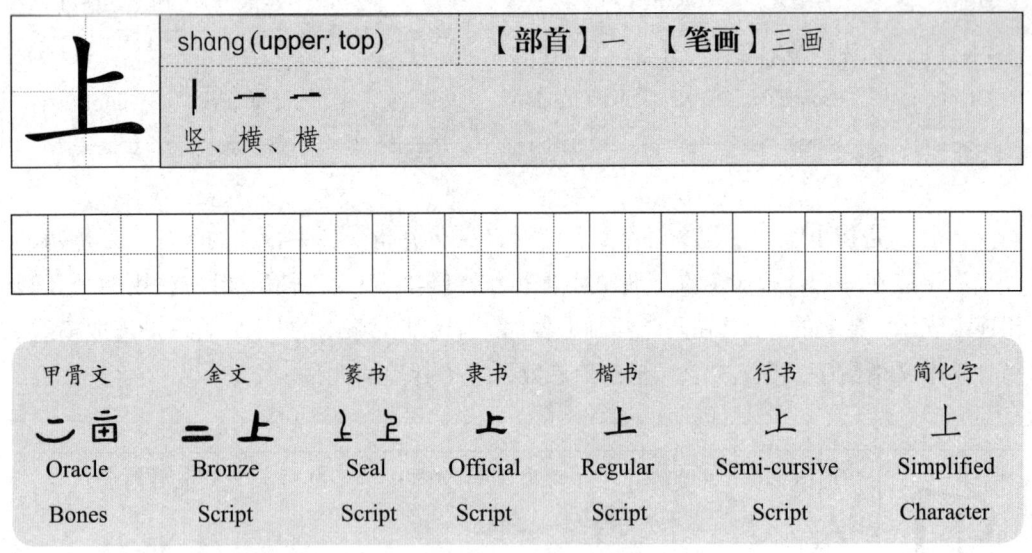

甲骨文	金文	篆书	隶书	楷书	行书	简化字
Oracle Bones	Bronze Script	Seal Script	Official Script	Regular Script	Semi-cursive Script	Simplified Character

"上"在古文字中是指事字。甲骨文和金文的"上"形似"二",下部较长的横画代表地平线,上部较短的横画是指事符号。"上"本义指位于上方,表示天或朝天的方向。为了和"二"字互相区分,篆书的"上"在中间加了一笔竖画"丨",后来逐步演变成今天的"上"字。"上"与"下"相对。

词或短语　Words & Phrases

上午	shàngwǔ	a.m.; forenoon
上班	shàngbān	go to work; start work; be on duty
上课	shàngkè	go to class; attend class
马上	mǎshàng	immediately; at once
晚上	wǎnshang	night; evening
上面	shàngmian	above; upside
上级	shàngjí	superior

锦言妙语　Proverbs & Witticism

上当只有一回　shàngdàng zhí yǒu yì huí
A fox is not taken twice in the same snare.

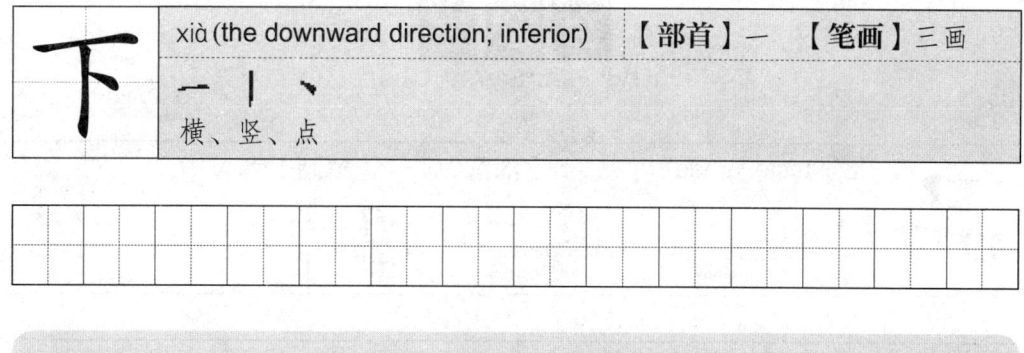

"下"是指事字。甲骨文的"下"字写作⌒,将表示"地"的南端横线写得较短,指代处在下面,表示地或朝地的方向。"下"的本义为地、底部。"下"与"上"相对。

词或短语 Words & Phrases

下午	xiàwǔ	afternoon
下雪	xià xuě	snowing
下半月	xià bàn yuè	the second part of a month
下楼	xià lóu	go downstairs
放下	fàngxià	lay down
下等	xiàděng	inferior; low-grade
下不为例	xiàbùwéilì	not to be repeated

锦言妙语 Proverbs & Witticism

下功夫 xià gōngfu

Devote time and effort. || Concentrate one's efforts.

大树底下好乘凉 dà shù dǐ xia hǎo chéngliáng

Great trees are good for shade.

会意字
Associative Compound Characters

品 pǐn (taste; grade) 　【部首】口　【笔画】九画

丨 フ 一 丨 フ 一 丨 フ 一
竖、横折、横、竖、横折、横、竖、横折、横

甲骨文	金文	篆书	隶书	楷书	行书	简化字
Oracle Bones	Bronze Script	Seal Script	Official Script	Regular Script	Semi-cursive Script	Simplified Character

　　"品"是会意字。甲骨文的"品"写作 ，由三个 (口，嘴巴)构成，表示吃好几口，并非(fēi)一口吞下，而是慢慢地品着味(wèi)道(dào)，享(xiǎng)受(shòu)美食，即品尝(cháng)，如品茶、品酒。

　　"品"由三个"口"字上下叠合而成，也可表示人多嘴杂。"品"本义指人多嘴杂，引申泛指众多。人一多，就会有各种各样的人，由各种各样的人，又引申指人的道德、风貌，如人品、品行、品格、品德；由各种各样的人，还可引申指事物的种类、类别和等级，即事物在质量上的优劣之分，如上品、下品、次品；由品类可引申指物品、物件，如商品、产品、赠品。

　　现在，"品"既可以表示人的道德修养、品行，也可以表示一种物品的质量或品质，还可引申作动词，指辨别高下、分出等级，特指品尝、辨别，如品茶。

品(pǐn)茶(chá)图(tú)

Words & Phrases

品尝　　pǐncháng　　taste

商品	shāngpǐn	commodity
产品	chǎnpǐn	product; commodity
品质	pǐnzhì	quality
赠品	zèngpǐn	gift; freebie
人品	rénpǐn	moral quality; personal character
品德	pǐndé	moral character
品学兼优	pǐnxuéjiānyōu	excellent in character and learning

锦言妙语　Proverbs & Witticism

万般皆下品，唯有读书高　wàn bān jiē xià pǐn, wéi yǒu dú shū gāo
To be a scholar is to be the top of society. ‖ All occupations are base, but book-learning is exalted.

吞 tūn (swallow)　　【部首】口　【笔画】七画

一 一 丿 乀 丨 ㇆ 一
横、横、撇、捺、竖、横折、横

金文	篆书	隶书	楷书	行书	简化字
Bronze Script	Seal Script	Official Script	Regular Script	Semi-cursive Script	Simplified Character

"吞"是会意字。从"口"，其字形像张开的口，表示以口吞食；从"天"，天有大的意思，表示口张得像天那么大，大口地吞，也表示动物吞咽食物时常将口朝天，以便咽下食物。"吞"本义指不经咀(jǔ)嚼(jué)成块吞咽食物或吞咽完整食物。

吞 (tūn)

词或短语 Words & Phrases

吞咽	tūnyàn	swallow
吞并	tūnbìng	merger; annex
吞吞吐吐	tūntūntǔtǔ	be hesitant in speaking; hesitate in speech

锦言妙语 Proverbs & Witticism

人心不足蛇吞象 rén xīn bù zú shé tūn xiàng
Be as greedy as a snake trying to swallow an elephant.

古　gǔ (age-old; ancient times)　【部首】十　【笔画】五画

一 丨 丨 𠃍 一
横、竖、竖、横折、横

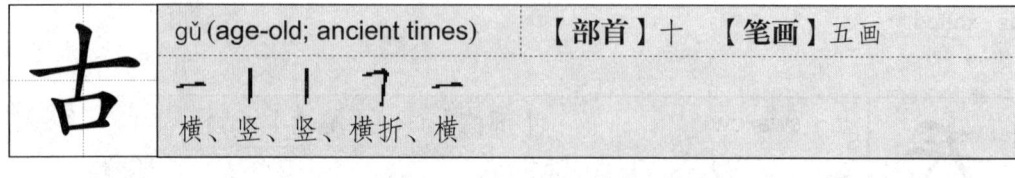

"古"是会意字。甲骨文的"古"写作 ， 由 （口，表示说）和 （十，表示数量很多）构成，表示祖祖辈辈流传下来的人和事。"古"从"十"、从"口"，由这两个字连接而成，表示通过许多人的口流传下来的故事。"古"本义指年代久远、古代，引申指古代的事情和人。现代汉语中，"古"常用来表示一个人思想僵化、不知变通，如古怪、古板。

西 (xī) 安 (ān) 古 (gǔ) 城 (chéng) 墙 (qiáng)

LESSON 4 What Is Seen and Heard • 第四课 目见耳闻

词或短语 Words & Phrases

古人	gǔrén	the ancients
古代	gǔdài	ancient times
古老	gǔlǎo	age-old
古迹	gǔjì	historical site
考古	kǎogǔ	engage in archaeological studies; archaeology
古板	gǔbǎn	old-fashioned and inflexible
古今中外	gǔjīn-zhōngwài	at all times and all over the world
古为今用	gǔwéijīnyòng	make the past serve the present

锦言妙语 Proverbs & Witticism

前无古人，后无来者 qián wú gǔrén, hòu wú láizhě
A record that has never been approached and will never be approached again.

古为今用，洋为中用 gǔwéijīnyòng, yángwéizhōngyòng
Make the past serve the present and foreign things serve China.

人生七十古来稀 rénshēng qīshí gǔ lái xī
It is seldom that a man lives to be seventy years old.

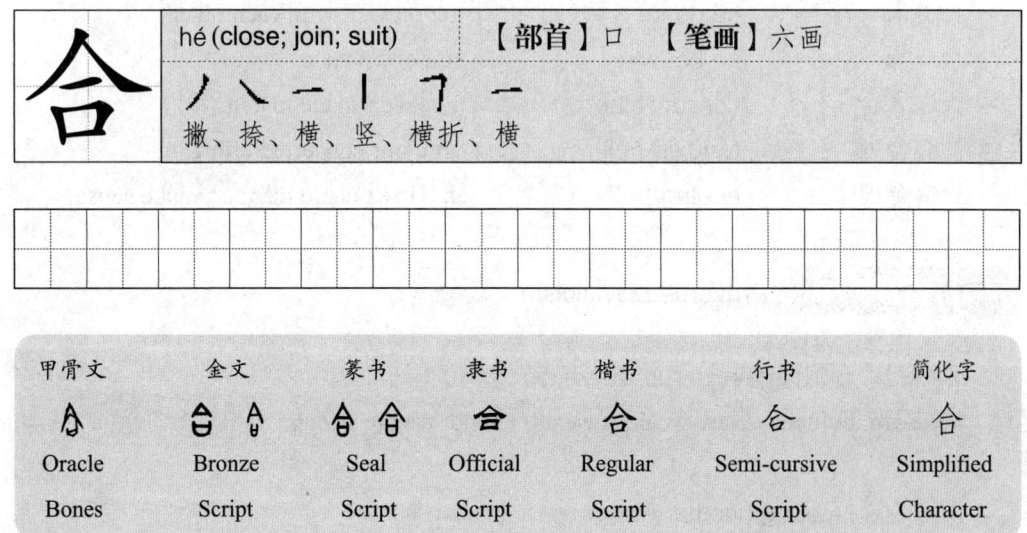

"合"是会意字。甲骨文的"合"写作 ᗡ，上部的 ᐱ 由一撇、一捺、一横构成，表示三画会合在一起，加上 ᒍ（口）字，表示闭合，像盖子盖在器物上。"合"本义指闭合，引申为聚合、会合、集合、结合、合并，又引申为匹配、配偶，如天作之合。现在，"合"大多表示合作。

盖(gài)子(zi)

词或短语　Words & Phrases

联合国	Liánhéguó	the United Nations
合适	héshì	suitable; fit
配合	pèihé	coordinate
合理	hélǐ	reasonable; rational
合同	hétong	contract; agreement
合作	hézuò	cooperation; collaborate; teamwork
合法	héfǎ	legal
合得来	hé de lái	get on well with each other
合口味	hé kǒuwèi	suit one's taste
天作之合	tiānzuòzhīhé	a heaven-made match
同心合力	tóngxīn-hélì	with our concerted effort
合情合理	héqíng-hélǐ	in a reasonable manner; make sense

锦言妙语　Proverbs & Witticism

分则弱，合则强 fēn zé ruò, hé zé qiáng
If we are divided, we are weak; if we are united, we are strong.

两好合一好 liǎng hǎo hé yì hǎo
Friendship cannot stand always on one side.

LESSON 4 What Is Seen and Heard • 第四课 目见耳闻

人有悲欢离合，月有阴晴圆缺 rén yǒu bēihuān-líhé, yuè yǒuyīn qíng-yuánquē
As people have their sorrows and joys, separating and reuniting, so has the moon its bright and dark, waxing and waning.

甜	tián (sweet)	【部首】甘　【笔画】十一画
	ノ 一 丨 丨 フ 一 一 丨 丨 一 一	
	撇、横、竖、竖、横折、横、横、竖、竖、横、横	

金文	篆书	隶书	楷书	行书	简化字
甜	甜	甜	甜	甜	甜
Bronze Script	Seal Script	Official Script	Regular Script	Semi-cursive Script	Simplified Character

"甜"是会意字。金文的"甜"字写作甜，由味觉器官 (舌) 和像口中含着甘美食物的 (甘) 会意。"甜"从"舌"、从"甘"，表示口中含着食物，舌头能感知食物的甜美，合起来指味道甘甜。"甘"是"甜"的本字。"甜"本义指味甘甜，形容词，多用来形容美好如蜜的味觉，如甜美。

甜 (tián) 葡 (pú) 萄 (tao)

词或短语　Words & Phrases

甜葡萄	tián pútao	sweet grape
甜食	tiánshí	sweetmeat; dessert
香甜	xiāngtián	fragrant and sweet
甜言蜜语	tiányán-mìyǔ	one's honeyed tongue and sugary words

锦言妙语 Proverbs & Witticism

强扭的瓜不甜 qiáng niǔ de guā bù tián
You can take a horse to the water but you cannot make him drink.

家乡水甜，家乡人亲 jiāxiāng shuǐ tián, jiāxiāng rén qīn
Water from the homeland is sweet; the people there are most dear.

见	jiàn (see; meet with; opinion)	【部首】见　【笔画】四画
	丨㇆丿乚 竖、横折、撇、竖弯钩	

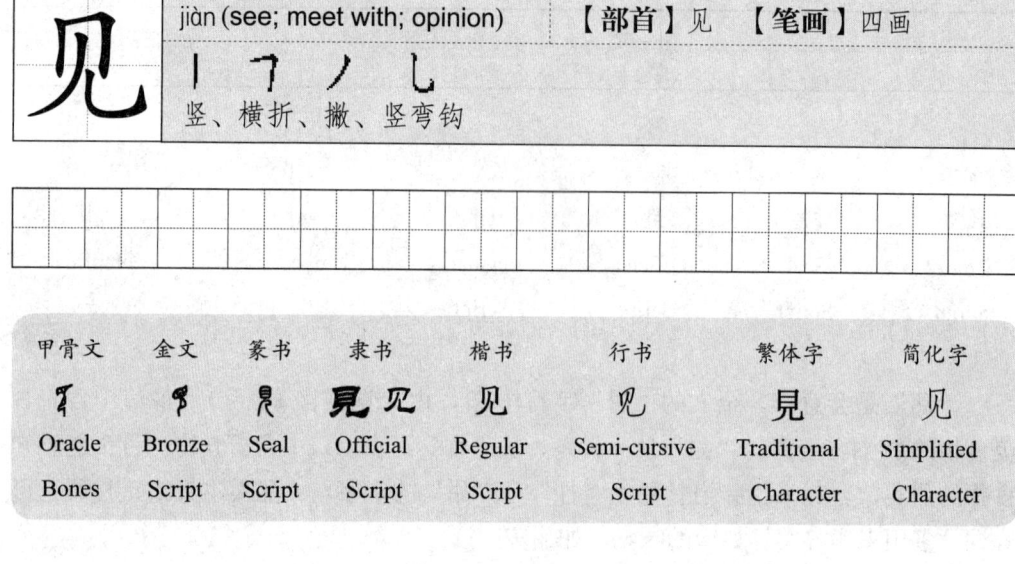

"见"是会意字。甲骨文的"见"写作 ，由 （目）和 （人）构成。字形突出眼睛的作用，表示一个人睁大了眼睛看，也表示一个人正用眼睛看。"见"本义指看见、看到，后引申为会见、觐见。

"见"也可用作名词，意为见解、看法、主张。在古代，"见"通"现(xiàn)"，意思是露出来、被看到。

词或短语 Words & Phrases

看见	kànjiàn	see
见面	jiànmiàn	meet
会见经理	huìjiàn jīnglǐ	meet with the manager
明天见	míngtiān jiàn	see you tomorrow
再见	zàijiàn	good-bye; see you later
见解	jiànjiě	opinion
意见	yìjiàn	idea; comment; suggestion

见多识广　　　　jiànduō-shíguǎng　　　well-informed
见钱眼开　　　　jiànqiányǎnkāi　　　　care for nothing but money

锦言妙语　Proverbs & Witticism

耳听为虚，眼见为实　ěrtīngwéixū, yǎnjiànwéishí
Seeing is believing, but hearing about it is not.

不见真佛不烧香　bú jiàn zhēn fó bù shāo xiāng
Don't burn incense on strange altars.

抬头不见低头见　tái tóu bú jiàn dī tóu jiàn
Meet regularly or frequently.

眼	yǎn (eyes; key point)	【部首】目　【笔画】十一画
	丨　𠃍　一　一　一　𠃍　一　一　𝗟　丿　㇏	
	竖、横折、横、横、横、横折、横、横、竖提、撇、捺	

金文	篆书	隶书	楷书	行书	简化字
𥃲	眼 眼	眼	眼	眼	眼
Bronze Script	Seal Script	Official Script	Regular Script	Semi-cursive Script	Simplified Character

"眼"是会意字。金文的"眼"写作𥃲，由⊖(目)和𠂆(艮，表示回头张望)构成。"眼"本义指眼睛，是用于张望的视觉器官。"眼"从"目"(眼睛)，从"艮"(gěn; gèn)，表示互相注视，又比喻要害或关键之处，如节骨眼儿。

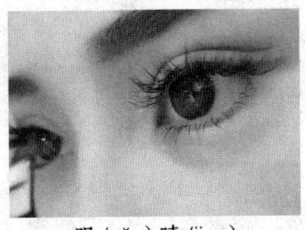

眼 (yǎn) 睛 (jing)

词或短语　Words & Phrases

眼睛	yǎnjing	eye
眼镜	yǎnjìng	glass
眼疾手快	yǎnjí-shǒukuài	have sharp eyes and quick hands

锦言妙语　Proverbs & Witticism

眼不见，心不烦　yǎn bú jiàn, xīn bù fán
Far from eyes, far from heart. ‖ Out of sight, out of mind.

眼睛是心灵之窗　yǎnjing shì xīnlíng zhī chuāng
Eyes are the heart's windows.

好汉不吃眼前亏　hǎohàn bù chī yǎnqián kuī
A wise man does not fight when he finds himself no match for his opponent.

一个心眼儿　yí gè xīnyǎnr
Of one mind; stubborn.

泪　lèi (tear)　【部首】氵　【笔画】八画

丶、丶、提、竖、横折、横、横、横
点、点、提、竖、横折、横、横、横

金文	篆书	隶书	楷书	行书	简化字
眔	𣽶	泪	泪	泪	泪
Bronze Script	Seal Script	Official Script	Regular Script	Semi-cursive Script	Simplified Character

"泪"是会意兼形声字。"泪"的金文字形好似泪如雨下，十分形象生动；篆书形体像水流；隶书、楷书形体像三滴水，表示眼泪似水。"泪"从"氵"(水)、从"目"(眼

睛），表示泪是眼中流出来的水。"泪"本义指眼泪。

眼 (yǎn) 泪 (lèi)

词或短语 Words & Phrases

眼泪	yǎnlèi	tear
泪水	lèishuǐ	tear drops
泪如雨下	lèirúyǔxià	tears fall down like rain

锦言妙语 Proverbs & Witticism

一把鼻涕一把泪 yī bǎ bítì yī bǎ lèi
Weep so sorrowfully that one's snivel and tears come down simultaneously.

不见棺材不落泪 bú jiàn guāncai bú luò lèi
Not to accept defeat until at the end of one's rope. ‖ Refuse to be convinced until one is faced with grim reality.

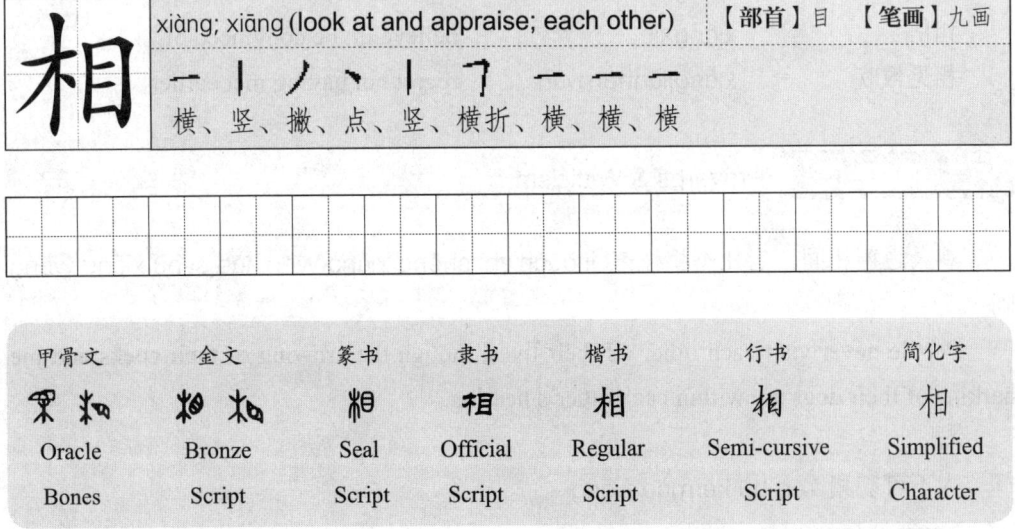

"相"是会意字。甲骨文的"相"可写作 ![img], 由 ![img] (木或树) 和 ![img] (目) 构成, 表示人爬上高树远眺侦 (zhēn) 察 (chá), 预警放哨; 甲骨文的"相"也可写作 ![img], 和金文的写法相似, 从"木"(树)、从"目"(眼睛), 左右组合而成, 表示人的一只眼睛正在盯着一棵树。由此可知, "相"本义指观看、察看 (kàn), 即观察情况, 加以判断, 如相 (xiàng) 面、相 (xiàng) 机行事。

"相"有时作官名, 如首相、丞相; 有时指人的相 (xiàng) 貌, 即面容、身材、衣着以及言谈举止, 如她相貌平平。

"相"还可读"xiāng", 如相 (xiāng) 亲、相见、相中、互相、相关、相信、好言相劝。

照 (zhào) 相 (xiàng) 机 (jī)

词或短语　Words & Phrases

照相机	zhàoxiàngjī	camera
长相	zhǎngxiàng	appearance
相似	xiāngsì	similarity
相同	xiāngtóng	the same; identical
相等	xiāngděng	equality
相反	xiāngfǎn	opposite
相信	xiāngxìn	believe in; be convinced of
相见恨晚	xiāngjiànhènwǎn	regret not having met earlier

锦言妙语　Proverbs & Witticism

鸡犬之声相闻, 老死不相往来　jī quǎn zhī shēng xiāng wén, lǎo sǐ bù xiāng wǎng lái

People never visit each other all their lives, though the crowing of their cocks and the barking of their dogs are within each other's hearing.

人不可貌相　rén bù kě mào xiàng

Never judge a person by his appearance.

宰相肚里能撑船 zǎixiàng dù lǐ néng chēng chuán
The prime minister's heart is big enough to sail a boat in – broad-minded.

冒 mào (risk; emit; head on; hat)　【部首】日　【笔画】九画

丨 ㇕ 一 一 丨 ㇕ 一 一 一
竖、横折、横、横、竖、横折、横、横、横

甲骨文	金文	篆书	隶书	楷书	行书	简化字
Oracle Bones	Bronze Script	Seal Script	Official Script	Regular Script	Semi-cursive Script	Simplified Character

"冒"是会意字。"冒"是"帽"的初文，本义指帽子。甲骨文的"冒"写作，是象形字，像一个帽 (mào) 子 (zi)，帽子上部有带球结的角饰，帽子下部是头套。金文的"冒"写作，省去甲骨文字形中帽子的角饰，增加眼睛，是会意字，表示人戴着帽子，露出眼睛。

由于"冒"后假借为顶着、不顾等含义，如冒雪、冒险，于是在"冒"左边加个"巾"字旁来代表帽子，使"帽"变成了左形(巾)右声(冒)的形声字。"帽"后来引申为各种形似帽子的物件，如笔帽。

帽 (mào) 子 (zi)

词或短语　Words & Phrases

冒险	mào xiǎn	adventure; risk
冒烟	mào yān	smoking
感冒	gǎnmào	catch a cold; sick
假冒伪劣	jiǎmào-wěiliè	fake and poor quality commodity

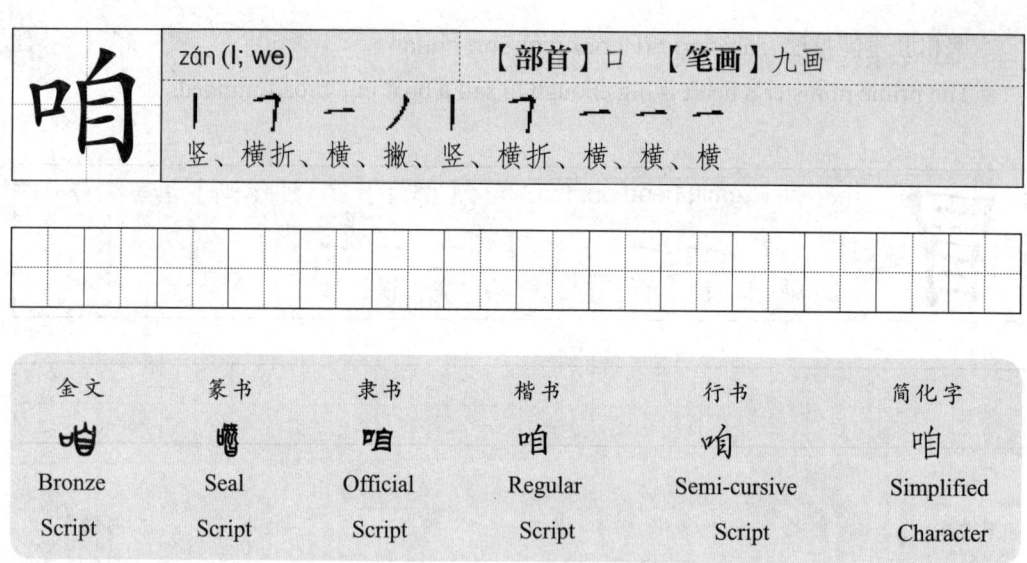

咱 zán (I; we)　　【部首】口　【笔画】九画

丨フ一ノ丨フ一一一
竖、横折、横、撇、竖、横折、横、横、横

金文	篆书	隶书	楷书	行书	简化字
Bronze Script	Seal Script	Official Script	Regular Script	Semi-cursive Script	Simplified Character

"咱"是会意字。"咱"从"口"(像张开的嘴)、从"自"(古文字形体像鼻子,表示自己),合起来用来称呼自己。"咱"是自己对自己的称呼,本义指我,又指说话的人和听话的人,如咱们是同学。

词或短语　Words & Phrases

咱们　　　　zánmen　　　　we
咱俩　　　　zánliǎ　　　　we; the two of us

锦言妙语　Proverbs & Witticism

咱们是一根绳子上的蚂蚱　zánmen shì yì gēn shéngzi shàng de màzha
We were all involved in the case and none of us could get away with it.

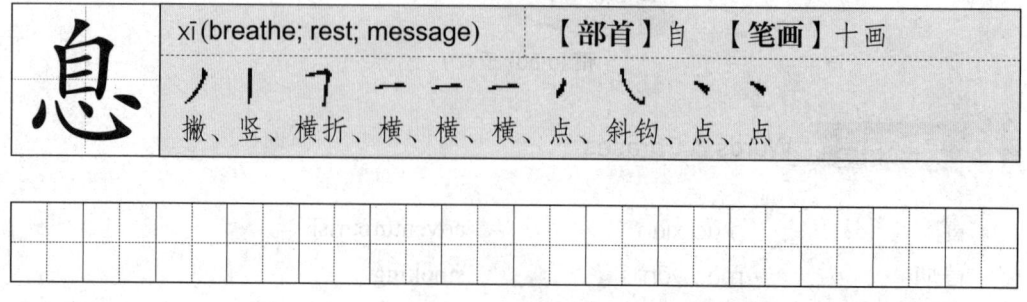

息 xī (breathe; rest; message)　　【部首】自　【笔画】十画

ノ丨フ一一一ノ乚丶丶
撇、竖、横折、横、横、横、点、斜钩、点、点

LESSON 4 What Is Seen and Heard • 第四课 目见耳闻

金文	篆书	隶书	楷书	行书	简化字
Bronze Script	Seal Script	Official Script	Regular Script	Semi-cursive Script	Simplified Character

"息"是会意字。金文的"息"写作，由（自或鼻子）和（心）构成，表示气息或心气从鼻孔中呼出。"息"本义指呼(hū)吸(xī)之气，如喘息。"息"又有停止之意，引申为歇息、休息、作息。

利钱是由本钱生出来的，于是"息"引申出利息、本息之义；现在又引申为音信，如消息、信息。

词或短语 Words & Phrases

叹息	tànxī	yammer
栖息	qīxī	inhabit
出息	chūxī	prospects; future; progress
信息	xìnxī	information
川流不息	chuānliúbùxī	never-ending; busy traffic
休养生息	xiūyǎngshēngxī	recuperate and build up strength; rehabilitation

锦言妙语 Proverbs & Witticism

日出而作，日入而息 rì chū ér zuò, rì rù ér xī
Go to bed with the lamb, and rise with the lark.

石沉大海，无声无息 shíchéndàhǎi, wúshēngwúxī
Just as a stone sunk into the sea, it has produced no reaction — failing entirely to attract any attention.

少说一句，息事宁人 shǎo shuō yī jù, xīshìníngrén
The least said, the soonest mended.

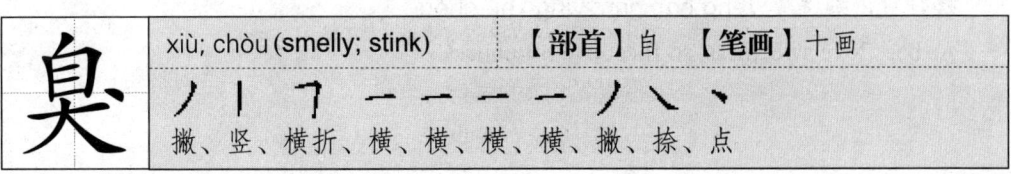

甲骨文	金文	篆书	隶书	楷书	行书	简化字
Oracle Bones	Bronze Script	Seal Script	Official Script	Regular Script	Semi-cursive Script	Simplified Character

"臭"是会意字。甲骨文的"臭"写作 ，形似一只站立的狗在用鼻子闻气味。因为狗的嗅(xiù)觉特别灵敏，所以古人用"犬"字来表示闻气味。"臭"本义为嗅(xiù)，即闻气味，如嗅(xiù)觉、嗅来嗅去。

现在，"臭"(chòu)字一般用作名词，指特别难闻的气味，如臭气、臭气熏天、臭味。人们常用"满身铜臭(chòu)"讽刺现代人过分看重金钱，视财如命，唯利是图。"臭"(chòu)与"香"(xiāng)相对。

嗅(xiù)

词或短语 Words & Phrases

嗅觉	xiùjué	sense of smell
臭味	chòuwèi	stink
臭架子	chòu jiàzi	hateful arrogance; the ugly mantle of pretentiousness
臭气熏天	chòuqì xūn tiān	reek with the stink of
臭名远扬	chòumíngyuǎnyáng	create a scandal far and wide

锦言妙语 Proverbs & Witticism

蜂好甘，蝇逐臭　fēng hào gān, yíng zhú chòu
As bees love sweetness, so flies love rottenness.

LESSON 4 What Is Seen and Heard • 第四课 目见耳闻

鱼放三日发臭，客住三天讨嫌 yú fàng sān rì fā chòu, kè zhù sān tiān tǎo xián
Fish smell after three days, and guests staying long are disgusting.

鱼烂头先臭 yú làn tóu xiān chòu
Fish begin to stink at the head. ‖ Corruption starts at the top.

闻	wén (hear; news story)	【部首】门　【笔画】九画
	、｜⺄一｜｜一一一	
	点、竖、横折钩、横、竖、竖、横、横、横	

甲骨文	金文	篆书	隶书	楷书	行书	繁体字	简化字
Oracle Bones	Bronze Script	Seal Script	Official Script	Regular Script	Semi-cursive Script	Traditional Character	Simplified Character

　　"闻"是会意字兼形声字。甲骨文的"闻"写作　，形似一个人跪坐在地上，专心地听着外界发出的动静。金文、篆书的"闻"字另造会意兼形声字，篆书的"闻"字由门(门)和⺹(耳)会意，表示在门里听门外的动静。"闻"本义指听到、听见。
　　关于听觉的描述，古代有两个字，一个是"听"，另一个就是"闻"。"听"本义指"往而听之"，就是主动跑过去听，如打听；而"闻"本义指"来耳闻之"，意思是声音传到耳朵里，如听见、听到。

听 (tīng)

 Words & Phrases

新闻　　　　　xīnwén　　　　　news

即时新闻	jíshí xīnwén	breaking news; live news; latest news
闻名	wénmíng	famous; well-known
丑闻	chǒuwén	scandal
传闻	chuánwén	rumor
默默无闻	mòmòwúwén	unknown to public

锦言妙语 Proverbs & Witticism

闻名不如见面 wén míng bù rú jiàn miàn
Knowing a person by repute is not as good as seeing him in the flesh.

闻声知鸣鸟，闻言见人心 wén shēng zhī míng niǎo, wén yán jiàn rén xīn
A bird is known by its note, and a man by his words.

视而不见，听而不闻 shì'érbújiàn, tīng'érbùwén
To look at but pay no attention to, and listen to but hear nothing.

奓 dā (big-eared; slouch) 【部首】大 【笔画】九画

一ノ丶一丨丨一一一
横、撇、捺、横、竖、竖、横、横、横

金文	篆书	隶书	楷书	行书	简化字
眘	夽	奓	奓	奓	奓
Bronze Script	Seal Script	Official Script	Regular Script	Semi-cursive Script	Simplified Character

"奓"是会意字，从"耳"(古文字形似耳朵)、从"大"(像人张开四肢)，"大"(dà)兼表声，合起来表示耳朵大。"奓"本义指耳朵大。奓拉表示向下垂(chuí)的意思，如一只奓拉着耳朵的狗。

LESSON 4 What Is Seen and Heard • 第四课 目见耳闻

耳 (ěr) 朵 (duo) 耷 (dā) 拉 (la)

词或短语 Words & Phrases

耷拉   dā la   droop; hang down; slouch

忐	tǎn (mentally disturbed; perturbed)	【部首】心 【笔画】七画
	 竖、横、横、点、斜钩、点、点	

忑	tè (mentally disturbed; perturbed)	【部首】心 【笔画】七画
	一丨丶丶ㄴ丶丶 横、竖、点、点、斜钩、点、点	

金文	篆书	隶书	楷书	行书	简化字
㐅	㐅	忐	忐	忐	忐
Bronze Script	Seal Script	Official Script	Regular Script	Semi-cursive Script	Simplified Character

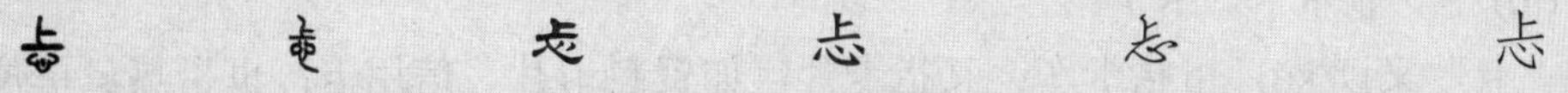

金文	篆书	隶书	楷书	行书	简化字
㐅	㐅	忑	忑	忑	忑
Bronze Script	Seal Script	Official Script	Regular Script	Semi-cursive Script	Simplified Character

- 199 -

"忐"是会意字，从"上"（表示向上、悬着、不踏实）、从"心"（古文字形似心脏，表示内心），合起来表示心神不宁，心好像悬着。

"忑"也是会意字，从"下"（表示向下）、从"心"（古文字形似心脏，表示与人的思维、心情有关），合起来表示心神不宁，心好像往下沉。

"忐忑"形容心神不宁、心虚，也表示畏惧、胆怯之义，如忐忑不安。

词或短语 Words & Phrases

忐忑不安　　　tǎntèbù'ān　　　be very upset; feel troubled and uneasy

qiǎ; kǎ (choke; be jammed; check-post; control)　　【部首】卜　【笔画】五画

丨一一丨丶
竖、横、横、竖、点

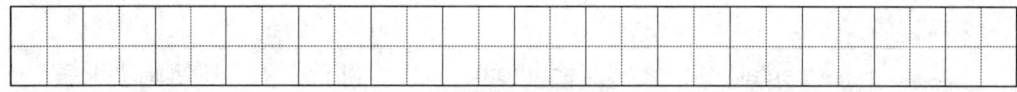

甲骨文	金书	篆书	隶书	楷书	行字	简化字
Oracle Bones	Bronze Script	Seal Script	Official Script	Regular Script	Semi-cursive Script	Simplified Character

"卡"是会意字。"上""下"合为一字，表示不上不下的意思。"卡"读qiǎ，本义指夹(jiá)在中间，不能上，也不能下；也指为了警戒(jiè)或收费而在交通要道设置的岗(gǎng)哨(shào)或检查站，如哨卡、关卡、税卡；还指夹在中间，不能活动，如卡壳(ké)、卡脖子、鱼刺卡在嗓(sǎng)子里。"卡"引申指夹东西的器具，如发(fà)卡、领带卡、卡子。

"卡"又读kǎ，可指卡车；又指卡片，如资料卡片、信用卡；也指热量单位，如卡路里的简称(calorie)。

词或短语 Words & Phrases

卡脖子　　qiǎ bózi　　　grip one's neck; seize sb. by the throat – put to death
关卡　　　guānqiǎ　　　customs pass; an outpost of the tax office

卡子	qiǎzi	clip; fastener
卡壳	qiǎké	stuck; jamming of cartridge or shell case
卡车	kǎchē	truck; lorry
信用卡	xìnyòngkǎ	credit card
卡片	kǎpiàn	card
卡通影片	kǎtōng yǐngpiān	animated cartoon film

锦言妙语 Proverbs & Witticism

鱼骨卡在喉咙里——吞不下吐不出　yúgǔ qiǎ zài hóulóng lǐ——tūn bú xià, tǔ bù chū
The fish bone is stuck in my throat — I couldn't swallow it and spit it out.

烦　fán (be annoyed)　【部首】火　【笔画】十画

丶ノノ丶一ノ丨フノ丶
点、撇、撇、点、横、撇、竖、横折、撇、点

金文	篆书	隶书	楷书	行书	繁体字	简化字
Bronze Script	Seal Script	Official Script	Regular Script	Semi-cursive Script	Traditional Character	Simplified Character

"烦"是会意字。篆书的"烦"字写作煩，由火(火)和頁(页、首或头)构成，表示因为有思想负担而焦躁不安。"烦"从"火"(像火苗)、从"頁"(页，像人头)，表示头发烧，像着火一样。今"煩"简化为"烦"。"烦"本义指发烧头痛，引申为苦闷、急(jí)躁(zào)。现在"烦"有时用作敬词，表示请、拜托，如麻烦、烦劳你帮个忙。

烦 (fán) 恼 (nǎo)

词或短语 Words & Phrases

烦恼　　　　　fánnǎo　　　　　be worried
烦闷　　　　　fánmèn　　　　　be unhappy
麻烦　　　　　máfan　　　　　 bother
心烦意乱　　　xīnfán-yìluàn　　be terribly upset
自寻烦恼　　　zìxúnfánnǎo　　 overcare

锦言妙语 Proverbs & Witticism

眼不见，心不烦 yǎn bú jiàn, xīn bù fán
What the eye doesn't see, the heart doesn't grieve for. || Out of sight, out of mind.

忍字家中宝，不忍惹烦恼 rěn zì jiā zhōng bǎo, bù rěn rě fánnǎo
"Bear and forbear" should be the motto in every family; want of forbearance produces discord.

钱财少，不烦恼 qiáncái shǎo, bù fánnǎo
Little goods, little care.

嚣　xiāo (noisy; clamour)　　【部首】口　【笔画】十八画

丨丨フ一丨フ一一ノ丨フノ丶丨フ一丨フ一
竖、横折、横、竖、横折、横、横、撇、竖、横折、撇、点、竖、横折、横、竖、横折、横

金文	篆书	隶书	楷书	行书	繁体字	简化字
Bronze Script	Seal Script	Official Script	Regular Script	Semi-cursive Script	Traditional Character	Simplified Character

"嚣"是会意字。金文的"嚣"写作 ，由 （頁或头）和 （四个"口"）构成。"嚣"从"頁"（页），其古文字形似头部突出的人；从四"口"，表示喧(xuān)哗、

吵闹。今"嚣"简化为"嚣"。"嚣"本义指吵闹、喧哗。

词或短语 Words & Phrases

喧嚣	xuānxiāo	noisy
气焰嚣张	qìyànxiāozhāng	swollen with arrogance
嚣张一时	xiāozhāngyīshí	be rampant for a time

锦言妙语 Proverbs & Witticism

吵吵嚷嚷,喧嚣一时 chāochaorāngrang, xuānxiāoyīshí
To raise a hue and cry for a while.

吹 chuī (blow; brag)　　【部首】口　【笔画】七画

丨 フ 一 丿 フ 丿 丶
竖、横折、横、撇、横钩、撇、捺

甲骨文	金文	篆书	隶书	楷书	行书	简化字
Oracle Bones	Bronze Script	Seal Script	Official Script	Regular Script	Semi-cursive Script	Simplified Character

"吹"是会意字。甲骨文、金文的"吹"字形似一个人蹲着用力吹气。"吹"从"口"(像张开的口)、从"欠"(表示人张口呼吸),表示用口吹气。"吹"本义指吹气,引申为吹奏(zòu)乐器,又引申出夸口、说大话、吹牛的含义。

现在人们常用"吹牛"这个词来形容说大话。另外,"吹"也表示关系破裂、事情失败。

吹 (chuī) 长 (cháng) 笛 (dí)

词或短语 Words & Phrases

吹牛	chuīniú	brag
吹捧	chuīpěng	flatter
吹牛皮	chuīniúpí	talk horse

锦言妙语 Proverbs & Witticism

野火烧不尽，春风吹又生 yéhuǒ shāo bú jìn, chūnfēng chuī yòu shēng
Even a prairie fire cannot destroy the grass, it grows again when the spring breeze blows – said of what cannot be suppressed.

不费吹灰之力 bú fèi chuīhuīzhīlì
As easy as blowing the dust off a table – need only a slight effort.

吹胡子瞪眼睛 chuī húzi dèng yǎnjing
Blow a fuse. ‖ Foam with rage.

形声字 Pictophonetic Characters

睛 jīng (the pupil of the eye; eye) 【部首】目 【笔画】十三画

丨 𠃍 一 一 一 一 一 丨 一 丨 𠃌 一 一
竖、横折、横、横、横、横、横、竖、横、竖、横折钩、横、横

金文	篆书	隶书	楷书	行书	简化字
睛	睛	睛	睛	睛	睛
Bronze Script	Seal Script	Official Script	Regular Script	Semi-cursive Script	Simplified Character

"睛"是形声字。"目"为形,表意,其古文字形似眼睛,表示眼珠在目(眼睛)中;"青"(qīng)表声兼表意,"青"有黑色之义,表示眼睛是黑色的。"睛"本义指眼珠、瞳子,后引申为眼睛、视力。

眼睛是心灵之窗,是一个人的神气所在。"画龙点睛"这个成语,本义指眼睛是龙的精髓,画完龙之后再点上眼睛,龙就更加神气活现,比喻写作文或说话时,在关键处加上几句话,使内容更加生动传神。

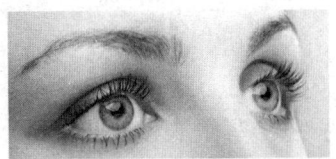

眼 (yǎn) 睛 (jing)

词或短语　Words & Phrases

眼睛　　　　　yǎnjing　　　　　　　eye
目不转睛　　　mùbùzhuǎnjīng　　　　gaze fixedly; fix eyes on
画龙点睛　　　huàlóngdiǎnjīng

Bring the painted dragon to life by putting in the pupils of its eyes — add the touch that bring a work of art to life.

眼高手低　　　yǎngāo-shǒudī

Have grandiose aims but puny abilities. ‖ Have sharp eyes in criticizing others but clumsy hands in doing things oneself.

锦言妙语　Proverbs & Witticism

相信眼睛比相信耳朵强　xiāngxìn yǎnjing bǐ xiāngxìn ěrduo qiáng
It is better to believe in the eyes than the ears.

画人难在画眼睛　huà rén nán zài huà yǎnjing
It is difficult to draw the eyes of a person.

- 205 -

金文	篆书	隶书	楷书	行书	简化字
想	想	想	想	想	想
Bronze Script	Seal Script	Official Script	Regular Script	Semi-cursive Script	Simplified Character

"想"是形声字。金文的"想"写作 ❀，由 ❀(相)和 ❀(心)构成。"心"表意，表示心有所思，心存其容其貌，追思、怀念；"相"(xiāng; xiàng)表声兼表意，表示用心思考问题，也可以理解为头脑中有影像，久久不能忘却。"想"本义指思索，如想法、感想、冥思苦想；可引申为希望、打算，如设想、妄想；又可引申为怀念、惦记，如想念；还可引申指推测、认为，如料想、推想。

词或短语 Words & Phrases

想念	xiǎngniàn	miss
思想	sīxiǎng	thought; mind
想法	xiǎngfǎ	idea
猜想	cāixiǎng	guess
梦想	mèngxiǎng	dream
理想	lǐxiǎng	aspiration; ideal
想当然	xiǎngdāngrán	assume (sth) as a matter of course
异想天开	yìxiǎngtiānkāi	whimsicality
想入非非	xiǎngrùfēifēi	let one's fancy run wild
想方设法	xiǎngfāng-shèfǎ	do everything possible

锦言妙语 Proverbs & Witticism

心往一处想，劲往一处使 xīn wǎng yī chù xiǎng, jìn wǎng yī chù shǐ
Think with one mind and work with one heart. || With everyone's thoughts and efforts directed towards the goal.

癞蛤蟆想吃天鹅肉 làiháma xiǎng chī tiān'é ròu

An ugly man hopes to marry a pretty girl like a toad on the ground trying to swallow a swan in the sky.

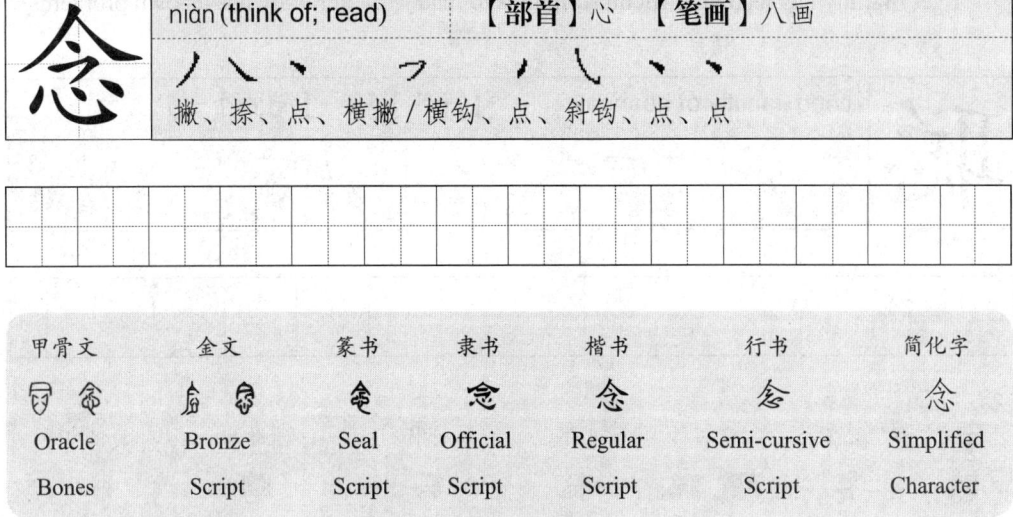

"念"是形声兼会意字。金文的"念"从"心"、从"今"(形似朝下的口,有的还画出了舌),意思是心中想、口中念叨,表示心中常惦念。《说文解字》："念,常思也。""念"本义指念叨、思念、想念,如念旧、怀念、念念不忘。

"念"用作名词,也指念头、想法,如一念之差、信念。由口中念叨,引申指诵读,如念书、念经、念诗;也指上学,如念小学、念大学。"念"还可用作数目字"廿"(niàn)的大写,表示二十。

词或短语 Words & Phrases

念叨	niàndao	talk about again and again in recollection or anticipation
念书	niàn shū	attend school
信念	xìnniàn	faith; belief; conviction
观念	guānniàn	idea; concept
念旧	niàn jiù	keep old friendship in mind
想念	xiǎngniàn	miss; remember fondly
怀念	huáiniàn	think of; cherish the memory of
一念之差	yīniànzhīchà	a great mistake made in a moment of weakness
念念不忘	niànniànbùwàng	keep in mind

锦言妙语 Proverbs & Witticism

家家有本难念的经　jiā jiā yǒu běn nán niàn de jīng
Every family has its own difficult scriptures to read. || Each family has its own problems.

聪　cōng (faculty of hearing)　【部首】耳　【笔画】十五画

一丨丨一一ノ丶ノ丨フ一丶乚丶丶
横、竖、竖、横、横、提、点、撇、竖、横折、横、点、斜钩、点、点

金文	篆书	隶书	楷书	行书	繁体字	简化字
Bronze Script	Seal Script	Official Script	Regular Script	Semi-cursive Script	Traditional Character	Simplified Character

　　"聪"是形声字。金文的"聪"写作 ，由 (耳朵，听) 和 (心脑，思) 构成，意思是耳听八方，听而能悟。"耳"为形，表意，表示听觉是耳朵的功能；"悤"(cōng) 表声兼表意，有迅速之意，表示耳朵能迅速听到声音。

　　简化字的"聪"从"耳"表意，"总"(zǒng) 表声兼表意，有聚合之义，表示"聪"是对聚合在耳中的声音产生的感觉。"聪"本义指人的听觉，引申指听觉灵敏，如耳聪目明；又引申指智慧，如聪敏、聪颖。

词或短语 Words & Phrases

聪明	cōngmíng	intelligent; clever; bright
耳聪目明	ěrcōng-mùmíng	can hear and see well
聪明好学	cōngmíng hào xué	be intelligent and fond of study
聪明活泼	cōngmíng huópō	be wise and active

锦言妙语 Proverbs & Witticism

聪明反被聪明误　cōngmíng fǎn bèi cōngmíng wù
A wise man can be ruined by his own wisdom.

LESSON 4 What Is Seen and Heard ● 第四课 目见耳闻

聪明一世，糊涂一时 cōng míng yī shì, hú tú yī shí
A lifetime of cleverness can be interrupted by moments of stupidity.

耍小聪明 shuǎ xiǎo cōngmíng
To play petty tricks.

闷	mèn; mēn (bored; depressed; tightly closed)	【部首】门　【笔画】七画
	、丨　㇆　丶　㇂　丶　丶	
	点、竖、横折钩、点、斜钩、点、点	

金文	篆书	隶书	楷书	行书	繁体字	简化字
Bronze Script	Seal Script	Official Script	Regular Script	Semi-cursive Script	Traditional Character	Simplified Character

　　"闷"是形声兼会意字，从"心"、从"門"（门），"門"（门 mén）兼表声，以门关闭表示心中憋闷。今"悶"简化为"闷"。"闷"本义指憋闷，引申为不痛快，如苦闷 (mèn)、烦闷。
　　"闷"发 mēn 音的时候，意思是空气不流通，如闷热、气闷；也有不显露、不出来的意思，如闷在家里。

 Words & Phrases

苦闷　　　　　kǔmèn　　　　　　depressed; anguish

沉闷	chénmèn	depressing; in low spirits
郁闷	yùmèn	gloomy; depressed
闷热	mēnrè	stuffiness
闷在家里	mēn zài jiā lǐ	boring at home
闷闷不乐	mènmènbùlè	moodiness; long face; gloomy

锦言妙语 Proverbs & Witticism

如同装进闷葫芦里——堵得慌 rú tóng zhuāng jìn mènhúlu lǐ——dǔ de huāng
It's like being stuck in an enigma — feeling something stuck in the heart.

二、注解 NOTES

(一) 孟子 (Mencius)

孟子(公元前372年—公元前289年)，名轲，山东人，战国时期伟大的思想家、政治家、教育家，先秦儒家的主要代表之一。据说孟轲出身于没落贵族家庭，父亲早逝，他由母亲抚养成人。孟母非常重视对孟子的教育，广为流传的"孟母三迁"的故事，足见孟母的良苦用心。长大成人后的孟子，曾"受业子思之门人"。子思是儒家创始人孔子的孙子，是战国初期有名的儒学大师。因此，作为子思学生的孟子，曾说"乃所愿，则学孔子也"，他将儒家学说当作自己的终身信仰。

中年时期的孟子以儒学大师的身份，曾效仿孔子游说各国近二十年，力求推行自己的政治主张。他倡导"民本""仁政""王道"三位一体，提出"民贵君轻"的民本思想，但不能为帝王所用。民本思想并非孟子首次提出，孟子以前的思想家，如老子、孔子、墨子等都曾提及民本思想。孟子的贡献在于深刻、系统地阐述了这一思想，进而将其发展成为仁政学说的理论基础。孟子深刻地意识到民心向背的重要性，认识到统治者要想巩固政权、治理好国家进而统一天下，就必须依靠民众的力量。他面对百姓处于水深火热之中的社会现实，痛心不已，呼吁统治者施行仁政，救人民于水火。在孟子的眼中，人民在国家政治中的作用是至高无上的。

孟子晚年归隐乡里，以著书立说为主，将"得天下英才而教育之"作为自己的人生志趣。有人曾总结孟子的生平与孔子有很多相似之处，都经历了读书、游历、教书，他们的思想主张都未能被统治者所采纳。正因为如此，孟子有"亚圣"之称，与孔子并称"孔孟",其著作《孟子》被后世列为儒家经典。

(二) 五官 (The Five Sense Organs)

五官指的是耳、眉、眼、鼻、口。人们常说的"五官端正""五官精致"是以容貌而言。五官对于容貌都很重要,而人们也常常以此评判一个人的容貌长相。

西医中的五官指的是眼、口、耳、鼻、喉;中医对五官有不同的解释,指的是耳、眼、唇、鼻、舌,它也指五种感觉,即听觉、视觉、触觉、嗅 (xiù) 觉 (jué) 和味觉。

有人相信第六感官,这个词与直觉大致吻合,其他类似的词还有预感、灵感、洞察力或预兆。直觉是指没有使用五官反射作用的感觉。

(三) 北京 (Beijing)

北京是中国的首都,位于华北平原,常住人口 2188.6 万人 (截至 2021 年末)。北京是历史文化名城,拥有众多历史名胜古迹和人文景观,如北京故宫、北京天安门、天坛、颐 (yí) 和 (hé) 园 (yuán)、明十三陵等。

贞元元年 (1153 年),金朝皇帝海陵王完颜亮正式建都于北京,称为中都。元朝时,北京被称为元大都,开始成为中国的首都。永乐十九年 (1421 年) 正月,明朝中央政府正式迁都北京。

北京故宫,旧称紫 (zǐ) 禁 (jìn) 城 (chéng),是中国明、清两代的皇家宫殿,是中国古代宫廷建筑之精华和中国传统建筑的杰出代表,是世界上现存规模最大、保存最完整的木质结构古建筑之一。北京故宫被誉为世界五大宫 (北京故宫、法国凡尔赛宫、英国白金汉宫、美国白宫、俄罗斯克里姆林宫) 之首。北京故宫于明成祖朱棣永乐四年 (1406 年) 开始建设,以南京故宫为蓝本,到永乐十八年 (1420 年) 建成。北京故宫南北长 961 米,东西宽 753 米,四面围墙高约 10 米,城外有宽 52 米的护城河。故宫有大小宫殿七十多座,房屋九千余间。

天安门 (Tian'an men) 位于能容纳百万人的天安门广场北面,面临长安街,对面是天安门广场以及人民英雄纪念碑、毛主席纪念堂、人民大会堂、中国国家博物馆。北京天安门是中国古代最雄伟的城楼,以其杰出的建筑艺术和独特的政治地位享誉世界。1949 年 10 月 1 日,伟大领袖毛泽东在这里庄严宣告中华人民共和国中央人民政府成立,并亲自升起了第一面五星红旗。北京天安门图案出现在中华人民共和国国徽中,成为中华人民共和国的象征。

(四) 茶 (Tea)

茶,中国传统饮品,植物学名:*Camellia sinensis* (L.)O.Ktze.,灌木或小乔木。
中国茶史的起源,众说纷纭,有的认为起于上古神农氏,有的认为起于周,还有的认为起于秦汉、三国。造成众说纷纭的主要原因是唐代以前无"茶"字,只有"荼"(tú)字的记载,直到唐代《茶经》作者陆羽将"荼"字减一画而写成"茶",因此有人说茶起源于唐代。

事实上,茶的历史要早于唐代很多年。在中国古代文献中,很早便有关于民间食茶的记载。在古代,茶本来是一种药,后来才发展成饮料。开始时,人们把新鲜的茶叶做成汤喝,后来为了方便保存和运输,才出现晒干的茶叶。

中国的茶早在西汉时便传到国外,汉武帝时曾派使者出使印度,所带的物品中除了黄金、锦帛外,还有茶叶。南北朝时,中国茶叶随出口的丝绸、瓷器传到了土耳其,在17世纪传到非洲和欧洲,在18世纪传到美洲。

《茶经》:"茶之为饮,发乎神农氏。"在中国的文化发展史上,往往把一切与农业、植物有关的事物起源都归于神农氏。相传神农在野外煮水时,刚好有几片叶子飘进锅中,煮好的水,其色微黄,喝入口中生津止渴、提神醒脑,神农以尝百草的经验,判断它是一种药。这是有关中国茶起源最普遍的说法。

茶叶的种类大体包括绿茶、红茶、乌龙茶、白茶、黄茶、黑茶。百姓眼中的十大名茶是指西湖龙井、洞庭碧螺春、黄山毛峰、安溪铁观音、君山银针、六安瓜片、信阳毛尖、武夷岩茶、祁门红茶、都匀毛尖。

现在,人们普遍生活压力较大,心肺脾胃之火多盛,茶苦而寒,饮茶有助于降火明目、宁心除烦、去痰热、消食去腻,对身体健康和舒缓精神都大有好处。据说用茶水洗脸,还能清除面部油脂、收敛毛孔、减缓皮肤老化。随着饮茶的人越来越多,茶文化逐渐形成。茶树生长于灵山,得雨露日月光华滋养,一枚茶叶,经采摘、晾晒、蒸、炒、烘焙、紧压等诸多工艺,方能成为可供人们冲泡的茶叶。沸水冲茶,温水沏泡,茶叶不停翻滚沉浮,不断舒展,溢出阵阵幽香,令人回味无穷。品茶正如品味人生,风雨磨砺,起起伏伏,苦乐年华中沉浮,方显英雄本色。

三、反义词 Antonym

上—下
甜—苦
长—短
远—近
快—慢
借—还

臭—香
新—旧

四、汉字的偏旁部首 The Structural Unit and Radical of Chinese Character

"心"字底和"忄"(竖心)旁

"心"是一个象形字，又可作部首字。"心"作部首时，在字的下面时写作"心"，称为"心"字底；在字的左侧时写作"忄"，称为竖心旁。"忄"是由"心"字演变而来的。

无论是由"心"字底还是由竖心旁组成的字，大多与人的思想和心理活动有关。例如，思想、怀念、急、恼、怕、怪，等等。

想	思想	sīxiǎng	thoughts
	想念	xiǎngniàn	miss
念	怀念	huáiniàn	cherish the memory of
	惦念	diànniàn	keep thinking about
忘	忘记	wàngjì	forget
怎	怎么样	zěnmeyàng	how
	怎么	zěnme	how
急	着急	zháojí	feel anxious
	急性子	jíxìngzi	short fuse; of impatient disposition
快	快乐	kuàilè	happy; joyful
慢	慢速	mànsù	low speed
	慢性子	mànxìngzi	slow coach; phlegmatic temperament
感	感情	gǎnqíng	emotion; feeling; affection
	感动	gǎndòng	touch; affect; move
	感慨	gǎnkǎi	sigh with emotion
	优越感	yōuyuègǎn	superiority complex
情	情绪	qíngxù	emotion; mood; feeling
惯	惯性	guànxìng	inertia
	娇惯	jiāoguàn	spoil
性	惰性	duòxìng	sluggishness

	性情	xìngqíng	disposition; temperament
悟	感悟	gǎnwù	inspiration
	悟性	wùxìng	power of understanding
意	意思	yìsi	idea; meaning; intention
	满意	mǎnyì	satisfaction
	同意	tóngyì	agree; consent
	愿意	yuànyì	be willing
	注意	zhùyì	attention; look out
怕	害怕	hàipà	fear; scare
	恐怕	kǒngpà	fear; be afraid of
怪	奇怪	qíguài	strange
	古怪	gǔguài	strange; oddball
忆	回忆	huíyì	recall
恶	恶劣	èliè	scurviness
恩	恩情似海	ēnqíngsìhǎi	Kindness is deep as the sea.
	感恩	gǎn'ēn	be thankful; owe; feel grateful
忠	忠诚	zhōngchéng	faithful; loyal
您	您好	nínhǎo	hello
忍	容忍	róngrěn	tolerate; put up with
	忍耐	rěnnài	endure
怨	怨恨	yuànhèn	hate; resentment
恨	怀恨	huáihèn	harbour resentment
息	叹息	tànxī	sigh
	休息	xiūxi	rest; take a rest
怒	愤怒	fènnù	rage; anger
	恼羞成怒	nǎoxiūchéngnù	be ashamed into anger
愁	愁苦	chóukǔ	feel gloomy; depressed
恐	恐惧	kǒngjù	fear
	惊恐	jīngkǒng	terrified
忧	忧虑	yōulǜ	anxious; worried
	忧愁	yōuchóu	sad; worried; depressed
	忧患	yōuhuàn	suffering; hardship
患	忧患意识	yōuhuàn yìshí	awareness of unexpected development
恋	恋情	liànqíng	amour
恼	烦恼	fánnǎo	annoyance; trouble

忐忑	忐忑不安	tǎntèbù'ān	be very upset; ill at ease
愚	愚忠	yúzhōng	foolish loyalty; blind loyalty
慈	慈悲	cíbēi	mercy
	慈悲为怀	cíbēiwéihuái	compassion
愉	愉悦	yúyuè	joyful; pleasure
	愉快	yúkuài	cheerful; pleasant
忙	慌忙	huāngmáng	in a great rush
	忙忙碌碌	mángmánglùlù	as busy as a bee
怯	胆怯	dǎnqiè	timidity; quail
悔	忏悔	chànhuǐ	confession
	悔悟	huǐwù	repentance
惭	惭愧	cánkuì	be ashamed of
懒	懒惰	lǎnduò	lazy; idleness
怜	怜悯	liánmǐn	pity; mercy; take pity on
惜	惋惜	wǎnxī	feel sorry for sb. or about sth.
惕	警惕	jǐngtì	vigilant
怖	恐怖	kǒngbù	terror; horrible; horror
惨	悲惨	bēicǎn	miserable

"口"字旁

"口"字是个部首字，由"口"字组成的字，其词义往往与嘴或方形物有关。"口"一般在字的左侧，有时也在字的上边或下边。例如，吃、喝、叫、喊、鸣、只、兄，等等。

吃	吃吃喝喝	chīchīhēhē	eat and drink
喝	喝茶	hē chá	drink tea
	吆喝	yāohe	call out
吩	吩咐	fēnfù	tell; order
号	号召	hàozhào	call upon
	号码	hàomǎ	number; code
叫	喊叫	hǎnjiào	shout; cry out
	鸣叫	míngjiào	tweet
呼	呼唤	hūhuàn	call
可	可能	kěnéng	possible
	可以	kěyǐ	may
只	两只耳朵	liǎng zhī ěrduo	two ears
听	听说读写	tīng shuō dú xiě	listening, speaking, reading and writing
	听力	tīnglì	hearing

味	味道	wèidào	taste
	口味	kǒuwèi	taste
啤	啤酒	píjiǔ	beer
品	品尝	pǐncháng	taste
叹	感叹	gǎntàn	sigh with emotion
唱	唱歌	chàng gē	sing
	鸣唱	míngchàng	sing
响	影响	yǐngxiǎng	influence
兄	兄弟	xiōngdi	brother
告	告诉	gàosù	tell
另	另外	lìngwài	in addition
哇	哇哇叫	wāwājiào	waul; wawl
叨	唠叨	láodao	jaw; nag; chatter
吐	呕吐	ǒutù	vomit; throw up
吸	吸收	xīshōu	absorb
	吸气	xī qì	inspired air; inspiration
咳	咳嗽	késou	cough
吞	吞咽	tūnyàn	swallow
否	否定	fǒudìng	deny; negate
呆	书呆子	shūdāizi	bookworm
吠	狗吠	gǒufèi	bark
吵	吵吵闹闹	chāochaonàonào	make a noise
咆	咆哮	páo xiào	roar
嚣	喧嚣	xuānxiāo	noisy
员	售货员	shòuhuòyuán	salesperson
	服务员	fúwùyuán	waiter or waitress
吻	吻合	wěnhé	be identical
吹	吹牛皮	chuī niúpí	hot air; brag
呻	呻吟	shēnyín	moan; groan
咱	咱们	zánmen	we
啃	啃咬	kěnyǎo	bite
啄	啄木鸟	zhuómùniǎo	woodpecker
叶	树叶	shùyè	leaf
	一片绿叶	yī piàn lǜyè	a piece of green leaf
兽	禽兽	qínshòu	birds and beasts

	喻	比喻	bǐyù	metaphor

"目"部，"目"字旁

"目"部字多和眼睛有关。例如，睡眠、相、盼、盯，等等。

眼	眼睛	yǎnjing	eye
	眼睁睁	yǎnzhēngzhēng	helplessly; unfeelingly
	眨眼	zháyǎn	blink; twinkle; wink
	着眼	zhuóyǎn	have sth. in mind
眉	眉毛	méimao	eyebrow
睡	睡眠	shuìmián	sleep
看	看书	kàn shū	read a book
盯	盯视	dīngshì	look at...fixedly
直	直线	zhíxiàn	straight line
	直视	zhíshì	look steadily at
	直觉	zhíjué	intuition; instinct
	一直	yìzhí	all the time; always; all the way
真	真切	zhēnqiè	clear
	天真	tiānzhēn	innocent; naive
瞒	隐瞒	yǐnmán	hide; conceal; cover up
相	相识	xiāngshí	acquaintance; be acquainted with each other
	相亲	xiāng qīn	blind date
	隐瞒真相	yǐnmán zhēnxiàng	conceal the truth; hide the truth
	照相	zhàoxiàng	take a picture; photo
盼	盼望	pànwàng	expect; look forward to
	期盼	qīpàn	look forward to; expect
眷	眷念	juànniàn	feel nostalgic about; think fondly of
盲	盲人	mángrén	blind person
瞎	瞎子	xiāzi	blind person; blind man
瞄	瞄准	miáozhǔn	aim; draw a bead on
盹	打盹儿	dǎdǔnr	nap; slumber; dogsleep
睹	耳闻目睹	ěrwén-mùdǔ	what is heard and seen
省	节省	jiéshěng	save; economize

五、HSK 试题选做 Sample Questions of the New HSK

(一) 根据对话选择正确的图片 (Choose the Corresponding Pictures Based on the Dialogues)

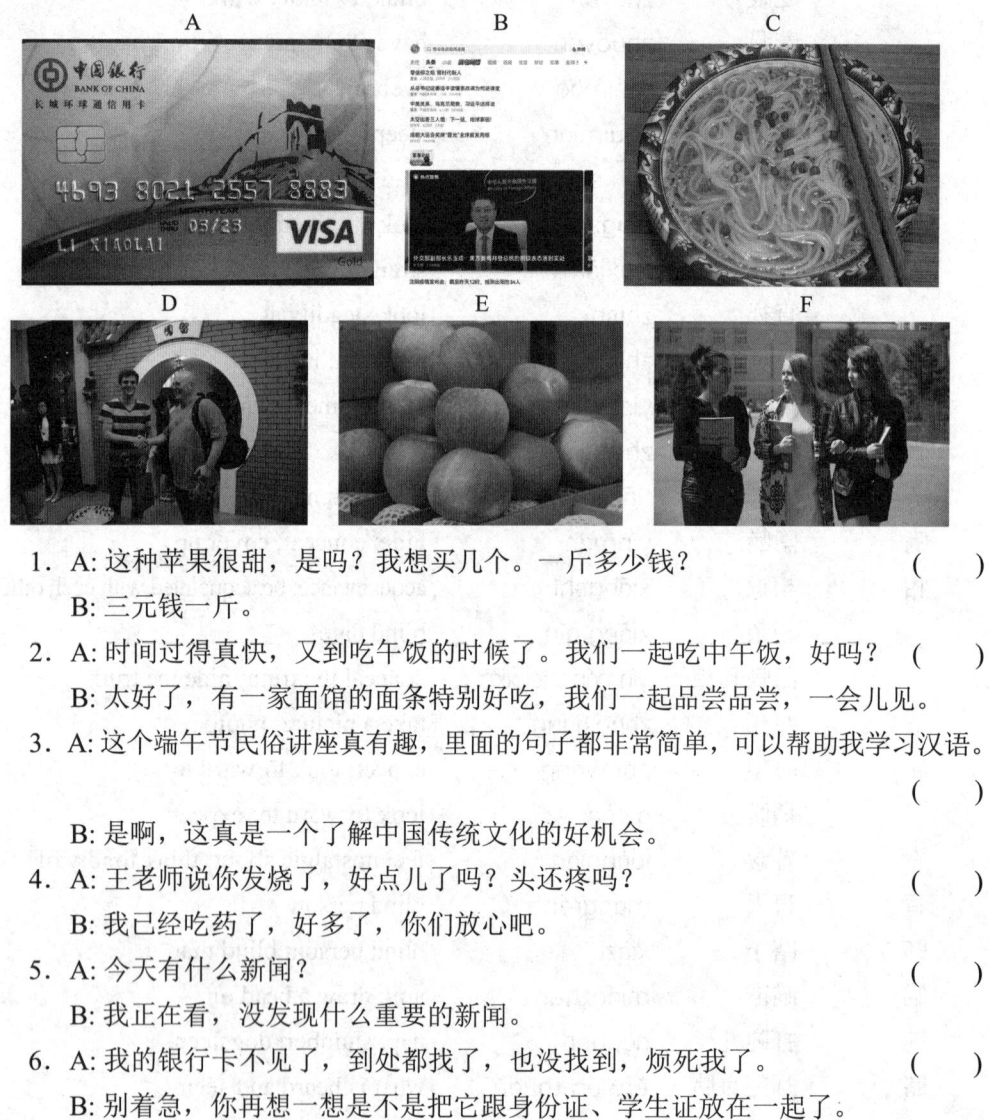

1. A: 这种苹果很甜,是吗?我想买几个。一斤多少钱? （   ）
   B: 三元钱一斤。
2. A: 时间过得真快,又到吃午饭的时候了。我们一起吃中午饭,好吗? （   ）
   B: 太好了,有一家面馆的面条特别好吃,我们一起品尝品尝,一会儿见。
3. A: 这个端午节民俗讲座真有趣,里面的句子都非常简单,可以帮助我学习汉语。
                                                               （   ）
   B: 是啊,这真是一个了解中国传统文化的好机会。
4. A: 王老师说你发烧了,好点儿了吗?头还疼吗? （   ）
   B: 我已经吃药了,好多了,你们放心吧。
5. A: 今天有什么新闻? （   ）
   B: 我正在看,没发现什么重要的新闻。
6. A: 我的银行卡不见了,到处都找了,也没找到,烦死我了。 （   ）
   B: 别着急,你再想一想是不是把它跟身份证、学生证放在一起了。

LESSON 4 What Is Seen and Heard • 第四课 目见耳闻

(二) 根据句子选择相应的图片 (Choose the Corresponding Pictures Based on the Sentences)

A　　　　　　　　B　　　　　　　　C

D　　　　　　　　E　　　　　　　　F

1. 不要躺着看书，对眼睛不好。　　　　　　　　　　　　　　　(　)
2. 我牙疼，想去看牙医，你能陪我去吗？　　　　　　　　　　　(　)
3. 你的自行车是新的还是旧的？　　　　　　　　　　　　　　　(　)
4. 我最不喜欢别人在我面前抽烟了。　　　　　　　　　　　　　(　)
5. 奶茶不仅讲究口味，而且还很注重颜色，因此最能吸引年轻人。(　)
6. 为了让自己更健康，他每天都花一个小时去锻炼身体。　　　　(　)

(三) 选词填空 (Choose the Corresponding Words Based on the Sentences)

A. 假新闻　B. 想　C. 看了　D. 烦闷　E. 身材　F. 眼睛

例如：与别人交流的时候，要看着对方的（ F ），这是基本的礼貌。

1. 新娘子长得很漂亮，就是（　）矮了点儿。
2. 我（　）一下午手机，太累了，想出去走走。
3. 和我们（　）的情况一样，他的面试成绩不算理想，现在一定很烦恼。
4. 电影明星看起来让人羡慕，可是她们也得面对很多问题，如婚姻、工作、身体健康，以及（　）带来的误会等，很多明星都去看心理医生。
5. 阴雨天让人（　），我从书架上随意拿了几本书看了看，觉得没啥意思，又放了回去。

- 219 -

六、朗读与书写练习 Reading and Writing Exercises

我家一共有三口人,都在医院工作。
贝宁卡宗同学会说一口流利的中文。
周末我又得去看牙医了。
在母亲的心目中,我一直是个孩子。
他看见这么一大笔钱,立刻眉开眼笑。
她工作不分主次,总是眉毛胡子一把抓。
老天给人双耳双眼一张嘴,为使我们多听多看少讲话。
今天午饭吃面条。
每个人都爱面子,尤其是男人。
中国的首都是北京。
妈妈是个心直口快的人。
一个人只有身心健康才会觉得快乐。
小心,别把笔记本丢了。
别担心,没事的。
我必须按时完成任务。
我为了她放弃了一切。
这儿的羊肉很好吃,而且也不贵。
不要自以为了不起,要甘当群众的小学生。
小朋友们对新年十分期待。
他去北京开会了。
要想学好外语,就得下功夫。
雨下得很大。
大家要学习这种高尚的品格,做一个有益于社会的人。
产品的质量太差。
你不要吞吞吐吐的,有话就直说吧。
西安有不少名胜古迹。
各族人民团结一心。
这苹果又红又甜。
好久不见,别来无恙。
我们很长时间没有见面了。
虽然好几年没见,但我一眼就认出是她。

他听到这个消息,顿时泪如雨下。
他的相貌吸引了她的注意。
他为什么要去冒这样的风险?
我又感冒了。
晚上咱们一起去看电影,好吗?
他整天工作,只在中午休息一会儿。
她的名声很臭。
他耷拉着头,一言不发。
考试成绩公布之前,我看得出她的忐忑不安。
一个人关在家里多烦闷呀!
麻烦没有来找你,不要去找麻烦。
我认为她完全是在吹牛皮。
她有一双明亮的大眼睛。
眼高手低,志大才疏,注定一事无成。
小姑娘的眼睛里闪烁着晶莹的泪花。
给我时间想一想,我会想出一个解决办法。
问题并没有大家想象的那么难。
我想知道您的电话号码,能告诉我吗?
新年快到了,我想家了。
他念念不忘自己的小学同学。
她坐在那里生闷气。

第五课
LESSON 5

母子情深
Great Affection between Mother and Son

老吾老，以及人之老；幼吾幼，以及人之幼；天下可运于掌。

——孟子

If everyone respects his own and then others' elders, loves his own and then others' children, it is as easy to run a state as to move balls in a hand.

—Mencius

一、读写基本汉字 Read and Write Basic Chinese Characters

象形字
Pictographic Characters

母	mǔ [mother;(of birds and animals)female]	【部首】母 【笔画】五画
	ㄥ ㇆ 丶 一 丶 竖折、横折钩、点、横、点	

甲骨文	金文	篆书	隶书	楷书	行书	简化字
Oracle Bones	Bronze Script	Seal Script	Official Script	Regular Script	Semi-cursive Script	Simplified Character

"母"是象形字。甲骨文"母"写作 ，整个字形可以使人联想到母亲正在给婴(yīng)儿哺乳的情形。"母"本义指母亲、妈(mā)妈(ma)。

在古文中,"母"常引申指能生子、哺乳的雌(cí)性(xìng)动物,如母鸡、母牛、母老虎;也可引申指能产生其他事物的本体,如母校、母亲河、母语、酵母。"母"与"公"相对。

哺(bǔ)乳(rǔ)图(tú)

词或短语 Words & Phrases

母亲	mǔqīn	mother
妈妈	māma	mom; mama

LESSON 5 Great Affection between Mother and Son • 第五课 母子情深

爸爸	bàba	father; dad
母爱	mǔài	motherly love; maternal love
母语	mǔyǔ	mother tongue
母子情深	mǔzǐqíngshēn	great affection between mother and son

锦言妙语 Proverbs & Witticism

一母生九子，九子各不同 yì mǔ shēng jiǔ zǐ, jiǔ zǐ gè bù tóng
A mother gives birth to nine children, each of whom is different.

儿行千里母担忧 ér xíng qiān lǐ mǔ dān yōu
When children travel far from home, mothers never stop worrying.

有其母，必有其子 yǒu qí mǔ, bì yǒu qí zǐ
Only such a mother could have had such a son.

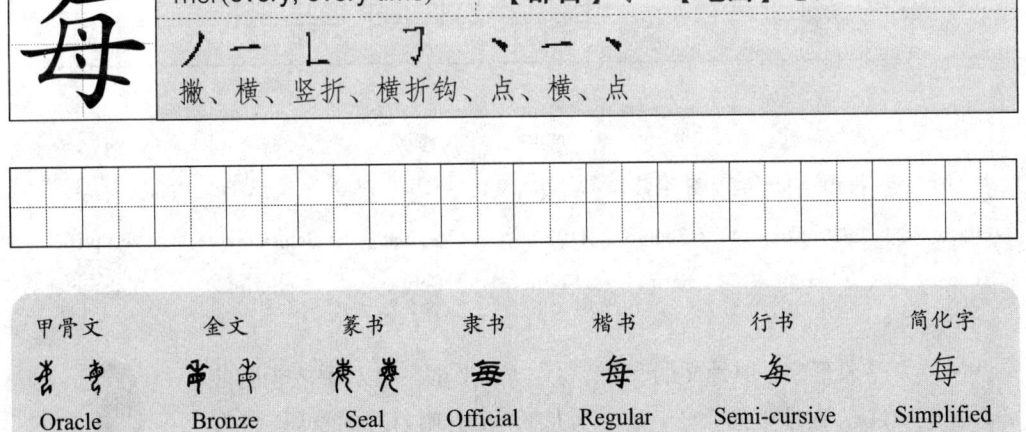

"每"是象形字。甲骨文和金文的"每"形似妇女头戴饰物，表示头饰华美的女子。"每"与"母"本为一字，"每"是"母"的异体字。"每"本义指头饰华美的母亲。

"每"字在古文中，还有草木初生或植物旺盛生长之义。后来"每"被借用，表示各个、逐(zhú)个、每次、凡是，如每月、每回、每战必胜、每况愈下。现在，"每"字通常用作副词，意为经常、常常。

词或短语 Words & Phrases

每天	měi tiān	every day
每年	měi nián	yearly; each year
每人	měi rén	everyone
每况愈下	měikuàngyùxià	The situation is worsening every day.

锦言妙语 Proverbs & Witticism

每逢佳节倍思亲 měi féng jiājié bèi sī qīn
At festival everyone misses his/her loved ones more and more.

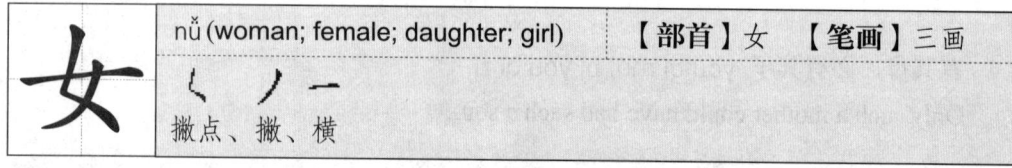

nǚ (woman; female; daughter; girl)　　【部首】女　【笔画】三画

撇点、撇、横

甲骨文	金文	篆书	隶书	楷书	行书	简化字
Oracle Bones	Bronze Script	Seal Script	Official Script	Regular Script	Semi-cursive Script	Simplified Character

　　"女"是象形字。甲骨文的"女"写作，形似一个双手放于胸前、跪 (guì) 坐 (zuò) 在地上的女子，表示听从吩 (fēn) 咐 (fù) 的意思。"女"本义指女性、女子、女人、妇女，与"男"相对，又指女儿。

　　国际妇女节是全世界女性共同的节日，它代表女性在政治、教育、经济方面与男子平等，代表公平、公正、和平与发展，是人类文明的巨大进步。

女 (nǚ) 人 (rén)

词或短语 Words & Phrases

女人	nǚrén	woman

LESSON 5 Great Affection between Mother and Son • 第五课 母子情深

女士	nǚshì	lady; madam
女儿	nǚ'ér	daughter
独生女	dúshēngnǚ	one's only daughter
女大当嫁	nǚdàdāngjià	A girl of age should be married.
女中豪杰	nǚ zhōng háo jié	woman of great capability

锦言妙语 Proverbs & Witticism

女大不中留 nǚ dà bù zhōng liú
A grown daughter cannot be kept unmarried for long.

女大十八变 nǚ dà shíbá biàn
A girl changes fast in physical appearance from childhood to adulthood.

皇帝女儿不愁嫁 huángdì nǚ'ér bù chóu jià
The daughter of an emperor does not worry about finding a husband.

| 丫 | yā (bifurcation) | 【部首】丶 【笔画】三画 |
| | 丶 丿 丨 点、撇、竖 | |

金文	篆书	隶书	楷书	行书	简化字
Bronze Script	Seal Script	Official Script	Regular Script	Semi-cursive Script	Simplified Character

"丫"是象形字，形似分叉的树枝。"丫"本义指树木或物体上端分叉的部分。由于女孩头上梳两个辫(biàn)子像"丫"形，称女孩子为丫头。

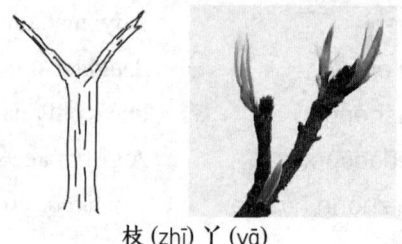

枝 (zhī) 丫 (yā)

词或短语 Words & Phrases

小丫头　　　　xiǎo yātou　　　　little girl

女 (nǚ) 孩 (hái) 子 (zi)

脚丫子　　　　jiǎoyāzi　　　　　foot

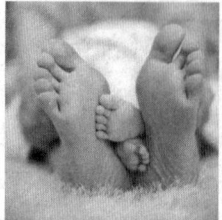

脚 (jiǎo) 丫 (yā) 子 (zi)

树丫　　　　　shùyā　　　　　　limb

锦言妙语 Proverbs & Witticism

黄毛丫头十八变　huángmáo yātou shí bá biàn
A girl changes all the time before reaching womanhood.

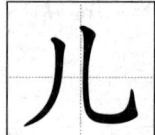	ér (child; kids; son)	【部首】儿　【笔画】二画
	ノ乚 撇、竖弯钩	

LESSON 5 Great Affection between Mother and Son • 第五课 母子情深

甲骨文	金文	篆书	隶书	楷书	行书	繁体字	简化字
𠒀 𠒃	𠒃	𠒀 𠒃	兒儿	儿	儿	兒	儿
Oracle Bones	Bronze Script	Seal Script	Official Script	Regular Script	Semi-cursive Script	Traditional Character	Simplified Character

"儿"是象形字。甲骨文的"儿"写作𠒃，形似婴儿的体形，上部很像囟(xìn)门还未闭合的婴儿头部，下部像一个"人"字。"儿"本义指儿童、小孩子。今"兒"简化为"儿"，引申为儿子。

婴(yīng)儿(ér)

词或短语 Words & Phrases

儿子	érzi	son; boy
女儿	nǚ'ér	daughter
儿童	értóng	children
儿童图书馆	értóng túshūguǎn	children's library
幼儿园	yòuéryuán	kindergarten
孤儿	gū'ér	orphan
生儿育女	shēngér-yùnǚ	bear sons and daughters
儿女情长	érnǚqíngcháng	the power of sexual love; be immersed in love

锦言妙语 Proverbs & Witticism

儿孙自有儿孙福，莫为儿孙做马牛 ér sūn zì yǒu érsūn fú, mò wéi érsūn zuò mǎ niú

The children can take care of themselves when they grow up, and the parents don't have to work too hard for their future.

好男儿志在四方 hǎo nán' ér zhì zài sì fāng
A good man sets his mind on the Four Seas.

儿不嫌母丑，狗不嫌家贫 ér bù xián mǔ chǒu, gǒu bù xián jiā pín
A son is not ashamed of his ugly mother, nor a dog of his poor family.

A good son does not covet the property of his ancestors, and a good daughter does not always wear the garments given to her at her wedding.

子	zǐ (child; baby; son)	【部首】子　【笔画】三画
	ㄋ 亅 一	
	横撇 / 横钩、竖钩、横	

甲骨文	金文	篆书	隶书	楷书	行书	简化字
Oracle Bones	Bronze Script	Seal Script	Official Script	Regular Script	Semi-cursive Script	Simplified Character

"子"是象形字。甲骨文的"子"写作 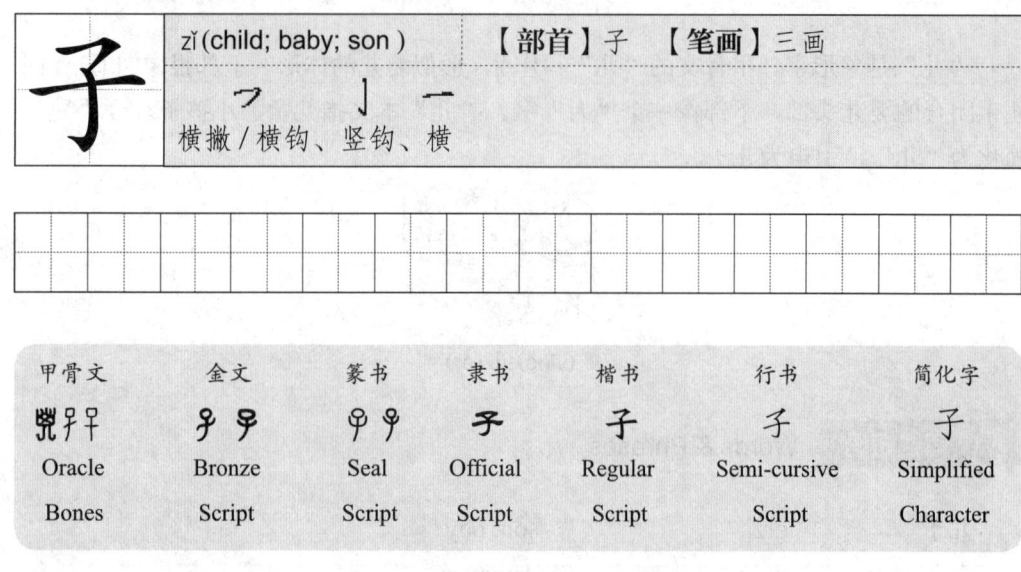，形似婴儿的脑袋 ⊙、头发 ⦙⦙⦙、两脚 儿，像一个有头发和囟(xìn)门(mén)未闭合以及两脚高高抬起的初生婴儿。甲骨文的"子"也可写作 孑，形似襁褓中的婴儿，其双腿被包裹着，两脚并拢在一起，只露出头和肩膀，两只手在空中摆弄。金文的"子"字基本延续甲骨文第二种字形。"子"本义指孩子、婴儿，现引申表示儿女、幼小、植物的种子和动物的卵。

由于婴儿头脑中没有杂(zá)念(niàn)，可用"子"来表示道德高尚的人，如老子、孔子、墨子、孟子；又引申指诸子百家的著作，如经史子集。

孩(hái) 子(zi)

词或短语 Words & Phrases

男孩子　　　　nánháizi　　　boy

LESSON 5 Great Affection between Mother and Son • 第五课 母子情深

男 (nán) 孩 (hái) 子 (zi)

女孩子	nǚháizi	girl
妻子	qīzi	wife
杯子	bēizi	cup; glass
盘子	pánzi	plate
胖子	pàngzi	fat person; obese person
句子	jùzi	sentence
裤子	kùzi	trousers
裙子	qúnzi	skirt
母子二人	mǔ zǐ èr rén	mother and child
子孙后代	zǐsūnhòudài	the coming generations; descendants

锦言妙语 Proverbs & Witticism

久病床前无孝子 jiǔ bìng chuáng qián wú xiàozǐ
A dutiful son is never found at the bedside of one who is ill for a long time.

为师不严，误人子弟 wéi shī bù yán, wù rén zǐ dì
Act as tutors without being properly strict, and thus mislead their pupils.

夫	fū (man; husband)	【部首】大 【笔画】四画
	一 一 ノ 乀 横、横、撇、捺	

甲骨文	金文	篆书	隶书	楷书	行书	简化字
夨 夫	夫 夫	夫 夫	夫	夫	夫	夫
Oracle Bones	Bronze Script	Seal Script	Official Script	Regular Script	Semi-cursive Script	Simplified Character

"夫"是象形字。甲骨文的"夫"形似一个正面站立、头上插发簪(zān)的成年人，上部的短横表示束(shù)发用的发簪(zān)。在中国古代，男子二十岁行加冠礼，将头发束起来插发簪，表示已经成人。"夫"本义指成年男子。

现在，"夫"引申为已经结婚的男子，女子的配偶叫丈夫；也可以表示从事某种体力劳动的人，如农夫、渔夫、马夫、船夫、伙夫。现代汉语中，"夫"大多指丈夫，与妻子相对。

束(shù)发(fà)图(tú)

夫(fū)

词或短语 Words & Phrases

孔夫子　　　　Kǒngfūzǐ　　　　Confucius

孔(kǒng)子(zǐ)画(huà)像(xiàng)

丈夫　　　　zhàngfu　　　　husband
大夫　　　　dàifu　　　　doctor

锦言妙语 Proverbs & Witticism

一夫当关，万夫莫开　yī fū dāng guān, wàn fū mò kāi
If one man guards the pass, then thousand are unable to get through.

LESSON 5 Great Affection between Mother and Son • 第五课 母子情深

夫妻本是同林鸟，大难临头各自飞 fūqī běn shì tóng lín niǎo, dà nàn lín tóu gè zì fēi
Birds in one grove as husband and wife, will each fly away when facing a disaster.

国家兴亡，匹夫有责 guójiā xīng wáng, pǐ fū yǒu zé
The rise and fall of the nation is the concern of every citizen.

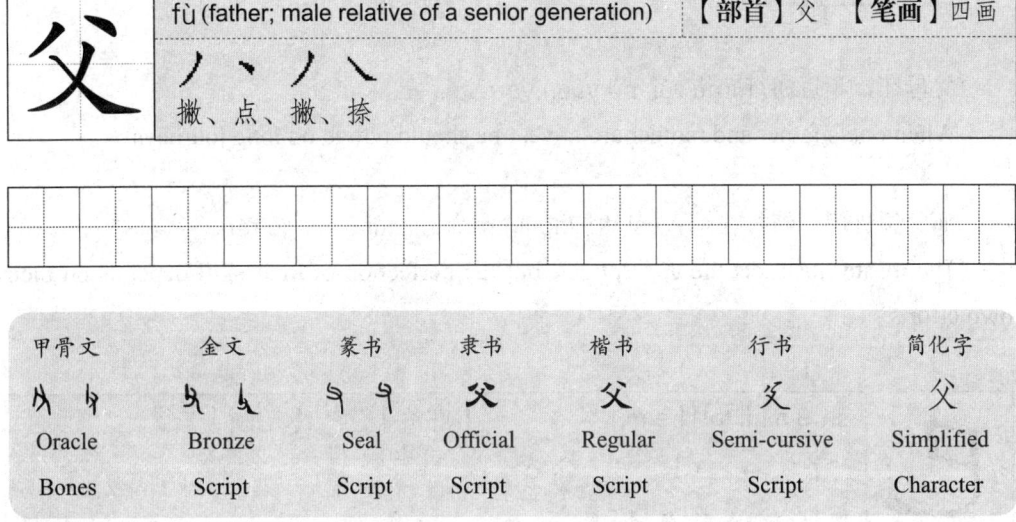

"父"是象形字。"父"是"斧"(fǔ)的本字。甲骨文和金文的"父"形似一个人手(彐)持石斧(fǔ)。"父"本义指石斧，也指劳动的男人。

在中国古代，持斧工作或作战一般是成年男子的职责。后来，"父"字常常指代父亲、家父，引申指男性长辈，如祖父、外祖父、岳父、叔父、姑父。

石(shí)斧(fǔ)

词或短语 Words & Phrases

父亲	fùqīn	father
爸爸	bàba	father
叔叔	shūshu	uncle
岳父	yuèfù	father-in-law

姑父	gūfù	uncle-in-law
父老乡亲	fùlǎoxiāngqīn	elders and folks

锦言妙语　Proverbs & Witticism

有其父，必有其子　yǒu qí fù, bì yǒu qí zǐ
Like father, like son.

父母在，不远游　fùmǔ zài, bù yuǎn yóu
When one's father and mother are alive, one should not go on long journeys.

师父领进门，修行在个人　shīfu lǐng jìn mén, xiūxíng zài gè rén
The master instructs the apprentices, but the perfection of their skill depends on their own efforts.

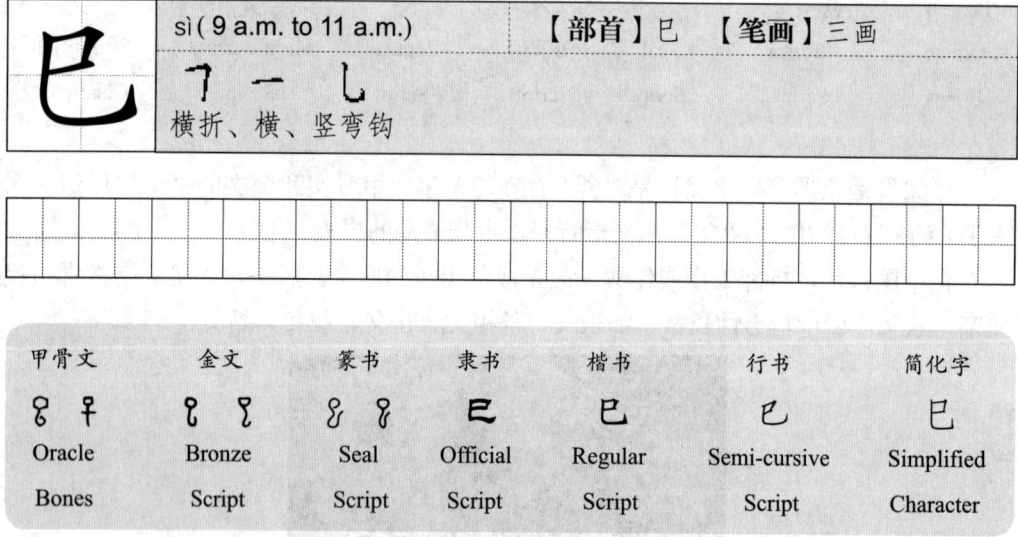

"巳"是象形字。甲骨文、金文、篆书的"巳"均形似母腹(fù)中未成形的胎儿。

在中国古代，人们把一天分为十二个时(shí)辰(chén)，每个时辰相当于现在的两个小时。简化后的十二地支为子、丑、寅、卯、辰、巳、午、未、申、酉、戌、亥。其中，巳时为地支的第六位，指上午九时至十一时。

LESSON 5 Great Affection between Mother and Son • 第五课　母子情深

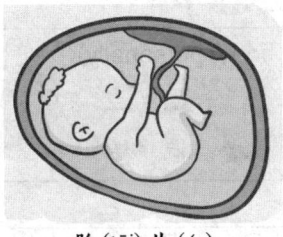

胎 (tāi) 儿 (ér)

词或短语　Words & Phrases

巳时　　　　sìshí　　　the period of the day from 9 a.m. to 11 a.m.

厶	sī (private)	【部首】厶　【笔画】两画
	撇折、点	

金文	篆书	隶书	楷书	行书	简化字
◊	ζ	△	厶	厶	厶
Bronze Script	Seal Script	Official Script	Regular Script	Semi-cursive Script	Simplified Character

　　"厶"是象形字。甲骨文的"厶"形似头朝下的胎儿，表示胎儿已经长成，将要降生，金文和篆书基本沿用此写法。"厶"是"私"的本字，"厶"本义指已经发育成熟的胎儿，由胎儿引申为男女隐私，又引申为个人的，如私事、私心、自私。

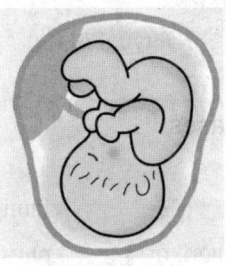

胎 (tāi) 儿 (ér)

　　"私"表示一个人的所思所想都围 (wéi) 绕 (rào) 着自己，所作所为只为自己。"私"与"公"(gōng) 相反。"厶"如今不单独用，只作偏旁，如允 (yǔn)、台、怠、能。

- 235 -

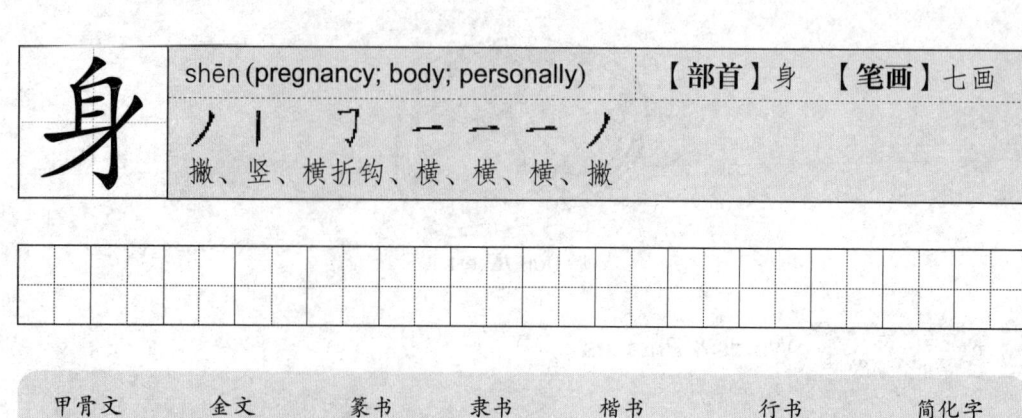

甲骨文	金文	篆书	隶书	楷书	行书	简化字
Oracle Bones	Bronze Script	Seal Script	Official Script	Regular Script	Semi-cursive Script	Simplified Character

"身"是象形字。甲骨文的"身"可写作 ，形似一个大肚子女人；甲骨文的"身"字也可写作 ，形似一个人（ ）隆起的腹（fù）部（ ）内有一个胎儿（ ）。

金文的"身"延续甲骨文字形，形似一个女人挺着大肚子，表示她有孕在身。"身"本义指身孕。

篆文的"身"形似人的躯干、身躯，引申为躯体，如身强力壮；也引申指亲自，如身体力行；又引申为本身、自己，如以身作则、身临其境、身先士卒。"身"现在也指人的生命或一生，如献身。"出身"则说的是人的社会地位，如身份、身价。

孕（yùn）妇（fù）

词或短语 Words & Phrases

出身	chūshēn	family background
身心健康	shēn xīn jiànkāng	physical and psychological health
设身处地	shèshēnchǔdì	put oneself in somebody else's position
以身作则	yǐshēnzuòzé	set oneself a good example to others
身败名裂	shēnbài-míngliè	lose all standing and reputation

LESSON 5 Great Affection between Mother and Son • 第五课 母子情深

锦言妙语   Proverbs & Witticism

身教胜于言教 shēn jiāo shèng yú yán jiāo
Practice is better than precept in the matter of educational effect.

身在福中不知福 shēn zài fú zhōng bù zhī fú
Growing up in happiness, one often fails to appreciate what happiness really means.

身正不怕影子斜 shēn zhèng bú pà yǐngzi xié
Stand straight and never mind if the shadow inclines.

牵一发而动全身 qiān yí fà ér dòng quán shēn
Pull one hair and the whole body is affected. ǁ A slight move in one part may affect the situation as a whole.

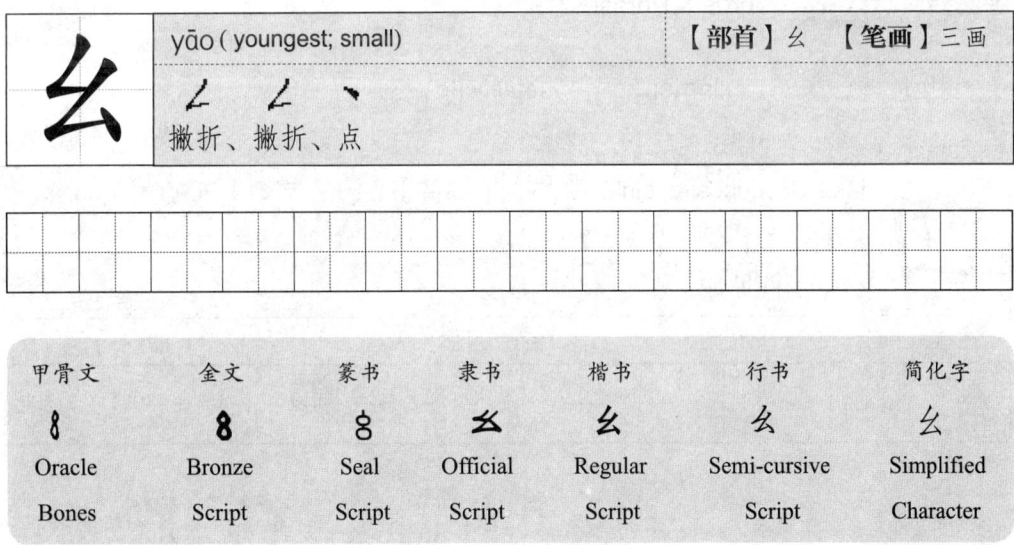

"幺"是象形字。甲骨文和金文的"幺"形似一束细(xì)丝(sī)。"幺"本义指一小把细丝。《说文解字》："幺,小也。""幺"像子初生之形,引申指幼小,家里排行最末的,如幺妹。

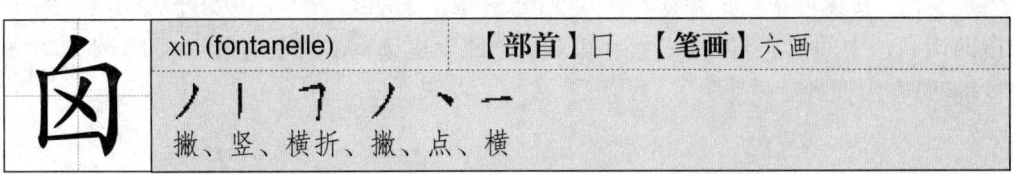

甲骨文	金文	篆书	隶书	楷书	行书	简化字
⊕	⊖	⊗	囟	囟	囟	囟
Oracle Bones	Bronze Script	Seal Script	Official Script	Regular Script	Semi-cursive Script	Simplified Character

"囟"是象形字,形似婴儿的囟(xìn)门(mén)。"囟"本义指囟门,即婴儿头顶骨未合缝的地方。

婴儿出生时有两个囟门,一个在头顶部,称为前囟,一般在一岁至一岁半闭合;另一个在头顶后部,称为后囟,一般出生时就很小,或已闭合。囟门为大脑的快速发育提供条件。

"囟"字图示

 Words & Phrases

囟门　　　　xìnmén　　　　fontanelle

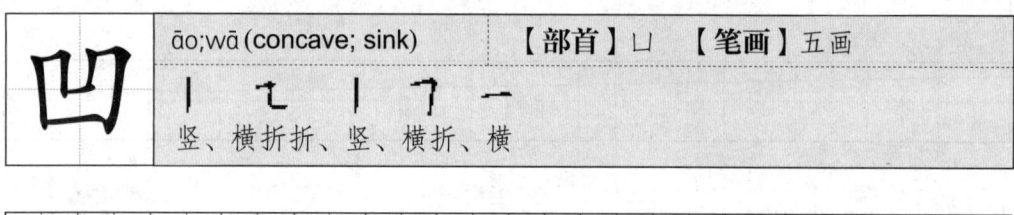

金文	篆书	隶书	楷书	行书	简化字
凹	凹	凹	凹	凹	凹
Bronze Script	Seal Script	Official Script	Regular Script	Semi-cursive Script	Simplified Character

"凹"是象形字,形似物体中间凹下去,也像平地上一个洼(wā)下去的坑。"凹"指四周高,中间低,与"凸"(tū)相对。"凹"也读 wā,同"洼",用于地名,如核桃凹(在山西省)。

LESSON 5 Great Affection between Mother and Son • 第五课 母子情深

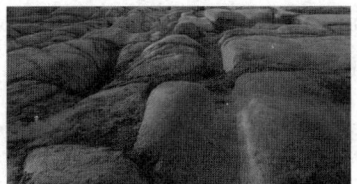

凹 (āo) 凸 (tū) 不 (bù) 平 (píng)

词或短语 Words & Phrases

凹面镜	āomiànjìng	concave mirror
凹凸不平	āotūbùpíng	rough and uneven in surface

凸	tū (protrude; bulge)	【部首】凵 【笔画】五画
	丨 一 丨 ㇋ 一	
	竖、横、竖、横折折折、横	

金文	篆书	隶书	楷书	行书	简化字
凸	凸	凸	凸	凸	凸
Bronze Script	Seal Script	Official Script	Regular Script	Semi-cursive Script	Simplified Character

"凸"是象形字，形似物体中间凸起，高于周围。"凸"与"凹"(āo) 相对。

凸 (tū) 峰 (fēng)

词或短语 Words & Phrases

凸出	tūchū	bulge
凸起	tūqǐ	bulge

- 239 -

凸显	tūxiǎn	give prominence to
凹凸不平	āotūbùpíng	rough and uneven in surface

指事字
Self-explanatory Characters

八	bā (eight) 八 撇、捺	【部首】八　【笔画】二画

甲骨文	金文	篆书	隶书	楷书	行书	简化字
八	八	八	八	八	八	八
Oracle Bones	Bronze Script	Seal Script	Official Script	Regular Script	Semi-cursive Script	Simplified Character

"八"是指事字。甲骨文、金文的"八"字形似一个物品被分(fēn)成两半。"八"由两个独立相对的笔画构成，表示分离(lí)、分别(bié)、划分。"八"本义是分开，后写作"分"，如把苹(píng)果(guǒ)分成两半。

因为"八"有分别的意思，所以，从"手"(扌)、从"别"，又造出个会意字"捌"(bā)，借用为"八"的大写字。现在，"八"一般只表示数字，因谐音"发(fā)"，被视为吉祥数字。

分(fēn)苹(píng)果(guǒ)

词或短语　Words & Phrases

八字胡	bāzìhú	mustache shaped like the Chinese character eight

LESSON 5 Great Affection between Mother and Son • 第五课 母子情深

八 (bā) 字 (zì) 胡 (hú)

八小时工作制	bā xiǎoshí gōngzuò zhì	eight-hour system of labor
八月	bāyuè	August
八折	bāzhé	twenty percent discount
八卦	bāguà	gossip
胡说八道	húshuō-bādào	nonsense
四面八方	sìmiàn-bāfāng	all directions
横七竖八	héngqī-shùbā	in disorder

锦言妙语 Proverbs & Witticism

八仙过海，各显神通 bā xiān guò hǎi, gè xiǎn shén tōng
Like the Eight Immortals (中国传统神话人物) crossing the sea, each one shows his or her special power.

八 (bā) 仙 (xiān) 过 (guò) 海 (hǎi)

八字没一撇 bá zì méi yī piě
Not even the first stroke of the character is in sight. ‖ Nothing tangible is yet in sight.

一方有难，八方支援 yī fāng yǒu nán, bā fāng zhī yuán
When one place is in difficulty, help comes from all quarters.

要 yāo; yào (important; want to; wish) 【部首】覀 【笔画】九画
一丨ㄱ丨丨一㇏ノ一
横、竖、横折、竖、竖、横、撇点、撇、横

甲骨文	金文	篆书	隶书	楷书	行书	简化字
🜛	🜛	🜛	要	要	要	要
Oracle Bones	Bronze Script	Seal Script	Official Script	Regular Script	Semi-cursive Script	Simplified Character

"要"是指事字。甲骨文的"要"写作🜛，其中间的🜛形似女人，两旁各有一只手🜛，合起来像一个女人双手叉(chā)腰，站在地上，展示好身材。《说文解字》：要，身躯的中段。""要"本义指人的腰部。后来，人们在"要"左边添加"月"(肉)，会意成"腰"，专指人体的腰部。

"要"可读作 yāo，引申为要求、强求、要(yāo)挟。

"要"也可读作 yào，由于腰部位于人身的中部，引申为关键、重大，如主要(yào)、重要、要事、要点、要紧、首要；又可引申为索取、希望得到，如要账、要强、需要；也可引申为应当，如要当心、要努力学习；还可引申为即将、将要，如花要开了、天要黑了。

词或短语 Words & Phrases

叉(chā)腰(yāo)

要求	yāoqiú	ask for; require; demand
重要	zhòngyào	important; significant
需要	xūyào	need
要点	yàodiǎn	main points
要面子	yào miànzi	be anxious to keep up appearances
要当心	yào dāngxīn	You should be careful.

锦言妙语 Proverbs & Witticism

打铁要趁热 dá tiě yào chèn rè
Strike the iron while it is hot.

只要功夫深，铁杵磨成针 zhǐ yāo gōngfu shēn, tiěchǔ mó chéng zhēn
If you work at it hard, you can grind an iron rod into a needle – perseverance spells success.

LESSON 5 Great Affection between Mother and Son • 第五课 母子情深

若要人不知，除非己莫为 ruò yào rén bù zhī, chú fēi jǐ mò wéi
If we don't want people to find out, then we shouldn't do it. || The day has eyes, the night has ears.

呆	dāi (silly; dull; stay)	【部首】口 【笔画】七画
	丨 𠃌 一 一 丨 丿 乀	
	竖、横折、横、横、竖、撇、捺	

甲骨文	金文	篆书	隶书	楷书	行书	简化字
Oracle Bones	Bronze Script	Seal Script	Official Script	Regular Script	Semi-cursive Script	Simplified Character

"呆"是指事字。"呆"由"木"和"口"两部分组成，"木"指树木，"口"表示树上的果(guǒ)实(shí)，意指张口结舌。"呆"本义是头脑迟钝、不灵敏，常用义为痴(chī)、蠢(chǔn)、傻(shǎ)，也有死板的意思。

"呆"是由"保"独立出来的分化字，用以表示婴儿呆头呆脑的样子，引申泛指傻、笨、不灵活、(头脑)迟钝，如呆头呆脑、呆板。"呆"又借作"待"，表示停(tíng)留(liú)，如待两天再走、待在那里不动。

果(guǒ)实(shí)

词或短语 Words & Phrases

呆笨	dāibèn	stupid; foolish
书呆子	shūdāizi	pedant
呆头呆脑	dāitóu-dāinǎo	to be muddle-headed; weak in the head
目瞪口呆	mùdèng-kǒudāi	stunned

锦言妙语 Proverbs & Witticism

整天用功不玩耍，聪明孩子成呆瓜

zhěng tiān yòng gōng bù wánshuǎ, cōngmíng háizi chéng dāiguā
All work and no play makes a child a dull boy.

会意字
Associative Compound Characters

好	hǎo; hào (good; friendly; enjoy)	【部首】女 【笔画】六画
	〈 ノ 一 フ 亅 一 撇点、撇、横、横撇、竖钩、横	

甲骨文	金文	篆书	隶书	楷书	行书	简化字
Oracle Bones	Bronze Script	Seal Script	Official Script	Regular Script	Semi-cursive Script	Simplified Character

　　"好"是会意字。甲骨文"好"写作 ，由 (女人)和 (孩子)构成,即由"女"和"子"两个字左右会意而成,呈现了女人抱着孩子的美好画面。

　　金文的"好"几乎沿用甲骨文的字形,从"女",从"子",也表示女子貌美。《说文解字》:"好,美也。""好"本义指容貌美,引申为美好、善良、优秀、和(hé)睦(mù),相关词汇如友好、好心、好意、完好、幸好、刚好。

　　现代汉语中,"好"常被用作形容词,读 hǎo,与"坏"(huài)相对;有时候也用作动词,读 hào,表示喜欢、喜爱,如好奇、好强、喜好、爱好。

女 (nǚ) 人 (rén) 抱 (bào) 着 (zhe) 孩 (hái) 子 (zi)

LESSON 5 Great Affection between Mother and Son • 第五课 母子情深

词或短语 Words & Phrases

好吃	hǎo chī	delicious
好成绩	hǎo chéngjì	good score
好新鲜	hǎo xīnxiān	very fresh
好玩儿	hǎo wánr	interesting; amusing; enjoyable
兴趣爱好	xìngqù àihào	hobbies and interests

锦言妙语 Proverbs & Witticism

好好学习，天天向上 hǎohǎo xuéxí, tiāntiān xiàng shàng
Study well and make progress every day.

好记性不如烂笔头 hǎo jìxing bù rú làn bǐtóu
It's practicable method to take a note of something and not talk from memory.

说得好不如做得好 shuō de hǎo bù rú zuò de hǎo
Actions are more effective than words.

孬	nāo (bad; cowardly)	【部首】女　【笔画】十画
	一 ノ 丨 丶 ㄑ ノ 一 ㄱ 亅 一	
	横、撇、竖、点、撇点、撇、横、横撇/横钩、竖钩、横	

金文	篆书	隶书	楷书	行书	简化字
孬	孬	孬	孬	孬	孬
Bronze Script	Seal Script	Official Script	Regular Script	Semi-cursive Script	Simplified Character

　　"孬"是会意字，由"不"和"好"两个字上下组合构成，合起来表示不好。"孬"本义指不好，引申指怯(qiè)懦(nuò)、没有勇气，如孬种(胆小无能的人)。

词或短语 Words & Phrases

孬种	nāozhǒng	coward
不孬	bù nāo	good

 xìng (surname; family name; common people)　【部首】女　【笔画】八画

ㄑㄧㄧㄧㄧ一丨一
撇点、撇、横、撇、横、横、竖、横

甲骨文	金文	篆书	隶书	楷书	行书	简化字
Oracle Bones	Bronze Script	Seal Script	Official Script	Regular Script	Semi-cursive Script	Simplified Character

"姓"是会意字。甲骨文的"姓"写作 ，由 (生)和 (女，母)构成，意思是指孩子的生母，即母亲。姓是母系社会的反映，故从"女"。在母系氏族社会，人们不在乎生父，崇(chóng)拜(bài)并纪念生母。姓是族号，随母亲，不能改变。"姓"本义是姓氏，家族的名称，如贵姓、姓名。在旧石器时代中、晚期，女性在社会中享有很高的地位，子孙归属母亲。

中国百家姓举例

词或短语 Words & Phrases

姓名	xìngmíng	surname and personal name; full name
老百姓	lǎobǎixìng	ordinary people; the populace; common people

LESSON 5 Great Affection between Mother and Son • 第五课 母子情深

尊姓大名	zūnxìng-dàmíng	honorable name
隐姓埋名	yǐnxìng-máimíng	conceal one's identity

妇 fù (woman)　　【部首】女　【笔画】六画

ㄑ ノ 一 フ 一 一
撇点、撇、横、横折、横、横

甲骨文	金文	篆书	隶书	楷书	行书	简化字
Oracle Bones	Bronze Script	Seal Script	Official Script	Regular Script	Semi-cursive Script	Simplified Character

"妇"是会意字。甲骨文的"婦"写作 ，由 (扫帚)和 (女子)构成,表示女子手里拿着扫(sào)帚(zhou)打扫卫生。"妇"的繁体写作"婦",今"婦"简化为"妇"。"妇"本义指已婚的女子。

在现代汉语中,"妇"字常作为女子的通称,如妇人、妇幼、少妇、媳妇、孕妇。中华人民共和国成立后,妇女的权利得到改善,社会地位显著提高。

扫(sào)帚(zhou)

词或短语　Words & Phrases

妇女	fùnǚ	woman
媳妇	xífù	daughter-in-law
家庭主妇	jiātíng zhǔfù	housewife
妇人之见	fùrénzhījiàn	short-sighted views not to be taken seriously
妇孺皆知	fùrújiēzhī	It is known even to women and children.

- 247 -

锦言妙语 Proverbs & Witticism

妇女能顶半边天 fùnǚ néng dǐng bàn biān tiān
Women can hold up half the sky.

巧妇难为无米之炊 qiǎo fù nán wéi wú mǐ zhī chuī
Even a clever woman cannot cook a meal without rice. || If you have no hand you can't make a fist.

幼	yòu (young; children)	【部首】幺 【笔画】五画
	ㄥ ㄥ 丶 𠃌 丿	
	撇折、撇折、点、横折钩、撇	

甲骨文	金文	篆书	隶书	楷书	行书	简化字
Oracle Bones	Bronze Script	Seal Script	Official Script	Regular Script	Semi-cursive Script	Simplified Character

"幼"是会意字。甲骨文的"幼"写作 ，由 (幺,小)和 (耒,力)构成，从"幺"(yāo)，像一束细丝，表示小；从"力"，像农具"耒"，表示力气，合起来表示力量弱小。金文、篆书的"幼"沿用甲骨文的基本写法。"幼"本义指力小、力量弱小，引申指初生、年幼、年龄小，如幼苗、幼儿、幼稚、幼虫；又引申指小孩儿，如扶老携幼。

幼 (yòu) 苗 (miáo)

LESSON 5 Great Affection between Mother and Son • 第五课 母子情深

词或短语   Words & Phrases

幼儿园   yòu'éryuán   kindergarten

幼 (yòu) 儿 (ér) 园 (yuán)

幼苗	yòumiáo	seedling; sapling
幼稚	yòuzhì	naive; childish
幼教	yòujiào	preschool education
扶老携幼	fúlǎo-xiéyòu	help the elderly people and children

 bǎo (protect; maintain)   【部首】亻   【笔画】九画

ノ 丨 丨 コ 一 一 丨 ノ ㇏
撇、竖、竖、横折、横、横、竖、撇、捺

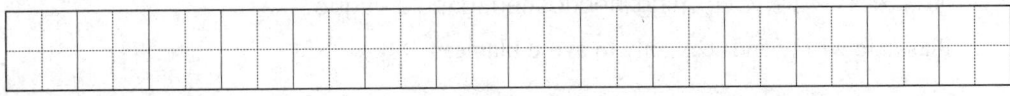

甲骨文	金文	篆书	隶书	楷书	行书	简化字
Oracle Bones	Bronze Script	Seal Script	Official Script	Regular Script	Semi-cursive Script	Simplified Character

"保"是会意字。甲骨文的"保"写作⺈、⺈、⺈，早期金文的"保"写作⺈、⺈，形似大人用手抱婴儿或者背 (bēi) 负 (fù) 婴儿。《说文解字》："保，养护幼儿。""保"本义指养育、抚养，引申为保护、爱护、守卫、维护等。

- 249 -

背 (bēi) 小 (xiǎo) 孩 (hái)

词或短语 Words & Phrases

保护	bǎohù	protect; safeguard
保险公司	báoxiǎn gōngsī	insurance company
担保	dānbǎo	guarantee
保密	bǎomì	keep secret
劳保	láobǎo	labour insurance
保持	bǎochí	keep; preserve
保国安民	bǎoguó-ānmín	

Defend the motherland so that the people can live and work in peace.

锦言妙语 Proverbs & Witticism

明哲保身，但求无过 míngzhébǎoshēn, dànqiúwúguò
Play safe wisely and seek only to avoid blame.

泥菩萨过河——自身难保 ní púsà guò hé, zìshēnnánbǎo
Like a clay idol fording the river — hardly able to save oneself.

舍车马，保将帅 shě jū mǎ, bǎo jiàng shuài
To sacrifice the knights in order to save the queen. ‖ To sacrifice the pawns to save the generals.

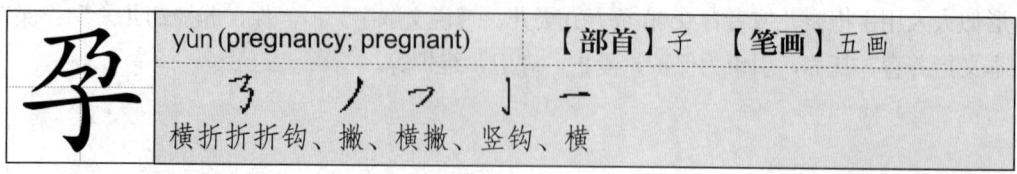

LESSON 5 Great Affection between Mother and Son • 第五课 母子情深

甲骨文	金文	篆书	隶书	楷书	行书	简化字
Oracle Bones	Bronze Script	Seal Script	Official Script	Regular Script	Semi-cursive Script	Simplified Character

"孕"是会意字。"孕"与"身"本同源。甲骨文的"孕"写作 ⚬、⚬，形似一个孕妇，腹(fù)中有胎儿，后来表示胎儿的 ⚬ 变作"乃"，表示孕妇为即将出生的婴儿贮(zhù)备(bèi)奶水。《说文解字》："孕，妇女怀胎。""孕"本义指怀(huái)胎(tāi)，引申指孕育。

现在，"孕"也常比喻新事物的产生，如成功可以孕育新的成功。

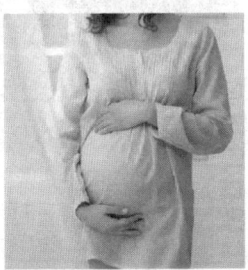

身 (shēn) 孕 (yùn)

词或短语 Words & Phrases

身孕	shēnyùn	pregnancy
孕妇	yùnfù	pregnant woman
孕育	yùnyù	be pregnant with

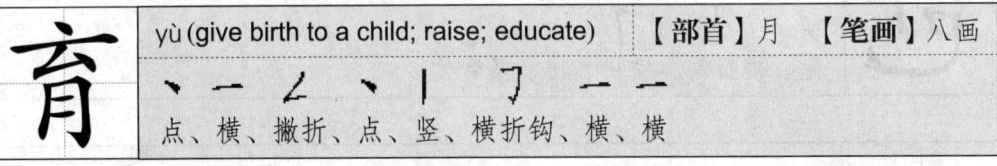

育　　yù (give birth to a child; raise; educate)　　【部首】月　　【笔画】八画

丶一 亠 丶 丨 𠃌 一 一
点、横、撇折、点、竖、横折钩、横、横

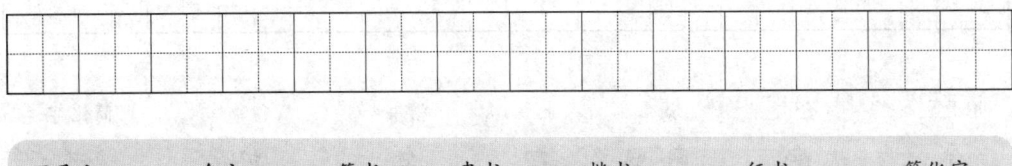

甲骨文	金文	篆书	隶书	楷书	行书	简化字
Oracle Bones	Bronze Script	Seal Script	Official Script	Regular Script	Semi-cursive Script	Simplified Character

"育"是会意字。甲骨文的"育"写作 ![img], 由 ![img](人, 母亲) 和 ![img](倒写的"子"字,表示头面朝下出生的婴儿) 构成, 表示孕 (yùn) 妇 (fù) 生下孩子。"育"在甲骨文和金文中是会意字, 形似妇 (fù) 女分娩 (miǎn)。篆书的"育"从"云"(倒子)、从"肉"(母体), 表示婴儿脱离母体。"育"本义指妇女生孩子、生育, 并悉心地养育孩子长大成人。

《说文解字》:"育,培养孩子,使之从善 (shàn)。""育"后来引申为教育、培育,如德育、体育。

词或短语 Words & Phrases

孕育	yùnyù	breed
教育	jiàoyù	education
体育运动	tǐyù yùndòng	sports; physical culture
教书育人	jiāoshū yùrén	imparting knowledge and educating people
生儿育女	shēng'ér-yùnǚ	give birth to children

锦言妙语 Proverbs & Witticism

发展体育运动,增强人民体质 fāzhǎn tǐyù yùndòng, zēngqiáng rénmín tǐzhì
Promote physical culture and build up the people's health.

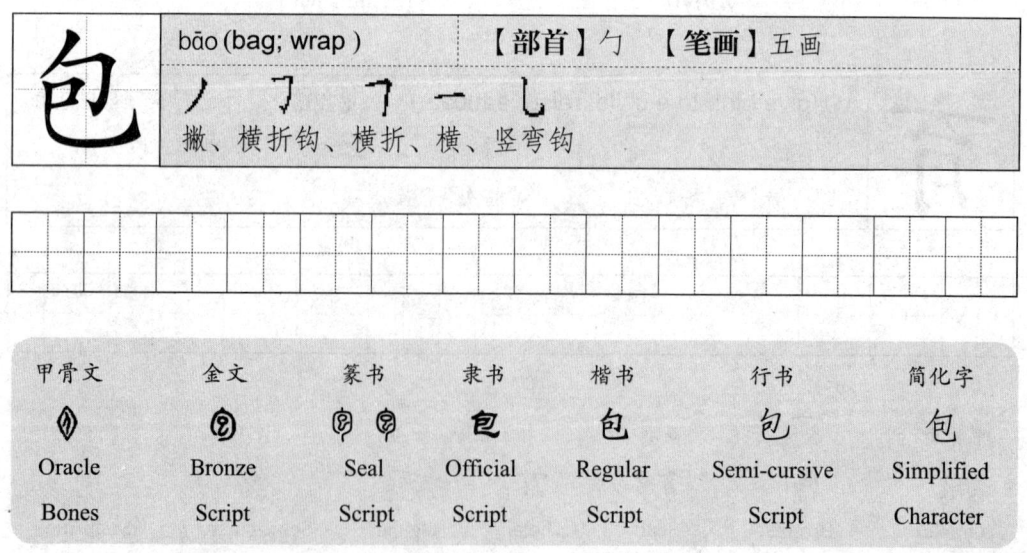

甲骨文	金文	篆书	隶书	楷书	行书	简化字
Oracle Bones	Bronze Script	Seal Script	Official Script	Regular Script	Semi-cursive Script	Simplified Character

包 bāo (bag; wrap)　【部首】勹　【笔画】五画
ノ 𠃌 フ 一 乚
撇、横折钩、横折、横、竖弯钩

"包"是会意兼形声字。甲骨文的"包"写作 ![img], 由 ![img](胎衣) 和 ![img](人) 构成,形似胎衣（◊）里包裹(guǒ)着一个胎儿（✧）。篆书的"包"看上去很像妇女怀孕的样子，中间为"巳"，像还没有成形的胎儿。"包"本义指裹、胎胞，即胎衣。"包"是"胞"的本字。同一父母所生的叫一奶同胞。"胞"也指同一祖国的人，如港澳台同胞。"包"引申指容纳在内，如包含、包括、包容。"包"还可用作名词，如书包、邮包、包裹、包装。

书(shū)包(bāo)

词或短语　Words & Phrases

蒙古包　　　　měnggǔbāo　　　　a Mongolian yurt

蒙(měng)古(gǔ)包(bāo)

包裹	bāoguǒ	package; parcel
包装	bāozhuāng	pack; package
背包	bēibāo	knapsack
钱包	qiánbāo	wallet; purse
包容	bāoróng	tolerate

锦言妙语　Proverbs & Witticism

包子好吃不在褶上　bāozi hǎo chī bú zài zhě shàng
It's not the pleats that taste good on the steamed stuffed buns.

精神空虚比钱包空虚更可怜　jīngshén kōngxū bǐ qiánbāo kōngxū gèng kělián
A poor spirit is poorer than a poor purse.

guī (rule; the tool for drawing circles)	【部首】见　【笔画】八画
一 一 丿 丶 丨 𠃍 丿 乚　横、横、撇、点、竖、横折、撇、竖弯钩	

金文	篆书	隶书	楷书	行书	繁体字	简化字
Bronze Script	Seal Script	Official Script	Regular Script	Semi-cursive Script	Traditional Character	Simplified Character

"规"是会意字。金文和篆书的"规"字从"夫"(成人)、从"见"。篆书的"规"写作 ，由 (夫)和 (见)构成，表示青(qīng)年(nián)向长辈观摩学习，用心见习。古人认为"女智莫如妇，男智莫如夫。夫也者，以智帅人者也"。"規"今简化为"规"。

《说文解字》："规，有法度也。""规"本义为法度，又指画圆的工具，即圆规，引申指约束人们言行的准(zhǔn)则(zé)、成例、典范，如规则、常规、法规。"规"用作动词，表示谋划、设法，如规划、规定、规避；进而引申指劝告，如规劝、规诫。

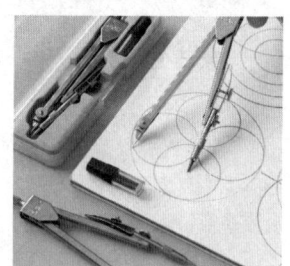

圆(yuán)规(guī)

词或短语 Words & Phrases

圆规	yuánguī	compass
规则	guīzé	rule; regulation
规划	guīhuà	project; plan
规劝	guīquàn	advise
规模	guīmó	scale
规范	guīfàn	standard; normal
规律	guīlǜ	law; regular pattern
规规矩矩	guīguījǔjǔ	be well-behaved

锦言妙语 Proverbs & Witticism

没有规矩，不成方圆 méi yǒu guīju, bù chéng fāng yuán
Nothing can be accomplished without norms or standards.

国有国法，家有家规 guó yǒu guófǎ, jiā yǒu jiāguī

LESSON 5 Great Affection between Mother and Son • 第五课 母子情深

A family has family rules, and a country has its laws.

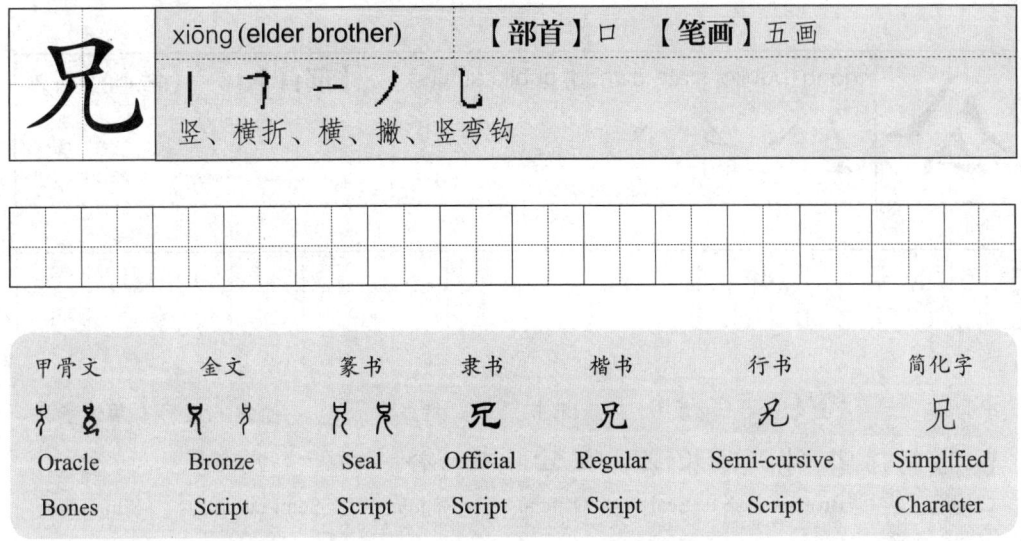

"兄"是会意字。"兄"是"祝"(zhù)的本字。甲骨文的"兄"写作𠈔，由 ᗡ(口，说) 和 𠔁(人) 构成，表示祝祷(dǎo)。

"兄"的古文字从"口"、从"儿"(人)，像人张口发号施令。过去一个家庭中兄弟姐妹比较多，长兄如父，兄长在大家庭中的地位较高，可以支使和吩(fēn)咐(fù)弟弟、妹妹做事。甲骨文、金文、篆书的"兄"字，对"口"进行了夸张的描绘，生动地表现了"嘴巴大"这一点，因为指派他人多用嘴巴。"兄"本义指兄长、哥哥，引申指亲戚、同辈中年龄比自己大的男子，同时也是对男性朋友的敬称。

词或短语 Words & Phrases

兄长	xiōngzhǎng	elder brother
哥哥	gēge	elder brother
兄弟	xiōngdì	brother
弟弟	dìdi	younger brother
兄弟姐妹	xiōngdì jiěmèi	brothers and sisters

锦言妙语 Proverbs & Witticism

亲兄弟，明算账 qīn xiōngdì, míng suàn zhàng
Even among brothers, accounts should be settled clearly.

兄弟同心，其利断金 xiōngdì tóng xīn, qí lì duàn jīn
When brothers are of the same mind, they have the power to cut through metal.

公	gōng (public; state-owned; public affairs) ノ八ム丶 撇、捺、撇折、点	【部首】八　【笔画】四画

甲骨文	金文	篆书	隶书	楷书	行书	简化字
Oracle Bones	Bronze Script	Seal Script	Official Script	Regular Script	Semi-cursive Script	Simplified Character

"公"是会意字。甲骨文的"公"写作 ，由 (八，平分) 和 (口，吃) 构成。八是"分"的本字，表示平 (píng) 均 (jūn) 分配 (pèi) 食物或物品。"公"本义指公平分配。《说文解字》："公，平分也。从"八"(相背)、从"厶"(私)，背私为公。"在原始社会，由于社会生产力水平低下，人们共同劳动，只有平均分配，才能保证社会成员的共同生存。

"公"，由本义"平分"引申泛指公平、公正；由"公正"引申为公然、公开，如公布、公告；又引申为共同的、公认的，如公害、公约、公议、公式；由"共同"引申为公家、公众的、国家的、大家的，如公事公办、一心为公、大公无私、公款、公共汽车、公园、公安局；还引申对男子的尊称，如周公 (周恩来)、邓公 (邓小平)；由男性尊称又引申指雄性禽兽，如公牛、公鸡、公狗。公与"母"相对。

分 (fēn) 蛋 (dàn) 糕 (gāo)

词或短语 Words & Phrases

公共汽车　　　　gōnggòng qìchē　　　　　　bus

LESSON 5 Great Affection between Mother and Son • 第五课 母子情深

公 (gōng) 共 (gòng) 汽 (qì) 车 (chē)

公园   gōngyuán   park

公 (gōng) 园 (yuán)

公路	gōnglù	highway
公民	gōngmín	citizen
公平	gōngpíng	fair; justice
公开	gōngkāi	open
公害	gōnghài	public hazard
办公室	bàngōngshì	office
公务员	gōngwùyuan	government officials; public servant
公司	gōngsī	company; corporation
公斤	gōngjīn	kilogram
公里	gōnglǐ	kilometer
公私分明	gōngsīfēnmíng	make a clear distinction between public and private interests

锦言妙语 Proverbs & Witticism

是非自有公论 shìfēi zì yǒu gōng lùn
Public opinion will decide which is right and which is wrong.

关公面前耍大刀 Guāngōng miànqián shuǎ dà dāo
Show off before an export. ‖ teach one's grandmother how to suck eggs.

张公吃酒李公醉 Zhānggōng chī jiǔ Lǐgōng zuì
Mr. Zhang drinks the wine and Mr. Li gets drunk. || One is mistaken for a wrong-doer and is punished for him.

| 分 | fēn; fèn (divide; distribute) ㄅㄱノ 撇、捺、横折钩、撇 | 【部首】八 【笔画】四画 |

甲骨文	金文	篆书	隶书	楷书	行书	简化字
Oracle Bones	Bronze Script	Seal Script	Official Script	Regular Script	Semi-cursive Script	Simplified Character

"分"是会意字。"八"是"分"的本字,从"八"、从"刀",像刀把物剖(pōu)开(kāi),将物体一分为二。"分"本义指分开,这个含义沿用到今天,如物以群分、分类、分工、区分、分配、分担、分别、分散、分离、分割等。

"分"字的引申含义是辨别,如分辨、分清、区别、分析。《论语》:"四体不勤,五谷不分,孰为夫子?"意思是说一个好吃懒做、连粮食都分辨不清的人,怎么能做别人的老师呢?分则成两半,故又引申指半,春分、秋分是春季和秋季的一半。

"分"又读 fèn,由"划分"引申指划定的范围、界限、责任和权利的限度,规定给每个人的本分、义务;又引申为成分,如水分、养分、盐分。

切 (qiē) 面 (miàn) 包 (bāo)

LESSON 5 Great Affection between Mother and Son • 第五课　母子情深

词或短语　Words & Phrases

分给	fēn gěi	share out
分配	fēnpèi	distribution
分享	fēnxiǎng	share
十分	shí fēn	extremely; very
一小时等于六十分钟	yì xiǎoshí děngyú liùshí fēnzhōng	one hour is equivalent to sixty minutes
本分	běnfèn	one's duty; obligation
水分	shuǐfèn	moisture
社会分工	shèhuì fēngōng	social division of labour
分秒必争	fēnmiǎobìzhēng	seize every minute and second

锦言妙语　Proverbs & Witticism

一分钱，一分货　yì fēn qián, yì fēn huò
The higher the price, the better the quality of the merchandise.

一分耕耘，一分收获　yì fēn gēngyún, yì fēn shōuhuò
One reaps no more than what he has sown.

物以类聚，人以群分　wùyǐlèijù, rényǐqúnfēn
Birds of a feather flock together.

天下大势，分久必合，合久必分　tiānxià dàshì, fēn jiǔ bì hé, hé jiǔ bì fēn
The general trend under heaven is that there is bound to be unification after prolonged division and division after prolonged unification.

脑　nǎo (brain; head; mind)　【部首】月　【笔画】十画

ノ 乛 一 一 丶 一 ノ 丶 乚 丨
撇、横折钩、横、横、点、横、撇、点、竖折、竖

金文	篆书	隶书	楷书	行书	简化字
𦞦	𦞦	脑	腦	腦	脑
Bronze Script	Seal Script	Official Script	Regular Script	Semi-cursive Script	Simplified Character

　　"脑"是会意字。从"月"(肉)，表示脑属于肉体；从"甾"(nǎo)，"甾"是"腦"的本字，形似"囟"(xìn，脑形)与"巛"(头发)的组合；"甾"(nǎo)兼表声。今"腦"简化为"脑"。"脑"本义指头脑、脑髓、大脑。

　　大脑是神经系统的最高级部分，会产生思想、记忆等心理活动，所以"脑"引申指思维能力，如脑力劳动、脑筋、脑海；也表示像脑的东西，如电脑；还可表示形状或颜色像脑的东西，如豆腐脑儿。

词或短语　Words & Phrases

大脑	dànǎo	brain
电脑	diànnǎo	computer
脑力劳动	nǎolì láodòng	mental work; brainwork
呆头呆脑	dāitóu-dāinǎo	idiotic

锦言妙语　Proverbs & Witticism

动脑筋，想办法　dòng nǎojīn, xiǎng bànfǎ
Use one's brains to find a way out. ‖ use one's head to think of a way.

脚打后脑勺　jiǎo dǎ hòu nǎosháo
Run so fast one's heels hit the back of his head-very busy.

面包滋养身体，书本充实头脑　miànbāo zīyǎng shēntǐ, shūběn chōngshí tóunǎo
Bread nourishes the body, and books enrich the mind.

LESSON 5 Great Affection between Mother and Son • 第五课 母子情深

形声字
Pictophonetic Characters

奶 nǎi (milk; grandmother) 【部首】女 【笔画】五画

ㄑ ノ 一 ㄋ ノ
撇点、撇、横、横折折折钩、撇

金文	篆书	隶书	楷书	行书	简化字
㚤	㚤	奶	奶	奶	奶
Bronze Script	Seal Script	Official Script	Regular Script	Semi-cursive Script	Simplified Character

"奶"是形声字。"乃"是"奶"的本字。古代"乃""奶"通用。"奶"从"女"为形，表意，从"乃"(nǎi)为声，兼表意。"奶"本义指乳房，引申为乳汁，又引申为喂奶。奶奶指祖母。

词或短语 Words & Phrases

牛奶	niúnǎi	milk
奶奶	nǎinai	grandma
爷爷	yéye	grandpa

锦言妙语 Proverbs & Witticism

有奶便是娘 yǒu nǎi biàn shì niáng
Whoever suckles me is my mother. || Obey anybody who feeds one || Ready to serve anyone for material benefit.

牛吃的是草，挤出来的是奶 niú chī de shì cǎo, jǐ chū lái de shì nǎi
The cow eats grass but gives milk.

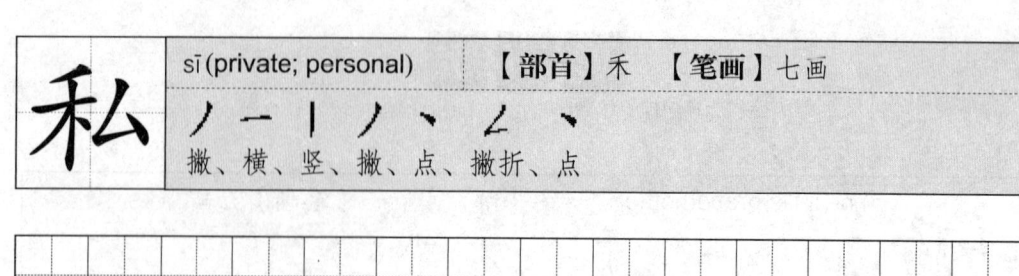

sī (private; personal)　　【部首】禾　【笔画】七画

丿 一 丨 丿 丶 厶 丶
撇、横、竖、撇、点、撇折、点

金文	篆书	隶书	楷书	行书	简化字
Bronze Script	Seal Script	Official Script	Regular Script	Semi-cursive Script	Simplified Character

"私"是形声字。金文的"私"字写作𥝢，由禾(禾)和厶(厶)构成，从"禾"。金文、篆书的"私"形似禾稻(dào)；"厶"(sī)为声，形似头朝下的胎儿。"厶"是"私"的本字。"私"最早由"厶"字演变而来。无论是禾稻，还是腹中胎儿，都属于私人所有，由此产生个人的、私有的含义，如私事、私心、私营、私塾、公私分明。"私"本义指个人的、自己的。"私"与"公"(gōng)相对。

私(sī)塾(shú)

词或短语 Words & Phrases

自私	zìsī	selfishness
无私	wúsī	selfless
隐私	yǐnsī	privacy
走私	zǒusī	smuggle
私立学校	sīlì xuéxiào	private school
私有财产	sī yǒu cáichǎn	private property
公私分明	gōngsīfēnmíng	be scrupulous in separating public from private interests
假公济私	jiǎgōng-jìsī	

use an official position to gain undeserved advantage for oneself

锦言妙语 Proverbs & Witticism

公是公,私是私 gōng shì gōng, sī shì sī
Business is one thing, friendship is another.

勇于私斗,怯于公愤 yǒng yú sī dòu, qiè yú gōng fèn
Ever ready for private fights, but leaning backwards in public cause.

无私才能无畏 wú sī cái néng wú wèi
Only the selfless can be fearless.

雹 báo (hail)　　【部首】雨　【笔画】十三画

一丶フ丨丶丶丶丶ノフフ一乚
横、点、横撇/横钩、竖、点、点、点、点、撇、横折钩、横折、横、竖弯钩

甲骨文	金文	篆书	隶书	楷书	行书	简化字
Oracle Bones	Bronze Script	Seal Script	Official Script	Regular Script	Semi-cursive Script	Simplified Character

"雹"是形声兼会意字。甲骨文的"雹"写作🝆,是会意字,其上部表示"雨",下部形似冰雹随雨降落。金文和篆书的"雹"变成形声字,上部的"雨"是形旁,表意;下部的"包"(bāo)是声旁,兼表意。"包"有疙(gē)瘩(da)之意,表示"雹"是冰疙瘩。《说文解字》:"雹,雨冰也。从雨,包声。""雹"本义指冰雹,俗称雹子,指从天空降下的冰块或冰粒。雹子形成于强对流天气,对农业、牧业、林业的危害很大,雹灾是严重灾害之一。

冰 (bīng) 雹 (báo)

词或短语　Words & Phrases

雹子	báozi	hail
冰雹	bīngbáo	hail; hailstone
雹害	báohài	damage by hail
雹灾	báozāi	disaster caused by hail

饱	bǎo (full)	【部首】饣 【笔画】八画
	ノ　フ　乀　ノ　フ　フ　一　乚	
	撇、横撇/横钩、竖提、撇、横折钩、横折、横、竖弯钩	

金文	篆书	隶书	楷书	行书	繁体字	简化字
飽	餚	飽 饱	饱	饱	飽	饱
Bronze Script	Seal Script	Official Script	Regular Script	Semi-cursive Script	Traditional Character	Simplified Character

　　"饱"是形声兼会意字。篆书的"饱"写作 饱，由 食(食，吃)和 包(包，孕妇)构成。在食物不充足的古代，人们会让婴儿或孕妇先吃饱。"饱"从"饣"(食)，表示食物或能吃的东西；从"包"，"包"有容纳、疙瘩之义，表示肚子容纳了食物就会饱，而且会隆起。包(bāo)兼表声。现"飽"简化为"饱"。

　　《说文解字》："饱，猒也。从食，包声。""饱"本义指吃足，引申为饱满、满足。"饱"与"饿"相对。

词或短语　Words & Phrases

半饱	bàn bǎo	half-full
温饱	wēnbǎo	adequate or ample food and clothing
饱和	bǎohé	saturation
饱经风霜	bǎojīngfēngshuāng	having experienced the hardships of life
酒足饭饱	jiǔzú-fànbǎo	have dined and wined to satiety

LESSON 5 Great Affection between Mother and Son • 第五课 母子情深

锦言妙语 Proverbs & Witticism

饱食终日，无所事事 bǎoshízhōng rì, wúsuǒshìshì
Full up and sit around every day.

饱汉子不知饿汉子饥 bǎo hànzi bù zhī è hànzi jī
Those on a full stomache wouldn't know what starvation was.

吃饱了就骂厨子 chībǎole jiù mà chúzi
Curse the cook after you're full.

份	fèn (portion)	【部首】亻 【笔画】六画
	ノ丨ノ丶フノ	
	撇、竖、撇、捺、横折钩、撇	

金文	篆书	隶书	楷书	行书	简化字
彸	朌朌	份	份	份	份
Bronze Script	Seal Script	Official Script	Regular Script	Semi-cursive Script	Simplified Character

"份"是形声字。篆书的"份"写作朌，由亻(人)和分(分或分给)构成，意思是分配到每个人的那一部分。"亻"(人)表意，"分"(fēn)表声。"份"本义指整体中的一部分或几个部分，每一部分为一份，如股份、凑份子；用在省、年、月后面，表示划分的单位，如省份、年份、月份；"份"也可用作量词，如一份报纸、两份礼品。

词或短语 Words & Phrases

准备几份礼物	zhǔnbèi jǐfèn lǐwù	prepare a few gifts
凑份子	còu fènzi	club together to present a gift to sb.
身份证	shēnfènzhèng	identification card
份儿饭	fènr fàn	one serving for selling
人人有份	rénrén yǒu fèn	something for everyone

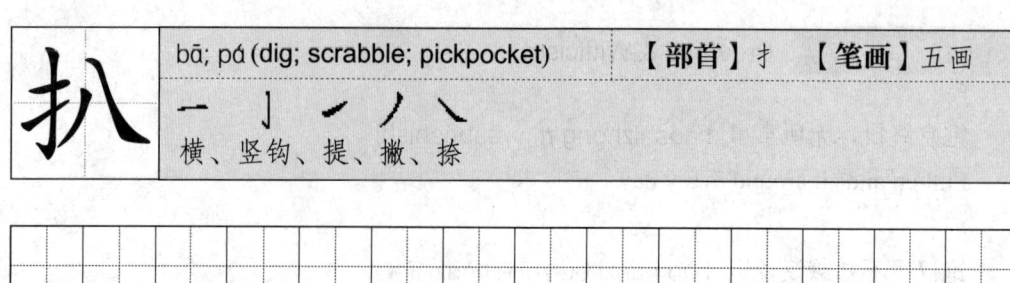

bā; pá (dig; scrabble; pickpocket) 　【部首】扌　【笔画】五画

横、竖钩、提、撇、捺

金文	篆书	隶书	楷书	行书	简化字
扒	扒	扒	扒	扒	扒
Bronze Script	Seal Script	Official Script	Regular Script	Semi-cursive Script	Simplified Character

　　"扒"是形声兼会意字,从"扌"(手),表示动手刨(páo)挖(wā);从"八"(bā),表声兼表意,"八"有分开的意思,表示刨开、扒开。"扒"本义指刨挖。

　　"扒"着重表示将物掏出时,读音为"pá",常用来表示小偷趁人不注意把别人口袋里的东西据为己有,即从他人身上窃取钱物,如扒(pá)手、扒窃。

扒(pá)窃(qiè)

词或短语　Words & Phrases

扒皮	bā pí	peel
扒手	páshǒu	pickpocket; shoplifter
扒窃	páqiè	steal

锦言妙语　Proverbs & Witticism

扒了皮的癞蛤蟆——活着讨厌,死了还吓人
bā le pí de làiháma——huózhe tǎo yàn, sǐle hái xià rén
A skinned toad — a nuisance alive, a horror dead.

LESSON 5 Great Affection between Mother and Son · 第五课 母子情深

吆 yāo (cry out)

【部首】口　【笔画】六画

丨 フ 一 ㄥ ㄥ 丶

竖、横折、横、撇折、撇折、点

金文	篆书	隶书	楷书	行书	简化字
吆	吆	吆	吆	吆	吆
Bronze Script	Seal Script	Official Script	Regular Script	Semi-cursive Script	Simplified Character

　　"吆"是形声字。"口"表意，形似张开的口(嘴)，表示用嘴吆喝；"幺"(yāo)表声，"幺"有小的意思，吆喝的对象大多地位低、辈分小。"吆"本义指高声呼(hū)喝(hè)。吆喝，意为大声喊叫，多用于小商小贩沿街售卖货物，叫卖东西，或者赶牲口、斥(chì)责(zé)人。

吆(yāo)喝(he)

词或短语　Words & Phrases

吆喝	yāohe	cry out; call; talk harshly; drive out
吆唤	yāohuàn	cry out; call
吆五喝六	yāowǔ-hèliù	hubbub of gambling

二、注解 Notes

（一）妻子 (Wife)

中国历史悠久，地域辽阔，语言丰富，例如对妻子的称呼就有很多种。

皇后：皇帝的妻子(多见于旧小说、戏曲)。

梓(zǐ)童：皇帝对皇后的称呼。

夫人：古代诸侯王的妻子称为夫人；明清(公元1368—1911年)时期，一、二品官的妻子封为夫人；在近代和现代为表示尊重，也可称一般人的妻子为夫人；现在"夫人"的称呼一般用于外交场合，有时也戏称朋友或同(tóng)事(shì)的妻子为"夫人"。

糟糠：糟糠之妻，男士用来形容与自己白手起家、共同患难和艰苦奋斗的妻子。

内人：这是过去男人在别人面前对自己妻子的称呼，书面语也称"内子""内助"。可尊称别人的妻子为"贤内助"。

内掌柜的：称男人为"掌柜的"时，可称其妻子为"内掌柜的"。

妻子：当妻子的"子"读第三声(shēng)时，"妻子"指的是妻子和儿女。当妻子的"子"读轻声(zi)时，妻子不包括儿女。

太太：古时候一般人称官吏的妻子为"太太"。有权势的富人对外也称自己的妻子为"太太"。

爱人：既可指妻子，又可指丈夫，现在普遍使用。

媳妇儿：中国北方部分地区方言口语(北方方言)中对妻子的亲昵称呼。

老婆：丈夫对妻子的称呼，过去在北方乡村较为普遍，现在南方年轻人也喜(xǐ)欢(huān)这种称呼，多用于口头语言。

老伴儿：老年夫妇的一方，一般多指女方。

（二）大夫 (Doctor; Physician)

在中国北方，人们习惯把医生称为"大夫(dàifu)"；在中国南方(尤其在农村地区)，人们习惯把医生称为"郎中"。唐末五代时期，朝政腐败，官吏多如牛毛，以官名互相称呼逐渐形成社会风气。医生是上至皇帝下至普通百姓都需要的人，受到人们的尊敬，因此人们就用官职中品级较高的"大夫""郎中"来称呼医生，并且沿用至今。

(三) 中国人的"百家姓" (The Book of Family Names in China)

中国姓的产生可以追溯到母系氏族公社(matrilineal commune),所以"姓名"的"姓"是"女"字旁。由于同一母系的后代不能通婚,为了区分不同的婚姻集团,便产生了姓。中国一些较古老的姓,在构字上大多有"女"字旁,如姜、姚、姬、嬴等。这正是母系社会 (matriarchal society) 在姓上的遗迹。

中国有一本供儿童识字用的通俗课本,叫《百家姓》,是宋代人编写的。因为宋代的皇帝姓赵,这本书便以"赵"字开头。据宋代学者王明清考证,排在前四位的姓——赵、钱、孙、李代表了当时最重要的家族,周、吴、郑、王次之。这本书虽叫百家姓,但收录的姓不止一百个,而且中国人的姓也远远超出一百个。据统计,最初中国人的姓有411个,后来增加到504个,其中单姓444个,复姓60个。较常见的姓有100多个,这100多个姓中有19个姓较为常见,即李、王、张、刘、陈、杨、赵、黄、周、吴、徐、孙、胡、朱、高、林、何、郭、马。

(四) 春分 (Spring Equinox)

春季的节气:立春、雨水、惊蛰、春分、清明、谷雨
夏季的节气:立夏、小满、芒种、夏至、小暑、大暑
秋季的节气:立秋、处暑、白露、秋分、寒露、霜降
冬季的节气:立冬、小雪、大雪、冬至、小寒、大寒

中国古代的日历把一年分成二十四个节气 (the 24 solar terms)。春分,是二十四节气之一,春季第四个节气。春分象征春天到半,且这一天昼夜平分,都是12个小时。

一年只有两天昼夜平分,即春分和秋分。这两天太阳直射在地球赤道,使得地球上大部分地区的白天和夜晚的时间接近相等。南北半球季节相反,北半球是春分,对南半球来说就是秋分。春分这天太阳从正东方升起,北半球从这一天开始,白天比黑夜一天长于一天,人们容易联想到光明占了上风。

春分将春天一分为二,春分后,气候温和,雨水充沛,阳光明媚,杨柳青青,草长莺飞。"一年之计在于春",说的就是这个时候。春天非常适宜人们出游,也适宜播种,培育农作物,这时候小麦拔节、油菜花香,农民开始忙碌。春分时节,中国民间有放风筝、吃春饼、立蛋等风俗。

三、反义词   Antonym

男—女
公—母
好—坏
公—私
凸—凹
饱—饿

四、汉字的偏旁部首   The Structural Unit and Radical of Chinese Character

"女"字旁

"女"部的字多与女人有关，"女"一般在字的左侧或下部。例如，妈、姥、好、娶、妻，等等。

妈	妈妈	māma	mom; mama
奶	奶奶	nǎinai	grandma
姥	姥姥	lǎolao	grandmother; grandma
姨	阿姨	āyí	aunt
姑	姑姑	gūgu	father's sister
婆	婆婆	pópo	mother-in-law
妻	妻子	qīzi	wife; other half
娶	娶媳妇	qǔ xífù	take a wife
嫁	婚嫁	hūnjià	marriage; take a wife or marry a man
她	她们	tāmen	they (female)
妇	妇女	fù'nǚ	woman
婚	结婚	jiéhūn	marry; get married
	婚姻	hūnyīn	marriage
姐	姐姐	jiějie	elder sister
妹	妹妹	mèimei	younger sister

LESSON 5 Great Affection between Mother and Son • 第五课 母子情深

娃	娃娃	wáwa	child
婴	婴儿	yīngr	infant; baby
好	好人	hǎorén	good person
姓	姓名	xìngmíng	full name
始	开始	kāishǐ	begin; start
如	如果	rúguǒ	if; in case
	例如	lìrú	for example
媒	媒人	méiren	matchmaker; go-between
	新闻媒体	xīnwén méitǐ	news media; press
娱	娱乐	yúlè	recreation; amusement
要	要求	yāoqiú	require; demand
妥	妥协	tuǒxié	compromise
奴	奴隶	núlì	slave
妄	狂妄自大	kuángwàngzìdà	be arrogant and conceited
妒	嫉妒	jídù	be jealous of
婪	贪婪	tānlán	greedy
妙	美妙	měimiào	wonderful

"子"部，"子"字旁

当"子"在字的左侧时，它由"子"变成"孑"，即"子"字旁。由"子"字组成的字，大多与小孩有关。例如，孕、孙、孩、学，等等。

孔	孔子	Kǒngzǐ	Confucius
孙	孙子	Sūnzǐ	grandson; Sun Tzu(中国古代军事家)
孩	孩子	háizi	child; kid
孺	孺子	rúzǐ	child
孕	孕育	yùnyù	breed; be pregnant with
孝	孝顺	xiàoshùn	filial piety
孤	孤独	gūdú	loneliness
字	汉字	hànzì	Chinese characters
学	学习	xuéxí	study; learn
存	保存	bǎocún	save; preserve; keep
季	季节	jìjié	season

"儿"字底

"儿"既是一个部首，又是一个独体字。"儿"部的字多和人有关，"儿"部一般在字的下部。例如，兀、元、先、兄，等等。

兀	兀鹫	wù jiù	griffon vulture
元	元旦	yuándàn	New Year's Day
	元首	yuánshǒu	head of a state; ruler; prime minister
	元凶	yuánxiōng	crime culprit
允	允许	yǔnxǔ	allow; permit; permission
兄	兄弟	xiōngdì	brother
见	见面	jiànmiàn	meet
光	阳光	yángguāng	sunshine
	光明	guāngmíng	light; sunshine
先	先生	xiānsheng	sir; Mr.; teacher
	先见之明	xiānjiànzhīmíng	foresight; foreknowledge
党	党派	dǎngpài	political parties and groups
	党员	dǎngyuán	party member
兜	兜圈子	dōu quānzi	beat around the bush; take a joy-ride
	衣兜	yīdōu	pocket
兆	卜兆	bǔzhào	omen
	预兆	yùzhào	omen; forebode

五、HSK 试题选做　　Sample Questions of the New HSK

（一）根据对话选择正确的图片 (Choose the Corresponding Pictures Based on the Dialogues)

A　　　　　　B　　　　　　C

 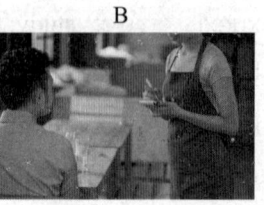 

LESSON 5 Great Affection between Mother and Son • 第五课 母子情深

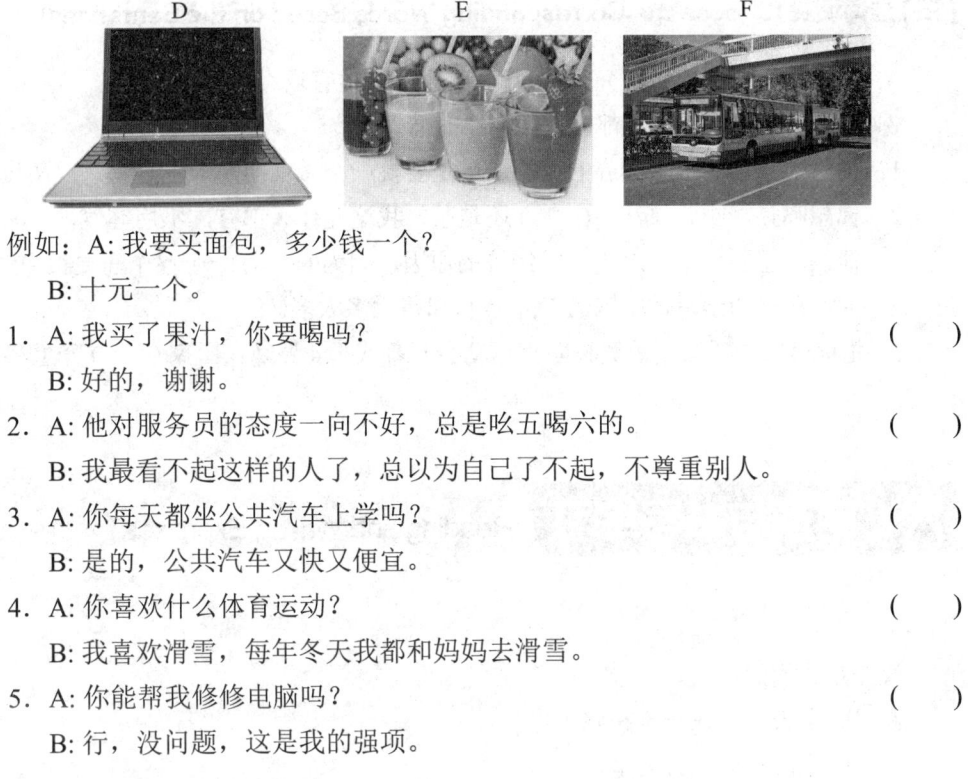

例如：A: 我要买面包，多少钱一个？
　　　B: 十元一个。

1. A: 我买了果汁，你要喝吗？　　　　　　　　　　　　（　）
   B: 好的，谢谢。
2. A: 他对服务员的态度一向不好，总是吆五喝六的。　（　）
   B: 我最看不起这样的人了，总以为自己了不起，不尊重别人。
3. A: 你每天都坐公共汽车上学吗？　　　　　　　　　（　）
   B: 是的，公共汽车又快又便宜。
4. A: 你喜欢什么体育运动？　　　　　　　　　　　　（　）
   B: 我喜欢滑雪，每年冬天我都和妈妈去滑雪。
5. A: 你能帮我修修电脑吗？　　　　　　　　　　　　（　）
   B: 行，没问题，这是我的强项。

(二) 根据句子选择相应的图片 (Choose the Corresponding Pictures Based on the Sentences)

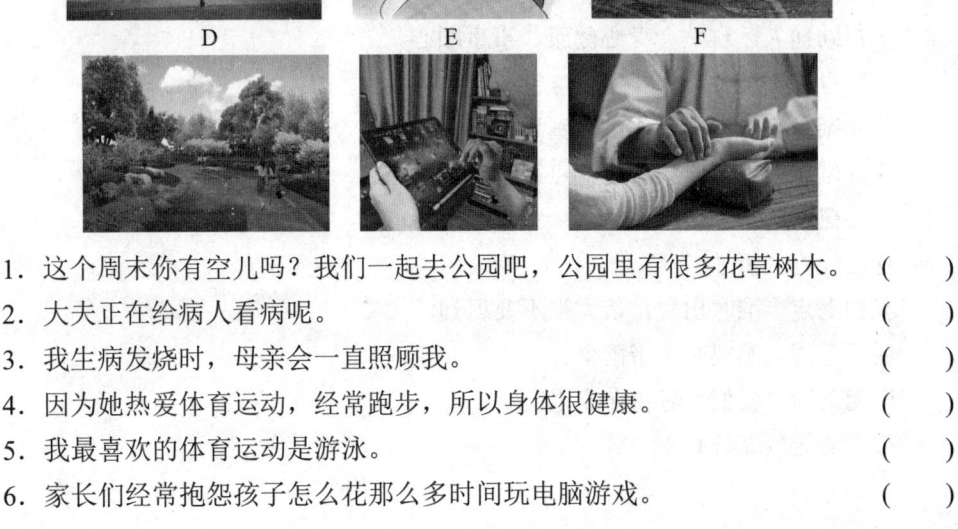

1. 这个周末你有空儿吗？我们一起去公园吧，公园里有很多花草树木。（　）
2. 大夫正在给病人看病呢。　　　　　　　　　　　　　　　　　　（　）
3. 我生病发烧时，母亲会一直照顾我。　　　　　　　　　　　　　（　）
4. 因为她热爱体育运动，经常跑步，所以身体很健康。　　　　　　（　）
5. 我最喜欢的体育运动是游泳。　　　　　　　　　　　　　　　　（　）
6. 家长们经常抱怨孩子怎么花那么多时间玩电脑游戏。　　　　　　（　）

(三) 选词填空 (Choose the Corresponding Words Based on the Sentences)

A. 鲜牛奶　B. 父母　C. 每天　D. 女孩儿　E. 体育场　F. 养育

例如：我们一般（ C ）都去打两个小时篮球。

1. 虽然他身边有很多漂亮（　　），可是要挑一个做女朋友却不容易。
2. 你想喝热咖啡、果汁、（　　）还是茶？我这儿什么都有，不用客气。
3. 他们不想要孩子，这主要是经济的原因，因为（　　）一个孩子需要很多钱。
4. 为了孩子的学习，中国的（　　）付出得太多太多。
5. 北京第二十四届冬季奥林匹克运动会开幕式于4日晚在国家（　　）隆重举行。

六、朗读与书写练习　Reading and Writing Exercises

汉语是我们的母语。

我母亲是大夫，在一家医院工作。

火车每小时行驶三百公里。

每到好天气，我们都会出去散步。

每个周末，我都去打篮球。

我每天步行去上班。

女儿是我一生最大的骄傲。

她是一个漂亮的姑娘。

这丫头几岁了？

我有一个哥哥、一个弟弟和一个姐姐。

多帮助他人，自然会身心健康、事事顺心。

祝您身体健康！

除非亲身体验，否则你不会真正理解。

保持健康的生活方式，这一点很重要。

天要黑了。

这已经打八折了。

我们七点半准时出发，请大家不要迟到。

明天有雨，不要忘了带雨伞。

因为下雨，我们只好待在家里。

今天的天气真好！

LESSON 5 Great Affection between Mother and Son • 第五课 母子情深

你汉语说得真好。
在过去，他们吃得孬、穿得孬。
你顺便帮我买两袋牛奶，好吗？
你有什么爱好？
好久不见，最近身体怎么样？
我弟弟是个音乐爱好者。
幼儿园是儿童的乐园。
保持艰苦奋斗的优良作风。
大家一定要保护好自己的眼睛。
春天万物复苏，孕育着生机与活力。
中国的父母特别重视孩子的英语教育。
请帮我取一下包裹好吗？
他生活没规律，身体每况愈下。
从这儿到公园大概有两公里，走路大约需要 30 分钟。
我每天早上八点钟走进办公室。
我的电脑坏了。
她忙得脚打后脑勺，哪有时间看电视？
早上我吃了两片面包和一个鸡蛋，喝了一杯牛奶。
自私的人只关心他们自己。
外面下雹子了。
把这个文件复制一下，每人一份。
我明年七月份就大学毕业了。
乘坐公共汽车时要小心扒手。
别老是吆喝人。

后　记

　　我们在传播中国传统文化的过程中，深刻认识到汉字的起源和发展与中华民族文明紧密相连。习近平总书记指出："没有高度的文化自信，没有文化的繁荣兴盛，就没有中华民族伟大复兴。"当中国人民的"文化自信"逐渐建立起来的时候，中华文化自觉将达到空前广泛和深刻的程度。当传统再一次被高度认同和充分肯定，汉字文化也逐渐被人们重视。本教材旨在帮助外国朋友通过汉字了解中国传统文化，提升汉语水平，使其成为华文朗读者，同时增进广大读者对中国古代文化的体悟和认识。

　　笔者在撰写本教材的过程中，参阅了诸多名师的著作，如张惠芬编著的《张老师教汉字》、云红茹所著的《看部首学汉字》、左民安所著的《细说汉字》等。他们从不同角度、不同方面深入研究汉字，提出许多真知灼见，笔者深受启迪。为了更好地完成中国传统文化教育系列教材的编写工作，实现既有实用价值又不乏趣味性的编写目标，笔者结合自己在学习外语过程中遇到的困惑，以汉字造字法为切入点，讲解汉字的构造，由形表意、由简到繁，将繁多的汉字梳理成一幅幅情境画卷，归纳为不同的主题，以话题形式，引导读者开展听、说、读、写全方位的练习。

　　《汉字入门》及其姊妹篇《汉字渐进1》和《汉字渐进2》的撰写工作是同时进行的，基于循序渐进原则，同时严格遵循国际中文教育教学词汇大纲要求，三册教材涵盖HSK(汉语水平考试)所需的全部三级词汇、大部分四级词汇和部分五、六级词汇。本教材在七年前就已经成稿，而后历经七次教学循环过程，不断完善。我们采用小班授课模式，每班来华留学生人数为2～8人，加上寒暑假海外短期汉语研修班的部分学员，共计200余名学生。可以说，本教材通过了实践教学的充分检验。多年以来，在编写、改写及教学使用过程中，本教材得到诸多领导、同事、学生和朋友的关注，笔者一直心存暖意和敬意。

　　生活是一种经历，思想的展开是一个过程。人有思想 (thoughts or minds)，所思所想的东西 (things or reality) 一般来说都是自己生活中的大事。汉字 (words) 起源于图画，不管以什么写法出现，都是中国人表达思想的工具。作为老师，必须拥有"深刻"的思想，必须铸就认知力和洞察力，必须有思想高度和维度。教学的过程就是与学生进行思想交流的过程。在教学过程中，老师应能融会贯通地举例、启发、说明、演示，设定语境，预留思考空间，引导学生思考汉字间的相互关联，指导学生解析汉字的字形结构，帮助学生准确、透彻地理解汉字的字义，将关联的汉字联系起来，灵活地将象形字或指事字，组合成会意字或形声字，尤其是形声字。"秀才识字认半边"，学生能做到举一反三、触类旁通，学习就会变成一种自觉行动，这样才能更深刻、更快速地认识汉字，记住汉字，从而熟练、正确地使用现代汉字。

中华传统文化源远流长、博大精深、浪漫包容，具有强大的生命力。汉字不仅是中华文明的载体，也是我们祖先生活智慧的写照。不管是初识汉字，还是研究中国传统文化，从汉字的起源开始，了解每个汉字的来龙去脉，以及与哪些词汇有关联，无疑是理解中华文化的好办法。

伴随实现中华民族伟大复兴的脚步，汉字正在走向世界。

李刚

2022 年 7 月